Fridtjof Nansen Land
Spitsbergen
ARCTIC OCEAN
New Siberian Islands
Greenland Sea
Novaya Zemlya
Kara Sea
North Cape
Barents Sea
CIRCLE
Iceland
Siberia
Lena
Dvina R.
URAL MTS.
R. Ob
Yenisei River
River
North Sea
Baltic Sea
EUROPE
ASIA
Sea of Okhotsk
Dnieper R.
Volga R.
Ob River
Irtish
Lake Baikal
Sakhalin
Amur River
R. Danube
ALPS
Black Sea
Caspian Sea
Aral Sea
Lake Balkhash
Mediterranean Sea
Amu Darya R.
HIMALAYA MTS.
Hwang-ho (Yellow R.)
Sea of Japan
JAPAN
Euphrates R.
Suez Canal
Indus R.
Brahmaputra R.
Yangtze Kiang
Ganges R.
Sahara Desert
Nile R.
Red Sea
Arabian Sea
Mekong R.
Salween R.
Irrowaddy River
Bay of Bengal
PACIFIC
L. Chad
Niger R.
AFRICA
South China Sea
Philippine Islands
Guam
OCEAN
Gulf of Guinea
L. Victoria
Ceylon
Sumatra
Borneo
Celebes
Ascension I.
River Congo
L. Tanganyika
Lake Nyasa
INDIAN
Java
New Guinea
ATLANTIC
Helena
Zambesi R.
Madagascar
OCEAN
Orange R.
AUSTRALIA
OCEAN
Cape of Good Hope
Murray R.
Tasmania
ANTARCTIC OCEAN
ANTARCTICA

# *Lands and Peoples*

THE WORLD IN COLOR

VOLUME I

THE GROLIER SOCIETY

NEW YORK TORONTO

## Editorial Staff

| | |
|---|---|
| HELEN HYNSON MERRICK | *Managing Editor* |
| L. ROBERT TSCHIRKY | *Associate Editor* |
| HELEN RIEHL HITCHCOCK | *Production Editor* |
| ROBERT P. BULLEN | *Staff Editor* |
| CHARLES P. MAY | *Staff Editor* |
| CATHERINE OWEN PEARE | *Staff Editor* |
| ETHEL K. WILHELM | *Staff Editor* |
| MURIEL R. ATKINS | *Staff Assistant* |

## Art Staff

| | |
|---|---|
| GLADYS D. CLEWELL | *Director* |
| GLORIA GRAY CLARK | *Assistant Director* |
| NAN A. HARVIE | *Artist* |
| MARCHELLE RUSH | *Artist* |
| JOYCE STUVE | *Artist* |
| ELAYNE VICTOR | *Artist* |
| CATHERINE O'DEA | *Picture Research* |
| HELEN D. SABBATINO | *Picture Research* |
| KATHARINE BROWN | *Picture Librarian* |

## Production

| | |
|---|---|
| GEORGE MAHLSTEDT | *Production Manager* |

## Special Contributors

| | |
|---|---|
| HARTNEY ARTHUR | *The Island Continent* |
| ROBERT BARRAT | *The Beautiful Land of France* |
| CHARLES BARRETT, C.M.Z.S. | *Australia's Aborigines* |
| CARLETON BEALS | *The Pageant of Modern Mexico* |
| GEORGE BRYANT | *The Maoris Today* |
| G. M. CRAIG | *The Atlantic Provinces* |
| N. E. DONOVAN | *South Sea Island Nation* |
| JOHN R. DUNKLE | *The Cities of the United States* |
| E. S. FERGUSON | *New and Old Lebanon* |
| | *The Troubled Land of Syria* |
| ANNE FREMANTLE | *Town and Country in England* |
| GUNNAR LEISTIKOW | *Europe's Oldest Kingdom* |
| | *The Heartland of Europe* |
| TRYGVE LIE | *The United Nations* |
| HENRY MICHAEL | *The Races of Mankind* |
| RICHARD L. NEUBERGER | *Lands of Treasure and Romance* |
| W. P. PERCIVAL | *Quebec, Once New France* |
| WHEELER B. PRESTON | *The British Isles* |
| B. K. SANDWELL | *Canada, Monarch of the North* |
| WALTER SULLIVAN | *Berlin in Eclipse* |
| JAMES RAMSEY ULLMAN | *Introduction* |
| C. LESTER WALKER | *The Millionth Map* |
| MORRIS ZASLOW | *The Roof of North America* |

E. V. McLOUGHLIN, *Editorial Director, The Grolier Society*

M

# Volume I

# TABLE OF CONTENTS

Photograph by James V. Lloyd

THE CALL TO THE GREAT SPIRIT AT MIRROR LAKE, CALIFORNIA

AN INDIAN LEGEND DEPICTED IN PAGEANTRY IN YOSEMITE NATIONAL PARK

# THE COUNTRY OF THE KANDEMOR

MANY years ago, when I was a boy in grade school, I had an atlas that contained a very special map. It was a map of Africa, and at first sight it seemed the same as any other map: blue and pink, green and yellow, with the countries and cities, coastlines and rivers all in their usual places. But then one day while studying it I found the thing that made it "special." Deep in the yellow Sahara, in a region that on other maps was labeled "desert" or "uninhabited," or simply left as a great blank, was written, in tiny letters, "The Country of the Kandemor."

I remember asking my teacher about it and that she shook her head in puzzlement. Everyone else I've ever asked has shaken his head. Never in any other atlas, in any geography, history or travel book, have I found mention of a place or a people called The Kandemor. What is it? Or what are they? I still don't know. And although I've tried hard to find out, I'm rather glad that I haven't been successful. In dreary fact The Country of the Kandemor might be only an empty waste or a heap of stones or, even worse, a map-maker's mistake. I prefer to keep it what it was for me as a boy and what it has remained for me ever since—the country of my imagination—strange and distant, full of mystery and wonder.

We all have our Country of the Kandemor. Some men, in days gone by, called it El Dorado. For others it was Cathay or the Northwest Passage or the Spice Islands. For us of today it can lie in the deserts of Africa, among the polar ice caps, beyond the Amazon jungles, on the great untrodden mountains of Asia. It does not matter where, or even what, it is. The facts and figures, population charts and trade tables will all come in due time. What does matter is that our imaginations are stirred by the lure of far places; that the world, in spite of all that has happened to it, is still a wide and wonderful place, with a new horizon beyond every old one.

Start at home. A boy (or why not a girl?) hears the whistle of a locomotive in the night. He watches a great ship move down a river to the sea, a plane be-

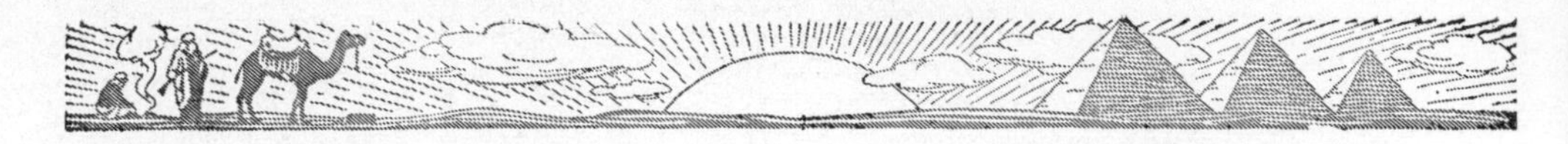

come a silver speck in the blue vastness of the sky. And in his imaginings he goes with them. That is the beginning. He is already a traveler and explorer in his heart. His next day's journey, alas, may be only as far as school, or possibly to the dentist's, but the desire to go, to see, to know, is already deep within him. And someday . . . someday . . .

### *A Mysterious City Beckons*

PERHAPS some of you have already read Joseph Conrad's wonderful story called YOUTH. It is told by an English seaman who has been almost everywhere and seen almost everything, and at the end of the story he thinks back to what he decides was the greatest of all his experiences. This had come when he was little more than a boy, on his very first voyage to the East. His ship had anchored at night off a great and mysterious city. Then the dawn came, a small boat was let down, and he and his shipmates rowed toward land. The sun came up. The palms and temples glittered. Bells rang, strange voices called out, strange faces looked out from the shore. And looking back at them, moving toward them, the young sailor was suddenly overcome with a feeling of wonder, mystery and excitement such as he was never to know again during the rest of his life. When he was older, this very same city might become for him nothing more than another port, another workaday place for loading or unloading cargo. But then, that first time, it was the unknown, it was adventure, it was magic. And, as Conrad makes clear, as much of the magic was in the boy's own heart as in the city to which he came. That was why he called the story YOUTH.

"But the world has become so small!" we hear people say. "There are no really strange or far places left in it." These people, I'm afraid, don't know the world very well. True enough, the development of transportation, communication —and unfortunately, of weapons—has brought us all closer together than would have been thought possible two thousand, two hundred or even twenty years ago. But this does not mean that they have made it all alike, or that the earth has become a dull, uniform and monotonous place. Look north, south, east, west. In the thirty-one square miles of Manhattan Island more than a hundred languages are spoken. In the forests of Brazil and New Guinea live tribes who have never heard of our civilization. The ten highest mountains in the world have not been climbed, and half of them not even explored. The dark floors of the oceans are less known than the surface of the moon.

### *The World's Endless Variety*

IF it is a small world it is also still a big world—big not only in mere miles but in its endless variety. Consider one city: Paris. It has been called "The City of Light." Depending on what one is looking for, it can be called the city of art, the city of restaurants, the city of strikes, the city of dressmakers, the city of the guillotine. It is all of these. Plus three million people. Plus two thousand years of history.

Or take, not a city, but a region: the great basin of the Amazon in South America. What is it? To the traveler flying over it, merely a wilderness of jungles and rivers. But to the Indians dwelling there it is home. To the early Spanish and Portuguese explorers it was the promise of riches and empire. In the years since, men have searched there for gold, for rubber, for oil, for strange plants and animals, for lost tribes, for lost cities.

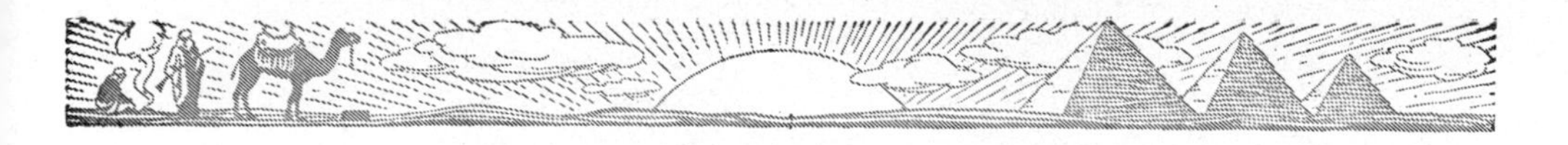

After the American Civil War a group of Southern families went there, looking for a new place to settle. Now scientists are hoping that it can be developed as one of the great sources of food for the whole world. The Amazon is not merely water, mud, trees, insects. It is what the imagination and will of men make of it.

In this mid-twentieth century we are apt to think of the world largely in terms of governments and politics. And for this there is, of course, good, if unfortunate, reason. But the world is more than just these things; and geography—the study of the world—is more than a listing of capitals, boundaries and populations. That, it seems to me, is the really fine and important thing that these books have to offer: that they go beyond today's headlines, today's news, today's problems and propaganda, to the deeper and more permanent world that stretches from yesterday to tomorrow. Here are earth's mountains and rivers, its farms and cities, its arts and sciences, its living men and women and children. Here is what the world is made of: lands and peoples.

### *Each to His Own Taste*

HUMAN tastes and interests differ, which (except perhaps in totalitarian countries) is a very good thing indeed. And no reader is going to be equally interested in everything in these pages. In my mind's eyes I can see David enthusiastically telling Susan about Eskimo seal hunters or Congo witch doctors, and Susan replying with a ladylike "Ugh." I can see Susan clapping her hands over the photograph of a Spanish lady in a beautiful mantilla, and David grunting, "Does it keep her warm?" But it is hard for me to imagine anyone with so little curiosity, so little imagination, that his mouth won't water over at least some of the many courses in this feast of wonders.

The whistle shrieks; the foghorn toots; the propellors whir. These books are your train, your ship, your silver plane, and they will take you not just to one destination, but everywhere. To—(well, let's open a page at random)—to Death Valley, in California, where you stand at the lowest point in the United States and look up at Mount Whitney, the highest. To Manaos, the old rubber capital of Brazil, where a great opera house rises out of the jungle. To the palaces of France, the temples of Siam, the Great Wall of China, the stilt-houses in the rivers of Borneo. To Arabia, land of the camel and the tractor, of ancient mosques and gleaming pipe lines. To Azizia, in Libya, where the thermometer goes up to 136 degrees (in the shade), and Verkhoyansk, in Siberia, where it goes down to 90 below zero.

### *Home Address—The World*

NOT interested? With all my heart I hope no one really feels that way; for anyone who says "not interested" to the world he lives in might as well turn up his toes. Naturally, we all love our own customs—but there's something very wrong about a man who is such a slave to habit that he has no interest in anything except what he is used to.

For most of us, happily, there is more to living than mere existence, more to the world than the little part of it that has become familiar. Home is good, no doubt about it. But the rest is good too; good in its broadness, its variety, its lure, its challenge. And we are not really strangers to that "rest"; we ourselves are part of it. Whatever our home address, we have another one besides. That address is—The World.

Small world—big world. A contradiction, but true. And you will see both its

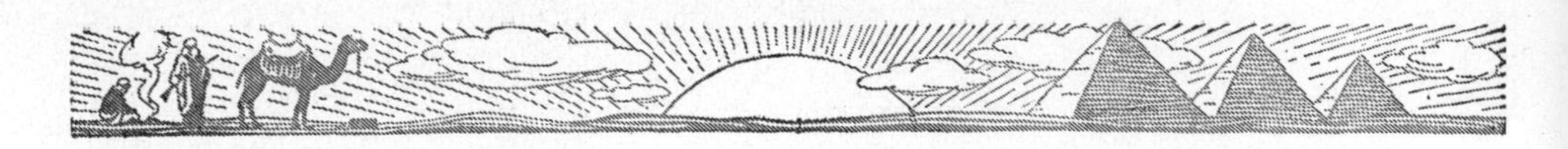

smallness and its bigness spread vividly before you as you read the stories and study the pictures in these books. Through most of human history it mattered little to people on one side of the globe what was happening on the other. The life of a person in America or England was scarcely touched by events in Russia, China, India or Africa. But that, as we know all too well, is no longer true. The earth has grown small. Nation jostles against nation, race against race, culture against culture, until we are almost as closely involved with people ten thousand miles away as with our next-door neighbors. It is enormously important that we know these people as they really are—as they live their lives—as they think and work and play. And that is exactly what these seven books of LANDS AND PEOPLES can bring to us: an understanding of the world we live in.

### *The Gift of Imagination*

BUT is understanding all of it? No, I don't think so. The other great and equally important thing that these books will do—and now we are back to the beginning—is to stir the imagination. There are dreary folk in the world who will tell you that living is a routine and dull business and that imagination is for poets and small children. Don't believe them for a minute. Instead, look through these books and then back into history at the men who made them possible. What was it but imagination that sent the old Phoenicians exploring in their galleys? That sent Columbus to the New World, Marco Polo to Cathay, Cartier to the St. Lawrence, Captain Cook to the Pacific, Livingstone to Darkest Africa, Peary and Amundsen to the Poles? What is it but imagination that drives men today to study the earth—to try to know it better, understand it better—and to try to make it a better place to live in?

### *Man the Adventurer*

IN our complex and organized world a man is known by many labels. He is called a citizen, a subject, a producer, a consumer, a student, a worker, a provider. Let us remember that he is also, in his heart, an adventurer. Beyond the fact, the thing, the number lies the hope and the dream. Beyond the school and the library, the city and the farm lies the whole wide earth. Beyond the mountains and the deserts lies The Country of the Kandemor.

JAMES RAMSEY ULLMAN

Explorer, mountain climber, author. Among his books are *The White Tower; High Conquest; Kingdom of Adventure: Everest* (Editor) ; and *River of the Sun.*

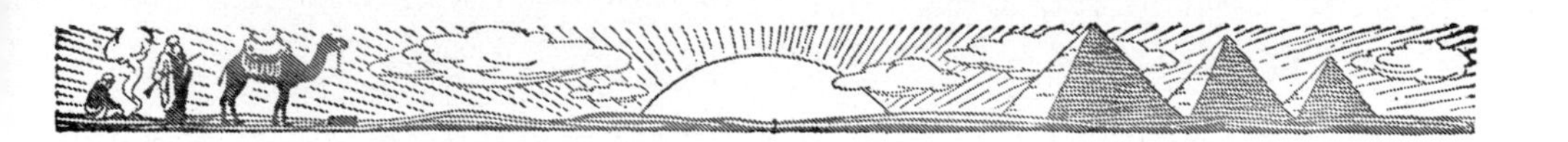

# General Arrangement

THE seven volumes of this work are so arranged that contiguous countries are brought together as nearly as possible. Where such groups as the Commonwealth of Nations, the French Union or territories far from the homeland are concerned, each region is placed according to its geographical location. For example, Algeria is described not under France but in the volume that includes Africa. The general scope of each volume in the set of books is indicated in the paragraphs that follow.

**VOLUME I**

*Western Europe*

IN this volume are included an Introduction giving the general aims of the work; an article on the Millionth Map, an international geographic project; two articles each on England and France; and one each on the British Isles as a whole, London, Wales, Scotland, Ireland (both the Republic and Northern Ireland), the Atlantic islands, the Netherlands, Belgium, Paris, Spain, Portugal and the Mediterranean islands. There are 107 illustrations in full color.

**VOLUME II**

*Central Europe*

IN this volume are included articles on Norway; Sweden; Finland; Iceland and Greenland; Denmark; Germany, with separate sections on Western and Eastern Germany; Berlin; Poland; Estonia, Latvia and Lithuania; Czechoslovakia; Austria; Hungary; Switzerland; "toy states"; Italy; Rome; Venice; and Sicily. There are 87 illustrations in full color.

**VOLUME III**

*The Middle East*

IN this volume are included three articles on the Union of Soviet Socialist Republics (both European and Asiatic territory) and one article each on Greece, Athens, Albania, Yugoslavia, Bulgaria, Rumania, Iran (Persia), Iraq, Bagdad, Turkey, Istanbul (Constantinople), Syria, Lebanon, Israel and Jordan, Bedouins and the states of Arabia. There are 88 illustrations in full color.

**VOLUME IV**

*Asia*

IN this volume are included three articles on the Republic of India and on Pakistan; two articles on China; and one article each on Afghanistan; Kashmir; Tibet, Nepal and Bhutan; Burma; Ceylon; Malaya; Thailand (Siam); Indochina; Formosa; Mongolia; Peking (Peiping); Japan; Tokyo; and Korea. There are 96 illustrations in full color.

**VOLUME V**

*Africa, Australia and Oceania*

IN this volume are included three articles on Egypt, ancient and modern; two articles each on Borneo, Australia and New Zealand; and one article each on Morocco; French territories; Algeria, Tunisia and Libya; Cairo; Ethiopia and Liberia; British territories; the Congo Basin; South Africa; Madagascar; Indo-

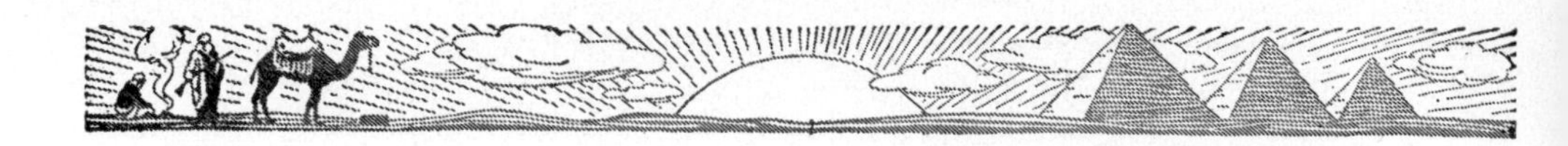

nesia; the Philippine Republic; and the South Sea islands. There are 72 pages in full color.

### VOLUME VI

*North America*

IN this volume are included articles on the North Pole region; North American Indians; a general survey of Canada; the Atlantic Provinces (Nova Scotia, Prince Edward Island, New Brunswick and Newfoundland and Labrador); Quebec; Ontario; the western provinces (Manitoba, Saskatchewan, Alberta and British Columbia); Canadian cities; the Yukon and the Northwest Territories; the Good Neighbor Policy; a general survey of the United States; the northeastern states; the southern states; the north-central states; the mountain and Pacific states; Hawaii and Alaska; the cities of the United States; the national parks and forests of the United States; and the national parks and reserves of Canada. There are 92 illustrations in full color.

### VOLUME VII

*Latin America and General Topics*

IN this volume are included articles on Mexico; Central America; Cuba; the West Indies; Haiti and the Dominican Republic; Venezuela and the three Guianas; Colombia and Ecuador; Bolivia and Peru; Chile; Argentina, Uruguay and Paraguay; Brazil; Antarctica; the United Nations; races of mankind; boats, ancient and modern; donkeys; hats; gipsies; transportation in remote areas; rivers; deserts; waterfalls; spinning and weaving; elephants; and volcanoes. There are 89 illustrations in full color.

*Each volume has its own index, and there is a combined index in Volume VII.*

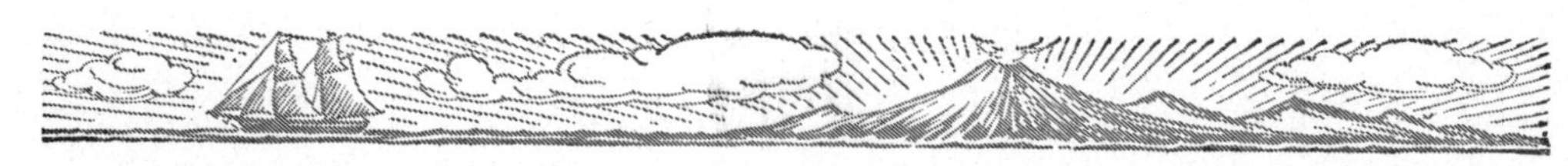

# The Millionth Map

## *Guide to the Broad Acres of the Whole Earth*

Maps of some kind are probably as old as man himself. To tell his fellows where there was water or good hunting, primitive man no doubt drew a rough chart on the ground with a stick. Two of the oldest maps in existence date back to the 1300's B.C. and were made in ancient Egypt. The maps of the ancient Mediterranean world that have come down to us were no mean achievement, though we may smile at their wildly imaginary drawings of the unknown lands beyond. Yet for all our present-day knowledge of the earth, our maps are still far from adequate. The Millionth Map is an attempt to fill this great lack.

IN the years ahead we are all going to hear more and more about the Millionth Map. It is a new map of the world in the process of being put together. Its official name is the International Map of the World (IMW for short). However, it is popularly called the Millionth Map because its scale is one to one million. This means that one inch on the map equals one million inches on the earth, or almost sixteen miles.

When the Millionth Map is completed, it will be the first map ever constructed to be standard for every part of the globe. Not only will it have the same scale throughout (making comparisons of different regions easier) but every part will have met the same severe tests for accuracy and workmanship. Thus it will be as accurate for one part of the world as for another.

It hardly seems believable that no such map was ever made before. To get a single dependable map of the whole world, many maps have had to be used, and each is different. Most countries have produced their own maps, using whatever scale and methods seemed suitable to them regardless of the maps of other nations. Naturally among all these maps there is great variation in the way they are drawn and in their general reliability.

Though the Millionth Map is spoken of as a single map, actually it consists of a number of sections, or sheets. The number of sheets for all the continents and islands of the earth—a total of about fifty-five million square miles of land surface—eventually will be 961.

Each sheet covers exactly six degrees of longitude by four degrees of latitude. (At the equator one degree of latitude or longitude is, roughly, seventy miles.) From this you can see that the sheets will disregard national boundaries. They will not stop, as do so many maps, where one country ends and another begins. A distinguishing name is given to each section, usually the name of some prominent town or feature of the region. For instance, sheet M-15, which includes part of Minnesota and parts of Manitoba and Ontario, is called "Lake of the Woods" sheet from the large lake that borders on the state and both provinces. Thus this section ignores a border and covers parts of both Canada and the United States.

As a further indication of its global character, the Millionth Map is being prepared under the sponsorship of the International Geographical Union, a group of geographers whose homelands include almost every country in the world.

The idea for the map was first proposed in 1891. This came about at a congress of geographers in Bern, Switzerland. One day a young professor of geography, Albrecht Penck of the University of Vienna, read a paper before the meeting that suggested the new world map and showed how seriously it was needed.

The idea was received with enthusiasm. Even then, before the airplane had arrived to shrink distances between the farthest countries, the necessity for such a map was recognized. The one-to-one-million scale was then proposed, and an international committee of leading geographers was selected to study the matter and to decide how such a map could be made a reality.

Yet for about eighteen years the Millionth Map remained little more than an idea. It received new impetus in 1909 when Great Britain called a meeting of ambassadors from a number of countries to consider the matter. This conference was able to agree on many practical details. Among other matters, the delegates decided what parts of the world should be mapped by what countries. Cartography is an exacting and highly complicated art, and even today there are many nations that lack trained map-makers. At the 1909 conference, France was given the task of mapping some parts of Asia, a project it had already begun. Germany was assigned the work on China; and Great Britain, the British sections of Africa.

Nevertheless jealousies and suspicions among nations have still slowed the map's progress. Wars have brought work on it almost to a standstill. During the second World War the permanent headquarters of the commission, at Southampton, England, was destroyed by bombs. Disputes among the geographers themselves as to the best ways to make the map sometimes have wasted months or years.

### *The Latin America Section*

Regardless of all these setbacks the map has been slowly progressing, a few sheets finished and published in one year, a few more in another. Like any great idea, that of the Millionth Map has refused to die. In 1945 it received a great boon. For some years the American Geographical Society had been working on a map of Latin America, and in that year it was completed. This map is on the same scale and has the same style as the Millionth. So it was decided to include the sheets of the Latin America project with the international one. Thus one-sixth of the land surface of the globe—from the Rio Grande to Cape Horn—was added in one fell swoop.

By the early 1950's the Millionth Map had arrived almost at the halfway post. About 50 per cent of its total number of sheets had been completed and published.

What will the Millionth Map look like? What will it be like to handle and to use? First, it will be a topographical map. This is a different kind of map from those with which you are probably most familiar, such as road maps for automobile driving. Road maps are usually what is called planimetric: they are flat-measure maps. They show the land on a plane, as though there were no hills or valleys. Such maps are useful chiefly for indicating distances, the measure of miles or kilometers from place to place.

### *How Land Height Is Shown*

In contrast, topographical maps such as the Millionth indicate not only distances from point to point but also how the land looks and what it does. They show where it rises and falls, how high the land is above sea level or how low. They also indicate the rate of the rise or fall, whether it is steep or gradual. From such a map you can tell which side of a river valley is gently sloping or which side of a mountain is the most sheer. Thus the picture of the land a topographical map gives you is in three dimensions—width, length and height.

The advantages of a topographical map over a planimetric one are self-evident. Leaving the Millionth Map aside for a moment, it may astonish many Americans to learn that large areas of the United States have never been mapped in this way at all and that their country is less completely mapped by any method than Japan or India. Great Britain, Germany, Holland, Belgium and Austria have the most thorough topographical maps of any countries in the world. In fact, during World War II, Britain had a striking demonstration of the value of its topographical mapping. The particular map in question was a land-use map. In the tiniest detail it showed what every section of the island is best suited for, from John o'Groats in Scotland to Land's End in Cornwall. Armed with this information, Britain was able to increase its cultivated fields by 60 per cent, and suffered less for lack of food during the war than it would have without this extremely useful map.

The work involved to get the precise information needed for an accurate topographical map is enormous and far-reaching. For one thing, the land must be surveyed—that is, accurate points of latitude, longitude and altitude must be established. This is called the "geodetic control." In some cases the points are fixed by markers that must be correct to one-half inch in seven miles. Hundreds of observation stations are set up by men working on foot. In one jungle area, a survey party had to hack its way through the dense growth for fourteen days to go a mere twenty miles.

### *Contour Lines and Colors*

On the Millionth Map the shape of the surface is shown by contour lines and colored tints. Each contour line indicates an exact number of feet or meters above sea level. Thus contour lines zigzag or curve according to the altitude of the land. The colors reveal at a glance the relative highs and lows. For instance, lowlands may be tinted green, areas a little higher yellow, still higher areas brown, and lavender for high mountains.

Most of the sheets of the map are twenty by seventeen inches (they are somewhat smaller for polar regions). This size is just about the area of a newspaper page, and so a sheet is quite easy to handle.

The Millionth Map will fill the gap that exists between the small-scale maps of most atlases (which are too small in scale for accuracy) and the big-scale topographical maps usually published by the official map-making departments of most advanced countries. These are of a scale much larger than the average person needs. The one-to-one-million scale can show clearly most of the important features of any region; and geographers consider this scale the one that is most generally practical.

The map shows distances in kilometers and miles, and some of its sheets may also give the Russian distance measure of versts. (A verst equals 0.6629 mile.) Names of places are printed in the Roman alphabet. However, where the country shown has no alphabet (as Japan) there are usually two editions of a sheet. One uses the native writing and the other Roman characters, the most widely used alphabet in the West.

When all the sheets of the Millionth Map are finally completed, they will offer to the peoples of the world a map that, for its scale, will be the last word in both accuracy and practicality. It will be the best map in existence, for example, for the average traveler. You and I will find it more useful and easier to read than any other map we are likely to get abroad.

The map will also be invaluable to people who use maps in their work—geologists, economists, engineers, conservation and irrigation specialists. For this map will be accurate to the point where it can serve as a basic or "mother" map to which any kind of specialized information (about water, soils, vegetation, populations) can be added without fear of error.

Looking ahead, can one see when the Millionth Map will be wholly finished? Not yet. In 1953 the map's European, South American and African sections were almost all completed. But elsewhere scattered around the world there were many blank spaces still to be filled. China, the lands of the Soviet Union and Australia were chief among these. Of the seventy sheets on which the United States is to appear, only nine had been completed.

### *The Millionth Map in Service*

In the meantime, the sheets that are already published are serving the world well. With their aid, troublesome boundary disputes have been settled between quarreling nations. In several countries —notably Ecuador, Panama and Colombia —the sheets have become the right hand of census-takers. Engineers have been guided in remote mountains and deserts. A novel use has been made of the Latin America sheets on the upper Amazon, where it is claimed that steamboat captains find them more helpful than their navigation charts.

By C. Lester Walker

Philip Gendreau, N. Y.

**KING RICHARD I—THE LION-HEARTED**

With sword upraised, the valiant Richard still seems to be leading his men on to the Holy Land, in the Third Crusade. Though his motives were different, he was a forerunner of later men from the British Isles who were to venture to the far places of the globe. This statue is in London, and on the right is a glimpse of the Houses of Parliament.

# THE BRITISH ISLES

## *Home of English, Irish, Scots and Welsh*

The British Isles take their name from the ancient Britons, or Brythons, one group of Celtic people who crossed the English Channel from the mainland of Europe probably about 1000 B.C. They established themselves in present-day England and Wales. Another group, the Gaels, settled in Scotland and later some of them crossed to Ireland. Though the cluster of islands is comparatively small, in it have developed distinctive stocks—English, Irish, Scots and Welsh; a culture with world-wide influence; a nation, Great Britain, that is among the greatest on earth; and a new state—the Republic of Ireland.

JUDGED from the standpoint of size the British Isles are not impressive, for no place in either Great Britain or Ireland is more than sixty miles from salt water. Moreover, though the islands are quite densely populated, their total number of inhabitants is not large. Yet these isles have for long bulked large in world history, always in the front rank and sometimes holding the foremost place.

Their unique location, in the Old World and yet stretching out to the New, with vast ocean areas to the west and south, has been a decisive factor in their history. However, the discovery in England of the remains of mammals like those once common in western Europe proves that Britain was once part of the continent. It did not become an island until the late Stone Age. For this reason, Paleolithic (Old Stone Age) peoples, who used tools and weapons of crudely chipped flint, were able to arrive in Britain by land. They are the first people known to have reached the country. Later, after Britain became separated from the European continent, other peoples occupied the British Isles—Neolithic (New Stone Age) and then Celtic. Julius Caesar acknowledged the skilled seamanship of the Britons who opposed his landing in 54 B.C.; and more seafaring blood was introduced into the islands by the invading Danes and Norsemen who came later.

It was these varied strains and their language, mingling in an isolated environment, that molded the national characteristics of the modern Briton. From the Rhine, the Elbe and the Norwegian fiords, Britain received her Teutonic language and the rudiments of her free institutions. From the Seine Valley of northern France and the western Mediterranean came Christianity and scholarship. Thus both northern and southern Europe made great contributions.

Nevertheless, for many centuries the surrounding seas gave Britain protection. Behind this strong frontier the British developed an insular viewpoint which became one of their most striking characteristics. Thus, though in her were fused the several elements of European civilization, Britain really never became "European," that is, Continental.

In the Middle Ages, British ships opened trade with the countries of western and southern Europe. Later, following the great geographical discoveries of the fifteenth and sixteenth centuries, British seamen began the long series of voyages, for exploration and trade, that took them ultimately into every continent of the world. Thus it was that people from the overcrowded British Isles came to establish new homes in, or at least to govern, a greater part of the earth's surface than any other people in history. At the same time they spread the influence of Europe as a whole to all the shores of the world. The spirit of initiative and enterprise of these pioneers was developed in the little islands that we are considering here.

Much the same causes that set British conditions apart from those of the continent of Europe tended also to separate conditions in Wales, Scotland and Ireland from those of England. In the case of

Wales, and of Scotland, bleak uplands form a barrier; and the Irish Sea rolls between England and Ireland. In due course, Wales did become largely assimilated with England. Then, when the Scottish and English parliaments were united in 1707, the three countries became the Kingdom of Great Britain. When Ireland was drawn into political union, the kingdom took the name United Kingdom of Great Britain and Ireland. Still later (1921), when southern Ireland secured her freedom, the realm was designated officially the United Kingdom of Great Britain and Northern Ireland. Since Wales, Scotland and Northern Ireland (six counties of Ulster) are important parts of the kingdom, it is incorrect to refer to the whole country as "England." Even more to the point, the Welsh, Scots and the "unionist" Ulstermen resent it.

### *Highlands, Downs and Cliffs*

Besides Great Britain, the largest island, and Ireland, next in size, there are many smaller islands and groups around the rocky coasts. Among them are the quaint little Isle of Man, midway between the two main islands, and the picturesque Channel Islands, close to the north coast of France. The northern and western parts of Great Britain—Scotland and Wales—are highland zones, while south-central England is largely lowland. Down the center of northern England runs the Pennines, the so-termed backbone of upland country; and in the southwest lie the Mendip Hills and the Exmoor and Dartmoor plateaus. In the southeast, rolling downs cover deep chalk deposits which end in the white cliffs of Dover. On the French coast, across the Straits of Dover, are similar chalklands.

### *An Unwritten Constitution*

The British system of government as it exists today developed gradually through a period of more than six hundred years. There is no such thing as a single document embodying the fundamental principles of the British Constitution. Instead the government is based on a long series of charters, unwritten understandings, adjustments and laws. The British system is, in fact, both complex and unique. While modern Britain is a constitutional monarchy, permitting the sovereign to reign and not to rule, the government is a political democracy.

Long periods of security and of great national wealth, coupled with centuries of political evolution, developed tolerance and compromise in the people. At the same time, a love of tradition has kept alive many relics of the past. In the next article we tell you about some of the picturesque costumes and customs that still remain.

### *Growth of the English Language*

Other peoples have copied the pattern of democratic government fashioned in Britain. From the British Isles have also come a language and literature whose influence is world-wide. The English tongue, developed from the Anglo-Saxon, was modified first by Norman French and later by words of Latin and Greek origin. Words from numerous European languages, as well as distinctive terms originating in North America, have been adapted to it. Amid this perpetual change, however, there still remains an impression of continuity from earliest times. As a medium of communication between people who speak less well-known languages, English is used today to a great extent. Through translations, English literature, more extensive than that of any other tongue, has found its way into every country. Welshmen, Scots and Irish have shared with Englishmen in the British contributions to science and the arts. From all four countries have come leaders in government, finance, industry and the defense services.

Many times in the course of Britain's long story the country has suffered adversity. It has been ravaged by civil wars, smitten by economic depressions, and weakened by long and arduous struggles against foreign foes. During and after World War II, Britain found herself in desperate straits. Much of the countryside and parts of many large cities were pitted and ruined by enemy assault, foreign trade dwindled and her financial resources were strained almost to the breaking point.

In important ways, the years following World War II have made enormous changes in the life of the British people. During her first two thousand years, as we have seen, changes in government and in the way of life developed steadily but slowly. Suddenly—as if the nation had come to the end of one history book and turned the page of a new volume—a different epoch began. In the elections of 1945 the Labor party came to power, with a program that promised to nationalize the country's chief resources and to revise many aspects of everyday life. The party made good on its promises. The basic industries, railroads and communications and the banks are controlled by the government. A network of social services without parallel anywhere in the world cares for the individual literally from the cradle to the grave.

The people of the British Isles are bracing themselves for a long struggle and great sacrifices. Drawing upon their experience of hard times surmounted in the past, the British do not doubt that they will win through in due time to their former strength.

By Wheeler B. Preston

Pan American World Airways

**WHERE ANCIENT ROMANS ONCE TROD IN BRITAIN**

This pavement in tessellated mosaic work is the remains of a Roman villa that once stood near the present-day village of Bignor, in Sussex. Tesserae are small cubes of marble, or glass, used to form the design in a mosaic pavement. Such floors were common in Roman homes; and the richer the Roman, the more elaborate the design of the mosaic.

**MERRIE ENGLAND.** King's Bodyguard of the Yeomen of the Guard is the proper title of these Beefeaters, on their way to the Maundy Thursday ceremony at Westminster. They were recruited by Henry VII from the Bosworth veterans of 1485. Since 1605, one of their duties is to search the vaults of Parliament, before its opening, for a second Guy Fawkes.

DONALD MC LEISH

**THE LIFE GUARDS** were organized by Charles II from the loyalists who had followed him in 1651 on his nine years' exile in Holland. These two regiments of Household Cavalry have a magnificent fighting record stretching from the Battle of Dettingen in 1743 right up to the present. This resplendent guardsman is on duty outside headquarters in Whitehall.

EUROPEAN

AMID TRADITIONAL POMP AND PAGEANTRY, QUEEN ELIZABETH II DRIVES TO THE OPENING OF PARLIAMENT

Royal traditions, with all the ceremony and splendor that often accompany them, hold a cherished place in the hearts of the British people. On this occasion Queen Elizabeth and her husband, the Duke of Edinburgh, are leaving Buckingham Palace in the handsome Irish State Coach.

# MERRIE ENGLAND

## *Picturesque Survivals of a Crowded Past*

There are other chapters dealing with the people who live in the British Isles. This one is a sort of pageant of customs that still persist though they originated long ago, many of them when the word "merry" had a different spelling and meaning from what it does today. "Merrie" comes from an old Saxon word meaning brisk or vigorous and at first had little to do with mirth. The "merrie men" of Robin Hood, who banded together in Sherwood Forest, were not comic fellows but nimble hunters and fighters. Among the delights of a tour through England today are the many reminders of its storied past.

SINCE the end of the seventeenth century England has changed from an agricultural to an industrial country. It was once a land of forests and pastures and fields with a few small towns scattered through it. It was a country of squires who lived on their manors and managed their land themselves; of yeomen who lived in comfort; of peasants who were well fed and housed; of hardy fishermen from whom sprang fine sailors; and of stout burghers who nursed the seeds of commerce and of political liberty.

Now spreading cities cover the green fields with brick and mortar. Over whole counties the sky is blackened with the smoke of furnaces, and the air is filled with the whir of machinery. Peaceful lanes have become roaring highways of commerce. Hollows once sleepy and isolated are peopled by teeming millions. The very face of the land has changed for modern methods of farming have given the fields a different appearance.

Before the seventeenth century the population of England remained for hundreds of years at something between two and four millions, the chief variations being due to war and plagues. In the seventeenth century the population began to increase; in the eighteenth century it doubled; and in the nineteenth century it trebled. About 1820 the population of England and Wales was 12,000,000. Today about 44,000,000 people live in England and Wales, and most of them are town-dwellers.

The history of man's occupation of England is long, and many stocks have occupied the country in turn. Flint tools and weapons used by those who lived before the dawn of history have been found in many places. Most students think that the strange monuments at Stonehenge were built by these prehistoric people and not by the later Celts.

When Julius Caesar came to Britain in 55 B.C., he found the country inhabited by Celts, who had probably crossed over from Gaul (present-day France). Some of them lived in towns, had coins of gold and of iron and showed considerable artistic ability. Nearly a hundred years later the Romans undertook the conquest of Britain in earnest, and soon overran a part of Scotland as well. They were unable to hold all of this territory, however, and retreated below the wall that had been built by the Emperor Hadrian about thirty years before.

While the Roman civilization flourished in Britain, there were many walled towns and luxurious country houses. Several modern cities, among them Colchester, Lincoln, York, Gloucester and St. Albans, stand on the sites of Roman cities. London was an important town even then, and the springs at the present city of Bath were developed.

Later emperors found it necessary to withdraw troops from Britain, and left the island to its fate. Barbarians swarmed in from every direction. Of these, three Germanic tribes, the Angles, the Saxons and the Jutes, were the most important, and in the course of time brought the whole country under their control. They built chiefly of wood, rather than of stone

PHILIP D. GENDREAU

**A COLDSTREAM GUARD AT THE GATE OF BUCKINGHAM PALACE**

Like the other famous regiments of Foot Guards, the Coldstreams wear bearskin caps. Each regiment is known by the way the buttons are placed—two by two on the Coldstream uniform. The name of "Coldstream" comes from the fact that the regiment crossed into England from Scotland at the village of Coldstream when it helped to restore the monarchy in 1660.

BY BURTON HOLMES FROM EWING GALLOWAY, N. Y.

**A LIVELY DISCUSSION BETWEEN ETON STUDENTS**

Eton College, the most famous of English schools, was founded in 1440 by Henry VI as "King's College of Our Lady of Eton beside Windsor." Many of England's most distinguished statesmen and soldiers were educated at Eton. One may recognize Eton boys anywhere by their formal dress. The waist-length jacket has been copied widely by designers of women's clothes.

PIX

**"OYEZ, OYEZ!" CALLS A TOWN CRIER**

In the days when most folks could not read, every town employed a bell-man, or crier, who went down the street calling "Oyez!—listen!" Then he read out important announcements. Newspapers and radio have taken the place of town criers today; but in some parts of England there are town criers' contests, when the men parade in picturesque eighteenth-century costumes.

as the Romans had done, so there are fewer relics of Saxon than of Roman England. Some of the Saxon names still survive in English counties, such as Essex and Kent. The land was made up of small kingdoms but finally, about the year 827, the King of Wessex was recognized as overlord of the whole country. Soon, however, the Danes were invading it in force and much of the land was given up to them. The territory they captured was governed under the ancient Danelaw; and the Danegeld, a land tax, was imposed.

For a time we find the king of Denmark also the king of England. Then, in 1066, came the invasion of the Normans from France. These Northmen from Scandinavia had settled in France centuries before and had become more French than the French themselves. To England they brought a new language, new laws, new customs, new methods of building—in short, a higher degree of civilization. The Saxons were stubborn, however, and the newcomers were finally swallowed up in the main stream of English life. The English language shows many words brought in by the Normans, the laws were affected, many Norman buildings still stand, and English architecture was permanently influenced by these Norman builders. The Normans also played an important part in establishing the feudal system in England.

In modern England much of the past remains firmly embedded. Mighty London, for instance, in its broad expanse is, for the most part, a creation of the nineteenth century. Old market gardens are now asphalt streets. London mushroomed very much as Chicago and other large cities in North America grew during the same period. Nevertheless, it is amazing how much of old England may still be found even in London.

It is not merely that old churches, such as Westminster Abbey, still survive as they have been for centuries. Old streets, such as those that we find in the square mile known as the City, and old institutions, like the Inns of Court are relics. There are still to be seen bits of the old life going on unchanged. The royal procession at the opening of Parliament, the Lord Mayor's procession, and the procession of judges from Westminster Abbey to the House of Lords at the beginning of the legal year—all are pageants that have survived from the time when London was a small town.

The beefeaters at the Tower of London are veritable Yeomen of the Guard of the fifteenth century. The Life Guardsman who stands mounted on his black horse in Whitehall has come from the gay court of Charles II, the Merry Monarch.

Rural districts, of course, have changed less than the towns, and here the features of old England may be most clearly traced. First of all there are the men and women themselves. In remote places one may still recognize the original types from which the modern mixed English people have been made up. These differences show themselves in physical traits, such as size of head and color of hair and eyes, and also in variations of accent, dialect and custom. The tall, fair-haired, blue-eyed descendants of the Vikings may still be found north of the Humber River. Farther south, on the east and south coasts and in the midlands, are the descendants of Danes, Angles, Jutes and Saxons, golden-haired, more sturdily built and, as we approach the Saxons, more rugged in features. In the heart of England and toward the west we also find the ancient Britons, whom Caesar found in possession. Scattered throughout the country, but chiefly toward the west, in South Wales and in Cornwall, we find the dark hair and smaller stature of a still more ancient stock, which preceded the others and probably came originally from the shores of the Mediterranean Sea.

The workers on the land and the fisher

BRITISH INFORMATION SERVICES

**JUDGES LEAVING WESTMINSTER ABBEY FOR THE HOUSE OF LORDS**

Lawyers divide the legal year into terms and vacations and consider that it properly begins on Michaelmas Day, September 29, when the judges attend services in Westminster Abbey. Afterward they walk, dressed in the same sort of wigs and robes that English judges have worn for hundreds of years, to breakfast in the House of Lords.

**POLPERRO'S SMUGGLERS** were once noted, for it was a quiet little Channel port to which French luggers would come on a dark night and lower bale and keg into a waiting rowboat. Now it is much frequented by artists and the view has often been painted. This type of fishing boat has almost disappeared. There are many fossils in the neighborhood.

HORACE W. NICHOLLS

**FOR SUFFOLK FISHERMEN** life is busy both ashore and afloat. When the boats come in, the nets must be taken off and hung up to dry. Then they are carefully examined, for they often get frayed and torn, and any breaks must be mended with a special needle. These fishermen are wearing oilskin hats, called "sou'-westers" after the stormy southwest wind.

folk have changed least of all the peoples of England. Men who thus earn their daily bread are in direct contact with the elements. Their minds are stored with the lore of the weather and of the soil, of the ways of beasts and fishes. The machine hand of the towns seeks distractions in his hours of leisure from the monotony of his daily tasks. He is quick, volatile, changeable, restless. The country man and the fisher think long, slow thoughts and love the peace of nature.

Sheep must still be tended, and the shepherd is a lonely man by habit and inclination. He is no chatterbox, but he has a retentive memory, and he can tell you tales of adventure among men and beasts upon the moors and fells and hills, which have never been written down in books, but have been handed from generation to generation. There is no better guide and companion in the country than the shepherd, whether he be of the Salisbury Plain, the South Downs, the Yorkshire moors or the Cumberland fells.

England was once mainly covered with forests, in which the scattered little hamlets each had its own clearing for tillage and pasture. The forest yielded timber and firewood and game. A bold hunter might find a living there, as did Robin Hood and his merry men. The clearings yielded bread, milk, butter, cheese, wool, mutton and beef. The folk needed nothing from the outside world. They lived in the most complete isolation, one hamlet hardly knowing what happened in the next.

Today most of the forests are cleared and the land is under the plow. Only some remnants of the ancient forests remain. Of these the chief is New Forest. Epping Forest comes right up to the confines of London. Richmond Park, forest and meadow, is also near by. Then there are the famous Tintern Woods, in Monmouth, and various woods strewn up and down the country, representing what were once great forests, such as Arden and Sherwood.

Many of the folk dances, such as the Morris dance, which so many young peo-

PIX

**THE SURVIVAL OF A MEDIEVAL FROLIC**

The Play of the Mummers is eight hundred years old. Dressed in shaggy costumes made of paper strips, the players parade around the village led by the town crier with his bell. There are sham fights with sticks among the mummers, who represent such characters as Old Father Christmas, King William, Little John, the Doctor and Beelzebub the Devil.

PIX

**AN ELIZABETHAN PAGEANT, THE HORN DANCE, HELD IN STAFFORDSHIRE**

There are twelve dancers—the Jester, a lad riding a hobby horse (the two shown here), an archer representing Robin Hood, a man dressed as Maid Marian, two musicians playing a triangle and a melodeon, and six men bearing huge reindeer antlers—who perform set "figures." The dance began as a symbol of the villagers' right to hunt in Needwood Forest.

ple enjoy today, have come down to us from old England. As one old jingle goes:

> When Tom came home from labor,
> Or Ciss from milking rose,
> Then merrily went the tabor,
> And nimbly went their toes.

Children's games are often survivals of ancient popular ceremonies, dating from before the time of Queen Elizabeth. Punch and Judy has been traced back to an old mystery play about Pontius Pilate and Judas Iscariot. Mystery plays, on religious subjects, were not "mysterious" but were given by a ministry, or mystery, the old name for a craft or guild.

Many of England's most famous food specialties also have a long history. The cheeses are as various as the dialects—Stilton, Cheshire, Cheddar. And when English fare is not restricted by rationing, there are the delicious Cornish pasties, Devonshire cream, Melton Mowbray pies, Bath buns, Yorkshire pudding. Worcestershire sauce and English biscuits and marmalade are prized everywhere.

OTTO HOLBROOK

**COB WALLS AND THATCH** make the cottages of Thurlstone and many another Devon village. Cob is a mixture of clay and straw, or sometimes of straw, earth and lime; it is noted for its warmth and is easier to work than stone or brick. It is an old-time building material but still found in the southern counties. The village is near Kingsbridge and stands beside Bigbury Bay, to the west of Prawle Point. Off the beach there is an enormous arch of rock, the "thirled" or pierced stone which gives the village its name. Prawle Point juts into the English Channel.

SYDNEY H. NICHOLLS

**THE VILLAGE BLACKSMITH,** in his smithy, dressed in a leather apron, still uses his hammer to shape horseshoes and the tools of agriculture. Most of the iron-work of to-day is manufactured in the great industrial establishments of the north, but before the discovery of the coal fields wood-smelted Sussex iron supplied almost all of England's needs.

BRITISH INFORMATION SERVICES

OFF FOR A BRISK CANTER THROUGH NEWTON TRACEY, IN DEVON

Away from the main travel routes, the lanes twist and turn, following centuries-old paths. At every bend there is a lovely vista of thatched cottage, walled orchard or ancient trees.

# TOWN AND COUNTRY IN ENGLAND

## *By Wood and Brook, in Hamlet and City*

The pleasant land of England is celebrated in song and story—winding lanes abloom with hawthorn in the spring, rolling downs, windswept moors, forest glades where rippling brooks murmur. Yet natural beauty is but the warp in a living tapestry in which human deeds form the vivid weft threads. Hardly a village is without a reminder of the dramatic story of England. Here it is the remains of a camp of the ancient Britons, there a Roman villa, in another place a Saxon stockade, a Norman church or a Gothic cathedral—records on every hand of the different peoples who have contributed to a colorful history.

THE English countryside is really a garden—the garden of the whole Commonwealth of Nations—and nowhere is it lovelier than on the South Coast. When Englishmen say "South Coast," they mean the shires that edge on the English Channel, from Dover, in Kent, to Lyme Regis, in Dorset. The southwestern part of England, Devon and Cornwall, is considered separate.

Starting with Dover, suppose we meander west along the South Coast. Dover, on the Strait of Dover, is the nearest point in England to the Continent. From the keep of Dover Castle on a fine day, you can see the coast of France, twenty-two miles away. The port lies in a little valley, interrupting the line of the famous White Cliffs. Of gleaming chalk, they rise straight up from the sea, four hundred feet high in some places. They have been a symbol of England ever since Julius Caesar first sighted them.

High on the cliffs to the east of Dover, the Romans built a fort and a pharos, or lighthouse. Remains of the pharos still stand, though Dover Castle, largely a relic of Norman times, took the place of the fort. Beneath the castle one may wander through passages and casemates (chambers) that were hewed into the cliff.

Dover did not become very important until the Norman period. Then, however, it was made one of the Cinque (Five) Ports which were granted considerable privileges as the most important ports of the kingdom. Hastings, Sandwich, Romney and Hythe were the other four; and nearby Winchelsea and Rye had a share in their glory with the title of "ancient towns." In return for their privileges, the Cinque Ports provided ships for the navy.

From then on Dover figures time and again in English history. Richard the Lion-hearted assembled his knights at Dover for the Third Crusade. It was at Dover that the Spanish Armada was first checked. During World War II, bombs from the air and shells from the French coast fell on the town day after day but the people refused to leave their town.

Twenty miles northeast of Dover is Canterbury. Through it runs the little Stour River, which drains grassland and hop fields. Towering over the town is Canterbury Cathedral, largely Gothic in design though it was begun under the Normans. Thomas à Becket was murdered in the cathedral in 1170. When the Archbishop was made a saint two years later, it became a shrine, drawing crowds of pilgrims. Chaucer wrote of such a band of pilgrims in *The Canterbury Tales*.

Southwest of Dover is Romney Marsh, once the haunt of smugglers. Much of it is now a fertile meadow, and cattle and sheep are brought from other parts of the country to pasture here.

Winchelsea and Rye, each of which is on a knoll, nestle close to each other farther along the coast. The sea has receded here, and though this ruined the towns commercially, it saved them artistically. The parish church of Winchelsea, built around 1300 in honor of Thomas à Becket, has some of the best modern stained glass in England. Winchelsea used to be walled, and still has three of its old gates.

Hastings is where William the Conqueror defeated King Harold in 1066. The old part of the town is a pretty fishing village, with boats drying on the sands.

In this vicinity are some enchanting medieval structures. Battle Abbey—a school today—was built on the very spot where Harold fell. Bodiam Castle is a bold fourteenth-century fortress complete with parapets, a portcullis and a moat where water lilies float.

Herstmonceaux Castle has two of its original great gateway towers. Today it is the home of the Royal (Greenwich) Observatory, moved here from Greenwich (London) in 1948–49. Standing among the Sussex oaks and bracken, in spring almost moated with wild hyacinths, Herstmonceaux is a thrilling example of what can be achieved in brick. Old buildings in the English countryside reflect the kind of soil they stand on. Where it is clay, cottages are of brick and roofed with thatch. In localities that were once largely forest, the houses are timbered. Wherever stone could be found, stone was used, even if it was only a tiny quarry.

At Bexhill-on-Sea, in contrast, there is a striking example of modern architecture, with much glass—the De La Warr Pavilion. Built in the early 1930's, it was designed by Eric Mendelsohn and Serge Chermayeff, who were considered daring architects at the time.

At Beachy Head, a chalk headland almost six hundred feet high, the South Downs begin. The downs are treeless chalk hills that roll back from the coast. Those between London and Dover—in the counties of Surrey and Kent—are called the North Downs. The South Downs, largely in Sussex, are much nearer the coast. On their gentle slopes graze the famous Southdown sheep. At

BLACK STAR

**THE SOUTH DOWNS IN SUSSEX, STRETCHING AWAY TO THE SKY**

Hardly a tree breaks the expanse of the South Downs, which seem to roll back like the swells of a calm sea. The cottages are homes of shepherds who tend the famous Southdown sheep.

THE UNITED KINGDOM—GREAT BRITAIN AND NORTHERN IRELAND

MARKET CROSS AND CATHEDRAL SPIRE IN CHICHESTER

The Market Cross stands where the town's two main streets meet. Such structures, usually cross-shaped, were erected in the center of many town market places in medieval times.

PHOTOS, BRITISH INFORMATION SERVICES

UNDER A LEAFY ARCH ON THE BRIDPORT ROAD NEAR DORCHESTER

The fine modern highway traces a military road constructed by the Romans. On most of the approaches to Dorchester there are avenues of trees, a plan begun early in the 1700's.

lambing time the hills are an entrancing sight, with thousands of little balls of wool frisking about on the springy turf.

In the South Downs at Wilmington, a strange figure—the Long Man—is cut out on the side of a hill. It is 240 feet high and carries a staff in each hand. The Celts are supposed to have gouged it out long, long ago and it may represent a god of journeys. There are other such figures wherever there are downs. Perhaps the best-known of all is the Giant of Cerne Abbas, in the Dorset Downs. This one is 180 feet long and carries a club.

Lewes, the charming seat of Sussex County, lies in the very heart of the South Downs. On a height in the center of the town is a Norman castle. Nearby are the ruins of the Priory of St. Pancras, founded by William the Conqueror's stepdaughter. On the downs above Lewes, Henry III was defeated by Simon de Montfort in 1264. Henry was taken prisoner, and Simon called a meeting of Parliament. From this meeting the House of Commons developed. Lewes is

BLACK STAR

**A PROMENADE OVER THE SEA: THE WEST PIER AT BRIGHTON**

On warm, sunny days the pier is a delightful place for a stroll. It extends out into the surf for 1,100 feet. A concert hall is in the center of the pier and a theater at the end.

a center for painters and has many art exhibitions. A few miles away is Glyndebourne, a beautiful estate, where opera festivals are held in the summer.

Brighton is the largest and best-known seaside resort in England. It is sometimes called "London by the Sea." The resort became fashionable in the late 1700's. Dr. Johnson and his circle came to stay; and the Prince of Wales (later George IV) built an imposing pavilion. Along the ocean front are piers for promenading, and dignified Georgian houses delight the eye along the streets.

### *The Tract Called the Weald*

Just outside Brighton is the Devil's Dyke, a natural amphitheater. From above it, standing on the remains of a camp of the early Britons, you can see the whole Weald. This is the dale enclosed by the ranges of the North and South Downs. *Weald,* or *wold,* is an Anglo-Saxon word meaning a wood. Here and there in the tract charcoal burners still ply their ancient craft. Once upon a time there were iron-ore mines, as many of the lovely old iron gateways and lampposts still found in Sussex attest.

In this part of Sussex in the spring, there are fields of wild daffodils, of primroses, cowslips, orchis. In the woods bloom bluebells, windflowers, cuckoopint, or lords-and-ladies. Gardens display a wealth of wistaria, laburnum, magnolia and even camellias.

Around Arundel in May, the beechwoods are breath-taking. This quiet little town is in a gap cut through the downs by the River Arun, which moats Arundel on two sides. The town grew up in the shelter of Arundel Castle, the seat of the Dukes of Norfolk. Whoever becomes Duke of Norfolk also becomes the first peer and the Earl Marshal of England. One of his duties is to act as "stage manager" of coronation ceremonies.

Chichester, about ten miles from Arundel, is one of the oldest and most attractive of English cathedral towns. It was called Regnum by the Romans, and the Roman ground plan is followed by today's streets. The ancient town walls can still be traced. When the Saxons came, they bestowed the name of Cissa Ceaster on the village. In Chichester Cathedral are two well-preserved Saxon sculptures: the Raising of Lazarus, and Christ at the Gate of Bethany. They have influenced many modern sculptors. The Saxon works probably are from the earlier church built on the site of the cathedral. Largely Norman, it was begun in 1085.

Between Portsmouth and Southampton (in Hampshire), there is no real country. Both cities have the bustle and tang of shipping centers. Portsmouth is England's biggest naval base, and Southampton is the biggest port in England after London. Their harbors are admirably sheltered by the triangular Isle of Wight. The channel on the northwest is called the Solent; the northeast channel entrance is called Spithead. Southampton has double tides, which prolong high water. The first tide comes in through the Solent; two hours later the second rushes in through Spithead. It was at Southampton, perhaps, that King Canute rebuked his flattering courtiers, who thought that he could command the sea to roll back. From Southampton sailed some of the Crusaders; and here the Pilgrims hired the Mayflower for their great venture.

### *The Isle of Wight*

The Isle of Wight is a beguiling mixture of rolling downs inland and sandy beaches and cliffs along the coast. Almost in the center of the island, on a hill with a commanding view, is Carisbrooke Castle. Here Charles I was imprisoned for a time before his trial and execution. The island abounds with stately Elizabethan manor houses. On the western side are the Needles, three pointed masses of white chalk, a hundred feet high. Cowes, on the Solent, is the yachting center of England. Thousands of sails gleam on the sparkling waters during the summer and autumn. During the first week in August—Cowes Week—the gayest regattas of all are held.

From Lymington, a yacht-building center on the mainland shore of the Solent, the New Forest extends to the northwest.

BLACK STAR

ARUNDEL CASTLE BATTLEMENTS, OVERLOOKING THE CASTLE PARK

Feudal times seem vivid on these ramparts. Archers drew their bows in the crenels (the open spaces) and knights paced the parapet. The ancient castle withstood siege twice in the 1100's.

EWING GALLOWAY

**REPAIRING SHIPS AT BRISTOL**

Bristol has a large harbor on the Avon River a few miles inland from the Bristol Channel.

These 140 square miles of woodland and heath were named New Forest by William Rufus, William the Conqueror's surly son, who claimed the land as a royal hunting ground. Though it is hardly a real forest today, there are great oaks, beeches, yews and hollies.

The South Downs (also called the Dorset Downs here) meet the sea again at the so-called Isle of Purbeck. It is really a little peninsula. Purbeck marble (shelly limestone) and potter's clay are found. Studland, a headland that rises up out of the moors, is aflame all summer with nutty-smelling gorse. On the Dorset Downs pasture small, horned sheep that lamb twice a year.

Thomas Hardy called Dorsetshire "Wessex" in his novels. The county seat, Dorchester, is the setting for his *Mayor of Casterbridge*. South of the town are the Maumbury Rings, the most perfect

GRAMSTORFF BROS., INC.

**WHERE THE MEMORY OF ANNE HATHAWAY STAYS GREEN**

The straw-thatched farmhouse with half-timbered walls was the home of William Shakespeare's wife. It is at Shottery, in Warwickshire, only about one mile from Stratford-on-Avon.

Roman amphitheater left in England. Nearby Abbotsbury is a long, meandering village with a ruined monastery and a famous swannery. About a thousand swans glide around the pond.

From Weymouth, on the coast, is the shortest passage to the Channel Islands—chiefly Jersey, Guernsey, Alderney and Sark. Though these are much closer to France than to England, they have been united with England for more than eight centuries. Their laws are somewhat different, however, and they have a large measure of self-government. Both French and English are official languages, and a Norman-French dialect is spoken by many of the people among themselves. The cattle bred in the islands are famous the world over.

As we said earlier, Devon and Cornwall are considered a region apart from the South Coast. In this extreme southwest-

BRITISH INFORMATION SERVICES

**HALL AT WADHAM COLLEGE, OXFORD**

The dining hall is celebrated for its hammer-beam roof and Jacobean screen (at far end).

EWING GALLOWAY

**THE CATHEDRAL TOWN OF TRURO IN THE HILLS OF CORNWALL**

Though the cathedral, in Early English Gothic style, looks very old, it was built between 1880 and 1910 on the site of an earlier church. The spires dominate a pleasant market town.

A QUIET VILLAGE AMONG THE FENS OF CAMBRIDGESHIRE

The low, marshy ground of the fens is a paradise for wild life. Near the village of Wicken Fen, the area is preserved as a sanctuary for birds and flowers—and for insects!

PHOTOS, BRITISH INFORMATION SERVICES

APPLEBY, ON THE EASTERN EDGE OF THE LAKE DISTRICT

The town is in the lovely Vale of Eden and is the county seat of Westmorland. Old whitewashed houses face the street and the gray-stone building at the end keeps a look of Norman days.

**HILLY STREETS AND GOTHIC TOWERS IN NEWCASTLE**

The city spreads out over slopes on the left bank of the Tyne. Here past and present are thoroughly mixed. A railway, for instance, goes through the remains of the city's old castle.

ern peninsula of England, the land is hilly and in places wild. The cliffs on the coast are not chalk, but rock. In fact, Land's End—the tip that projects out into the Atlantic—is a mass of granite. So are the little Isles of Scilly, which lie about thirty miles southwest of Land's End. The climate is exceptionally mild, and semi-tropical plants flourish.

Exeter, the county seat of Devon, is one of the oldest towns in England. Here the Britons came out of hiding in Dartmoor and Cornwall after the Romans left. They lived peacefully side by side with the Saxons for several centuries until they were driven out again by King Athelstan early in the tenth century.

Exeter Cathedral is justly celebrated. Though most of it is Gothic, it has two massive Norman towers. Inside the cathedral is a plaque in memory of Richard Blackmore, author of *Lorna Doone*. Though his name is associated with Devon, the scene of his novel is Exmoor—which is mostly in Somerset, not far from the Bristol Channel. There is a real Doone Valley in Exmoor, though it is not

PHOTOS, BLACK STAR

**CATHEDRAL ON A SUMMIT**

The great Norman bulk of Durham Cathedral looms over its city from the midst of woods.

BRITISH INFORMATION SERVICES

**DELICATE TINTS FOR FINE POTTERY**

Flower designs are typical of Staffordshire pottery. The best quality is hand-painted.

as rugged as Blackmore described it.

Dartmoor is a larger and really wilder expanse of treeless plateau, to the west of Exeter. Here masses of granite crop out in what are known as "tors." Through the moor race clear streams, which pause now and then to form quiet pools where wily trout lurk. But beware of bright green grass on Dartmoor; the vivid color indicates a swamp.

In the lovely valleys of Devon there are unspoiled villages, dreamlike in the spring when the fruit orchards around them are in bloom. Devon cattle are a prized breed; and the clotted cream of the shire is an epicure's delight.

Plymouth, on the coast, was the starting point for many expeditions of the Elizabethan sea rovers—Drake, Humphrey, Hawkins—as well as the later Captain Cook. It was on the Hoe—an elevated esplanade—that Drake is supposed to have been bowling when the Spanish Armada hove in sight. From the quay called the Barbican, the Mayflower set sail in 1620.

For many years Falmouth, on the Cornish coast, was a busy port, but since the middle 1800's it has become more a resort. One of its main attractions today is the subtropical garden of Penjerrick.

From Falmouth it is only a few miles to the peninsula called the Lizard. On its breezy downs blooms the Cornish heath. The cliffs here are particularly beautiful, and there are secluded coves.

Cornwall has many remains of the ancient Britons and the Druids. Heaps of stone still stand that were once baronial castles, and many of the legends of King Arthur are associated with Cornwall. The eldest son of the English monarch always bears the title Duke of Cornwall, as Prince Charles does today. The Cornish language, a Celtic one, is no longer spoken, though there are hints of it in the present-day speech of Cornishmen and its literature has been preserved.

No place in England is more than a hundred miles from the sea, but the most truly inland country lies among the Cotswold Hills. They form the watershed between the Thames and Severn valleys. Limestone ridges, their highest point is Cleeve Hill, 1,031 feet, above Cheltenham.

The Cotswolds were once the center of the wool trade, from around 1300 to Henry VIII's time. England's wool trade, then virtually a world monopoly, made her people the richest in Europe. English cottages were palaces as compared with the dwellings of workers in any other part of the known world. Many of these cottages, with modern improvements, are lived in now.

### *By Cheltenham's Waters*

Late in the 1700's the mineral waters of Cheltenham transformed it into a fashionable spa. George III helped to make it popular; and the graceful mansions that make it so charming were erected during his reign and in the Regency period that followed. A profusion of lime and chestnut trees gives them a verdant frame.

On the Severn River is Gloucester, the county seat of Gloucestershire and a cathedral city. It is also important commercially with a number of industries. The cathedral, which is magnificent, was built between 1097 and 1472. As one would expect from these dates, its core is Norman but its most noticeable features are Perpendicular Gothic.

Near Moreton-in-the-Marsh is Compton Wynyates, perhaps the most famous of English manor houses. Built of timber, brick and stone, its style is a bridge between Gothic and Renaissance.

Oxford University, Blenheim Palace (the Duke of Marlborough's vast mansion), Stratford-on-Avon and the Royal China Factory at Worcester are all on the edge of the Cotswolds.

The Lake District is not far inland from the Irish Sea. Though the tract—due east of the Isle of Man—is only thirty-five miles square, its mirror-like tarns and aloof mountains have an unexpected wildness. History has trod lightly here. It was not until the early 1800's that the Lake District was really appreciated. Then Wordsworth, Coleridge, Southey and their friends—the Lake school of poets—extolled the region's beauties.

The largest of the lakes, Windermere, is but ten miles long. Derwentwater is considered the most beautiful. Above it, to the north, rears Skiddaw, a peak 3,053 feet high.

In fact, the Cumbrian Mountains of this district are as celebrated as the lakes. Helvellyn, just over 3,000 feet, is one of the most perfect in shape. From the heights of Place Fell and St. Sunday Crag one can see the Scottish Border and the Irish Sea. Near Wastwater, the most savage of the lakes, Scafell Pike reaches 3,210 feet into the sky, the highest point in England. All are far more impressive than their rather low heights suggest; and they are so rugged that Alpine climbers practice on them.

The Scottish Border has a grandeur all its own—high, remote, almost grim, with yellow trefoil and heather on the slopes and verdant valleys through which brooks and waterfalls splash. It is romantic country; history or legend is associated with almost every spot. At Flodden Field

PHOTOS, BRITISH INFORMATION SERVICES

**BUSY FACTORIES THAT HELP ENGLAND'S FOREIGN TRADE**

On the left warp threads for wool fabrics are being spun. The operator is on the alert for any breaks. Right, motorcycles are given final adjustments as they move on the assembly line.

the "flowers of the forest" were mowed down in 1513, when the Scots met a disastrous defeat under James IV. Sir Walter Scott's *Marmion* and many of his *Tales from a Grandfather* and much of Rudyard Kipling's *Puck of Pook's Hill* were written about the Scottish Border.

The border begins on the east with dour Durham, and nowhere else is there such a solid satisfaction of a cathedral, with its round Norman pillars. Dr. Johnson said that it produced an impression of "rocky solidity and indeterminate duration." Durham is the center of smoky coal fields, but the cathedral towers above them.

Farther north, on the River Tyne, is Newcastle, known everywhere for its export of coal. It is also a center of engineering industries and shipbuilding.

A little west of Newcastle is one of the most delightful towns in north England —Hexham. From east to west it is divided by one long street, called Priestpopple in one section, Battle Hill in the center and Hencotes beyond. Hexham boasts a magnificent priory church, with Saxon remains, a building that was a medieval prison and a fine bridge.

From Hexham one can walk along part of the Roman wall and climb the fells—wild, high, almost uninhabited country. The fells are the northern end of the Pennine range, the spine of England.

The Roman wall is often called Hadrian's wall. It was planned by that Roman Emperor around 120 A.D., to keep the wild Picts out of England. It cut clear across England, a distance of seventy-three miles, between the estuaries of the Tyne and the Solway. It was eight feet thick and twenty feet high, with a rampart walk on top. Below the northern face was a thirty-foot moat, or fosse, and on the south side a military road. Along the wall were sixteen major forts, with many smaller forts—now called "mile castles"—in between, and a turret every three hundred yards. Only a small part of the wall still stands though the whole route can be traced. It remains clearly marked.

BRITISH TRAVEL ASSOCIATION

**HADRIAN'S WALL, WHICH ONCE CUT ACROSS NORTHERN ENGLAND**

Most of the old Roman wall has crumbled. Yet when it was built, around 120 A.D., it was a formidable barrier with forts at intervals and a wide ditch on the northern side.

North of the wall, only a few miles from the North Sea, is Alnwick. The town takes its name from Alnwick Castle, an imposing pile of medieval fortifications on a commanding site. The Scottish Border has perhaps more than its share of castles. For hundreds of years it bled in either outright war or in raids.

Nearby Chillingham Castle is a fourteenth-century structure remodeled in the 1600's by Inigo Jones, the great architect. The castle is the home of the Earl of Tankerville, who owns the last herd of wild cattle in England. They look something like the American bison, as woolly but perhaps not as humpy.

Bamburgh Castle, farther north, looks out on the North Sea from a lofty basalt crag. According to the Arthurian legends, this was Sir Lancelot's castle of Joyous Gard. The Norman keep dates from 1150.

The town of Berwick not only marks the eastern end of the boundary between England and Scotland but in all old documents has a sort of extraterritoriality. "England, Wales and the town of Berwick-upon-Tweed" runs many a writ. It did not become English until 1482.

Near the western end of the border is Carlisle, called "merrie Carlisle" in many a border ballad. The Roman wall went through a suburb to the north; and in the days of border strife the town was a formidable fortress. Mary Queen of Scots spent a brief interval of her long imprisonment in Carlisle Castle.

Some distance south, along the North Sea coast, embracing the Wash, is the Lincolnshire Fen Country. The fens were formed by the gradual silting up of a once great bay, of which only the Wash remains. (Here King John lost his baggage and treasure in 1216.) It is supposed that the Romans first tried to drain the fens. However, the deep drains and sluices constructed to reclaim the area were not completed until the 1800's. The region teems with wild fowl. Around Spalding, in the spring, one finds almost as many kinds of flowering bulb as in Holland.

The fen folk have a unique dialect, and

PHILIP GENDREAU

**A WINDING STREET IN LINCOLN**

Town and cathedral (a tower is visible) are on high ground in the flat Lincolnshire fens.

most families have lived for centuries in the same cottages. No English people are more sturdily independent. Lincolnshire village churches are among the loveliest in England. The whole history of English architecture may be studied here.

South of the Wash are the Norfolk Broads, as the flat, shallow lakes of Norfolk County are called. The region is a level tract of land in the shape of a triangle. It fans out from Norwich to Palling on the north and Lowestoft on the south. Within this area there are about a dozen large broads and twice as many small ones. These, together with numerous sluggish streams, drain into Breydon Water, near Yarmouth. House boats and river yachts ply them. Between Reedham, near Yarmouth, and Norwich, they are an angler's paradise, teeming with bream, roach, pike, perch and rudd. In the terrible storms of January 1953, the broads, being natural lagoons, did not suffer as much as the dykes of Holland.

Norwich, the county seat of Norfolk, was the center for the Norwich school of English landscape painters—Crome, Cotman and Constable being the most important. It is also the home of the Norwich *Mercury,* the oldest English newspaper (founded 1714) still appearing under its original name. The apse of Norwich Cathedral, which is largely Norman, is notable for its flying buttresses. Nurse Edith Cavell, World War I heroine, is buried in a plot by the cathedral called Life's Green.

Because Norfolk County is so level, one is aware of the broad expanse of sky—as at sea—and among the broads rainbows and sunsets flame with a special glory.

We have had space here to talk of only a few districts of England. There are many others each with its special charms. All of the country is inviting, and every Englishman cherishes his own corner. Rare is the visitor who can resist the spell of this storied land, no matter where he wanders on the "blessed plot."

BY ANNE FREMANTLE

*Facts and Figures are given on page 64.*

BRITISH TRAVEL ASSOCIATION

**A LITTLE THEATER IN NORWICH WITH AN ELIZABETHAN AIR**

The building is not really so old but it copies the theaters of Shakespeare's day. It has an apron (projecting) stage. Elizabethan dramas and other classics are performed here.

BRITISH OFFICIAL PHOTOGRAPH

**"OH, TO BE IN ENGLAND NOW THAT APRIL'S THERE"**

When an Englishman abroad grows homesick for his native land, more often than not his thoughts turn to some quiet little village. There hedgerows are white with hawthorn blossoms in the spring; and gabled Tudor houses, little changed since Elizabethan times, cling to the side of the road. This lovely view of Yalding was taken from the village church.

BRITISH INFORMATION SERVICES

**"AND AFTER APRIL, WHEN MAY FOLLOWS"**

It is hard to believe that this hamlet, in Essex, is only forty miles northeast of bustling London. Probably the loudest sounds the villagers ever hear are the bells in the steeple summoning them to church. It is possible that the inn, "at the sign of the fox," is even older than most of the village itself. The little bridge crosses the pond in the central green.

© CUTLER

**IN SOMERSET**, one of the mild western counties, the sunshine of early spring makes the air warm enough for sitting comfortably out-of-doors. Here at Luccombe, a village not far from Minehead, and on the fringe of Exmoor, the high hedges and the cottage gardens have put on their yearly mantle of snowdrops, primroses, violets and little wild daffodils.

REID

**WINDING LANES,** shadowed by hedges and tall trees are typically English, and are to be seen in almost every district. This one is in Herefordshire, a county on the Welsh border, famous for its cattle, its apples and its many castles. The whole width of the roadway is occupied by the three horses, harnessed tandem and the heavy load of timber.

PHILIP GENDREAU

**NORMAN TOWER AND ELIZABETHAN SCHOLAR**

It is fitting that a statue of Richard Hooker should stand on the grounds of Exeter Cathedral. He was born near the town of Exeter and, more than that, he was a great Church of England theologian. Exeter Cathedral, begun in 1112, is one of the glories of Gothic architecture in England. The massive tower is one of two, each 130 feet in height.

PAN AMERICAN WORLD AIRWAYS

**A PART OF THE LOVELY BACKS OF CAMBRIDGE UNIVERSITY**

The Backs are the grounds that slope down to the Cam River from the backs of some of the university buildings. In this section the stream flows past Trinity College Library. Framed in the trees beyond the bend is St. John's New Court. Out of sight there is a covered bridge, dubbed Bridge of Sighs, connecting this court with older courts of St. John's College.

COMBINE PHOTOS

**TERMINAL AT SOUTHAMPTON FOR TRANSATLANTIC LINERS**

The largest passenger ships that ply the North Atlantic dock at this pier, which was erected after World War II. Built of concrete, it is a two-story building 1,300 feet long. It has three double sets of gangways which can be telescoped, luxurious lounges, four escalators, twenty-one elevators and a large parking space for cars.

FRITH

**SEA AND COUNTRYSIDE** meet in the white cliffs of chalk which stand out to greet those who enter England from France whether they land at Dover, at Folkestone or Newhaven. They are found where the North and South Downs run into the English Channel, and end in Shakespeare's Cliff, near Dover, and Beachy Head, near Eastbourne. Between these come the flat Romney Marshes. We are looking here at the South Downs, near Seaford, and at the long, undulating stretch of cliff that is known as the Seven Sisters.

TAYLOR

**CORNWALL'S COAST** is very different from that of Sussex. Here we find jagged cliffs composed of gray granite or black slate, and broken into rocky coves, deep bays or short valleys running into the high land and each occupied by a seaside town. This winding channel filled with a swirl of white foam, is on the north coast, near Tintagel Castle.

BRITISH TRAVEL ASSOCIATION

**THE SPRING OF THE YEAR IN WORCESTERSHIRE**

A gracious old manor house, Priory Park, at Malvern. Its setting—old trees, flowering shrubs and borders, and velvety sward—gives us a little glimpse of the glory of spring, which seems to have a special quality in England. The west midland county of Worcestershire is a fertile region, noted for its beautiful orchards, and grows luscious apples, pears and plums.

BRITISH INFORMATION SERVICES

**A GARDEN SQUARE IN THE TEXTILE CITY OF MANCHESTER**

Sunlight and flowers add charm to a peaceful park oasis in Manchester's Piccadilly, surrounded by the industrial buildings that play so important a part in the city's busy life. The fourth largest city in England, Manchester is a great center of cotton manufacturing. It is noted for its deep ship canal and its high-ranking newspaper, the Manchester *Guardian*.

British Information Services

**YORK MINSTER, THE DIGNIFIED AND MASSIVE CHURCH OF ST. PETER**

Famous especially for its extensive and representative series of stained glass windows, the minster includes examples of the early English Decorated and the early and late Perpendicular styles. On both sides of the west façade rise two richly decorated towers, 201 feet in height; in the northwest tower hangs the bell, Great Peter The central tower rises 216 feet.

ABRAHAM

**BEAUTIFUL WINDERMERE,** between Lancashire and Westmoreland, is the largest lake in England, but that is far from being its only claim to fame. Its clear, unruffled waters, its islands and woodlands and the rocky fell country surrounding it make a lovely picture. Rarely do the fells exceed a thousand feet in height, nor do they rise precipitously from the water-side, but behind them, in many places, we can catch glimpses of far loftier and more rugged peaks and crags. We are here looking at the northern end of the lake, near Waterhead.

ABRAHAM

**THE LAKE DISTRICT** boasts innumerable lovely spots, and of them all many people give Grasmere pride of place. To the north, across the islet that lies practically in its centre, rises Helm Crag. If we took the boat and rowed around the island, we should find the village, Grasmere, in and near which dwelt Wordsworth, chief poet of England's countryside.

BRITISH INFORMATION SERVICES

THE SHAKESPEARE MEMORIAL THEATER AT STRATFORD-ON-AVON

If the shade of William Shakespeare visits his birthplace today, it is no doubt delighted with the modern theater erected in his memory. On the bank of the River Avon in a verdant setting, it is a far cry from the little Globe Theater that he knew in London. The great tragedies, comedies and historical plays are performed regularly in the Memorial Theater.

British Information Services

**DERBY DAY CRY: "I GOTTA HORSE!"**

An old-time tipster, in amusing regalia, coaxes the crowd with the promise of sure bets on the races at Epsom Downs. The most famous of these races is the Derby, named for the Earls of Derby; and Derby Day is around the beginning of June. Then kings, peers and commoners flock to the course, which is in Surrey, about fifteen miles from London.

TAYLOR

**THE RIVER THAMES** has many aspects. As it winds under the many bridges of London, it is a muddy river, dotted with shipping. Yet only a little way beyond the city, the Thames becomes a silver stream flowing between green banks. The little craft tied up are punts. Instead of oars, they have poles. So quiet and serene does this spot look, it is hard to believe that long centuries ago, near here, Julius Caesar and his legions tried to ford the river, only to find that the Britons had driven great pointed stakes into its bed.

ABRAHAM

**FROM NEAR KESWICK** we look south over Derwentwater, the most beautiful lake in Cumberland, toward Borrowdale and its misty distant fells. Behind us we have the great mass of Skiddaw. The long range of hills across the lake has the curious name of Catbells, and if in the autumn we scramble up its steep, bracken-covered sides we can gather bilberries in plenty. Among the fells to the left are the Falls of Lodore, whose waters come "pouring and roaring, and waving and raving," just as Robert Southey describes them in his poem.

## *ENGLAND: FACTS AND FIGURES*

*THE COUNTRY*

Is in the southern part of the island of Great Britain. On the north it is bounded by Scotland, on the east by the North Sea, on the southeast by the Straits of Dover, south by the English Channel and on the west by the Irish Sea, Wales and the Atlantic Ocean. The area is 50,874 square miles; population, 41,147,938. The area of Greater London, comprising the City and metropolitan districts, is 443,455 acres.

*GOVERNMENT*

England is part of the United Kingdom, the government of which is vested in a Sovereign and a Parliament, consisting of two houses—the House of Lords and the House of Commons. The House of Lords is made up of the peers of the United Kingdom and consists of 853 members. The House of Commons consists of 625 members elected by direct ballot. Women are eligible to the House of Commons, and since 1928 have the franchise on the same terms as men. England is united with Wales in a system of local government, for the purposes of which England alone is divided into 50 administrative counties, each with a county council. London, apart from the city area of one square mile which is under the City Corporation, includes 117 square miles under the control of the London County Council.

*COMMERCE AND INDUSTRIES*

Although a large portion of the area is under cultivation, manufacturing, mining and trade are the principal industries. Coal is by far the leading mineral product. All kinds of goods are manufactured, the most important of which are textiles (cotton, wool, silk, linen and rayon) and iron and steel goods (machinery, electrical apparatus, automobiles). Sheffield cutlery and Birmingham hardware are world famous; potteries distinguish Staffordshire; boot and shoe-making Northampton. Other manufactures are harness and saddlery, chemicals, paper and board, building materials, clothing, tobacco and glass. England has long been one of the greatest shipbuilding centers in the world. In a recent year, more than 1,000 orders were placed for new ships. The fishing industry is active. Cattle and sheep are raised in large numbers and many of the breeds now found throughout the world originated here. Poultry raising is done on a large scale.

The exports are chiefly coal and manufactured goods, and the imports are raw cotton, wool, timber, petroleum, oils, food, drinks, tobacco and gold. The trans-shipment of goods is an important industry. Many of Britain's industries which had once been in the hands of private owners were nationalized by the Labor Government of the late 1940's.

*COMMUNICATIONS*

Britain's communications systems were nationalized by the Transport Act of 1947. Railway mileage, including Scotland and Wales, is about 20,000 miles. In a recent year public highways in England, Scotland and Wales totaled 183,821 miles. Aviation is under the direction of the Minister of Civil Aviation. Postal, telegraph and telephone services also are owned by the Government.

*RELIGION AND EDUCATION*

The Church of England is the established church but there is absolute religious freedom. The educational system is organized as a continuous process by the Education Act of 1945. The Minister of Education now has effective power to develop a national policy on education. There are also technical schools, training colleges for teachers, agricultural colleges and polytechnic institutions. Education is both free and compulsory. There are 12 universities (Oxford, Cambridge, Durham, London, Manchester, Birmingham, Liverpool, Leeds, Sheffield, Bristol, Reading and Nottingham), with 6,736 instructors and 67,799 students.

*CHIEF TOWNS*

London, capital, population, 3,389,850; Greater London, 8,390,941. Other large cities, with populations: Birmingham, 1,113,300; Liverpool, 804,000; Manchester, 703,500; Sheffield, 514,300; Leeds, 507,700; Bristol, 442,100; Kingston-upon-Hull, 297,800; Newcastle-upon-Tyne, 294,400; Bradford, 292,500; West Ham, 173,600; Nottingham, 303,300; Stoke-on-Trent, 275,100; Leicester, 285,800; Portsmouth, 218,200; Croydon, 252,000; Plymouth, 192,100; Salford, 179,100.

*THE ISLANDS*

The Isle of Wight, to the south, has an area of about 147 square miles; population, 95,594. It is governed as a county. The air is unusually healthful, and the island maintains a number of watering places. The Isle of Man, lying in the Irish Sea between Great Britain and Ireland, has an area of 221 square miles and a population of 55,213. It is governed in accordance with its own laws and a lieutenant governor is appointed by the Crown. There are some rich lead and iron deposits. The Channel Islands, northwest of France, consist of Jersey, Guernsey, Herm, Jethon, Alderney, Sark, Brechou and Libou. The area is 75 square miles; population, 102,770. The islands are governed according to their own laws and customs. Jersey has a lieutenant governor appointed by the Crown. The Channel Islands export large quantities of vegetables, flowers and livestock to the English market.

# A LOOK AT LONDON

## *Glamour and Charm of the World's Greatest City*

Of all the great cities of the world, many people have found London the friendliest and the least pretentious. It is the largest collection of buildings ever erected on an equal area of the earth and most of these buildings are either the homes of the warmhearted people, or the factories, warehouses and offices in which they earn their livelihood. Many of its wonderful cathedrals and churches, and other buildings as well, are revered for their age and beauty and have been the subject of poem and song. Its streets are familiar to readers of Shakespeare, Dickens, Conan Doyle and other writers. London is a museum and a fair. The world comes to London to study and to play. It is a market where the whole world trades. It is a capital where world-changing decisions are made.

VISITORS to England are sometimes confused by references to the City, the L.C.C., and to Greater London. These three names only serve to show how the metropolis has grown. The City is an area only a single square mile in extent; it is the very heart of London. Once this was all of London. The City today is the "Wall Street" of London, the center of finance and banking and of great commodity markets. The Bank of England, "the Little Old Lady of Threadneedle Street," is here, and the Stock exchange, and Lloyd's, the insurance institution. St. Paul's dominates a broad space, especially since the war, for bomb and fire destroyed many old buildings which had clustered close to the cathedral, and almost hid the lower part of the structure from view.

Outside the borders of the City spreads a mighty urban ring, thickly populated, called the County of London, or familiarly, L.C.C. Beyond this ring are wide suburbs that are included in the Metropolitan Police District. The City, L.C.C. and these suburbs make up Greater London—almost seven hundred square miles in all, peopled by more than eight million souls.

The first men who settled here chose a position on rising ground above the River Thames, with a stream flowing on one side. This was about the place where Cannon Street Station, a railway terminus, now stands. When the Romans came they found a little fort on a hill, and when they departed, four hundred years later, they left behind them a compact and well-defended city, about a square mile in extent, with a wall all around it and a bridge across the river. Even to this day the line of that wall can be traced. There were gates in it where the principal roads went forth, but it is not believed that the names of existing streets—Aldgate, Bishopsgate, Moorgate, Aldersgate, Cripplegate, Newgate and Ludgate—correspond to these Roman gates. There are fragments of the wall itself existing—one at St. Giles', Cripplegate, and one at the Tower.

Houses were later built outside the walls, and the borders of the City were extended; so that there are wards Without—that is without the wall—as well as Within. In this way the City reaches westward as far as Temple Bar, though the old Lud Gate was about half way up Ludgate Hill. It is especially necessary to mention this because, when the king comes in state to visit the City, the procession halts at Temple Bar, near the Law Courts, and the Lord Mayor presents him with the Sword of the City. The City is not under the jurisdiction of the County Council; it has its Lord Mayor, its own government, its own courts of law and its own police.

It is a very remarkable thing that there should be two cities so near to each other that they are joined by houses—houses all the way. The other is the City of Westminster. When London proper was but an isolated fort, the district at Westminster was very marshy, and the river spread round an island called the

MC LEISH

**THE TOWER OF LONDON,** fortress, palace, prison, and now a barracks and museum. Beyond the Lanthorn Tower and the modern red-brick Guard House is the great White Tower, the oldest part of the fortress. This was built in the time of William the Conqueror. Its walls are fifteen feet thick. The tower was bombed in World War II.

**ST. PAUL'S CATHEDRAL** was hemmed in by buildings on every side, as this view, taken before World War II, shows. The neighborhood suffered severely from bombing and fire in 1940; and when the area is rebuilt the approaches to St. Paul's will be open, to give a clear vista of the great cathedral. The new London will be beautiful.

Courtesy, British Travel Association

BROADCASTING HOUSE AND ALL SOULS' CHURCH, AT LANGHAM PLACE

Where Upper Regent Street meets Langham Place is all Souls' Church with its classic portico and tapering spire. Behind, at the corner of Portland Place, is Broadcasting House, headquarters of the British Broadcasting Corporation. Many businesses in London still maintain a comfortable leisurely tempo but here the visitor notices crisp, modern methods, though many of the workers take time to enjoy afternoon tea.

**THE MONUMENT, BUILT TO COMMEMORATE LONDON'S GREATEST FIRE**

A visitor to England's capital is certain to see the Monument, a column 202 feet high, near the north end of London Bridge, which marks the place where the Great Fire of London started in 1666. Many people climb the 345 steps of the spiral stairway inside it, for the sake of the wonderful view. The top is meant to resemble or symbolize flames.

FELTON

**IN TRAFALGAR SQUARE** two fountains attract the loiterer with the music of their falling waters. We see here the church called St. Martin's-in-the-Fields, a short distance from Charing Cross. The nearest fields are now miles away, though once they surrounded the village of Charing, or Cherringe. This lovely old landmark was damaged in World War II.

EWING GALLOWAY

**WESTMINSTER ABBEY,** one of the most beautiful churches in England, also has a special place in the hearts of the English. For centuries their kings and queens have been crowned here. Between 1050 and 1065, Edward the Confessor built a church on the site. The main part of the Gothic structure was erected in the 1200's; and the towers were completed in 1739.

British Information Services

**IN COVENT GARDEN: LONDON'S MARKET FOR FRUIT AND VEGETABLES**

Billingsgate for fish, Smithfield for meat, Covent Garden for fruit, vegetables and flowers—these are the three great wholesale markets of London. Covent, or Convent, Garden, which was once a real garden belonging to the monks of Westminster, is thronged early every morning by all the florists, greengrocers, costers and flower girls of London.

Isle of Thorney. When a river widens, it almost always becomes shallow, so at this place there was a ford, over which travelers could pass with their pack-horses and goods. They came from the north by way of what is now Edgware Road and Park Lane, which lie over one of the oldest of the British track-ways. The monks founded a church on Thorney Island. This church grew through the ages into the magnificent Abbey of Westminster, which is the scene of the coronation of British kings and the burial place of the great dead.

St. Paul's Cathedral and Westminster Abbey can peep at each other over the curving reaches of the river, but at one time there seemed little likelihood of their both forming part of the same London, for Westminster and London, as cities, were separated by miles of horribly bad and robber-infested roads. It was much safer to go by river than to run the risk of your horse slipping in the mud, and throwing you down helpless at the mercy of footpads.

St. Paul's Cathedral was burned down in the Great Fire which followed the Great Plague, and was rebuilt by Sir Christopher Wren. The actual building is not so ancient as that of Westminster. In the terrible German air attack on London in the fall of 1940, the cathedral was again severely damaged.

Could we take an aeroplane view of London, beginning at the east end, the first thing we should notice would be numbers of ships, apparently enclosed by the land, lying in the great docks made in the bends of the river between the Pool of London and Limehouse Reach. Below these docks is Greenwich Hospital, formerly a home for disabled seamen, now the Royal Naval College. The buildings of the college are on the site of an ancient palace, in which King Henry VIII and Queen Elizabeth were born. Two great architectural minds have contributed to the splendor of the buildings. Charles II remade the old palace according to plans designed by Inigo Jones. Later additions such as the south colonnade were built by Christopher Wren.

**SEEN IN COVENT GARDEN**

The porters of Covent Garden, London's great fruit and vegetable market, are proud of their skill in balancing great piles of baskets and boxes upon their heads.

The river near the Tower Bridge is full of traffic. Passenger boats, tramp steamers and long strings of barges are tied up at the wharves, or else are bent on avoiding one another in the fairway. In and out among them, like water-beetles, dart the smart little launches of the River Police or the Customs officers. The Custom House is yonder above the Tower, and the Tower Bridge is one of the sights of London.

The Tower of London is a relic of Norman days. William the Conqueror pulled down an ancient fortress close by, and

BRITISH INFORMATION SERVICES

**MASTERPIECE OF EARLY NINETEENTH-CENTURY ARCHITECTURE**

Looking west at Park Crescent from Portland Place, near Regent's Park in Marylebone, London. The graceful, concave façade is one of the finest creations of John Nash, the greatest of the regency architects. Greek pillars, a continuous balcony and stucco front are prominent features of this English adaptation of Palladian and Directoire styles.

BURTON HOLMES FROM EWING GALLOWAY, N. Y.

**A BIT OF THE COUNTRY: LONDON'S KENSINGTON GARDENS**

Looking down from the fountains we see Long Water, the Kensington Gardens extension of the famous Serpentine. Queen Caroline, wife of George II, in the 1730's had numerous ponds of Hyde Park and the gardens made into this one long body of water, forty-one acres in area. Taking a rowboat out on the Serpentine is a favorite London pastime.

BRITISH INFORMATION SERVICES

**A WINGED EROS WATCHES OVER PICCADILLY CIRCUS**

Londoners have an amused fondness for the boyish figure poised on the Shaftesbury Memorial fountain. It is a meeting place for those bent on entertainment. Some stop to buy posies from the flower girls who are usually on the steps of the fountain. Piccadilly Circus is in the heart of the West End, which is the city's shopping and theater center.

Courtesy, Associated British and Irish Railways, Inc., N. Y.

**VICTORIA EMBANKMENT, SHOWING CLEOPATRA'S NEEDLE ABOVE THE TREETOPS**

Until 1864 the area now occupied by the Victorian Embankment was a mud bank. At high tide the water reached the end of those streets which run south from the Strand and at the end of one, Buckingham Street, there still stands the York Watergate as evidence. There is now nearly a mile and a half of roadway between Westminster and Blackfriars along which is a double car track forming an important connecting loop with the systems south of the river. Next to the new office building is the famous Savoy Hotel. The river is beyond the fence at the right.

**WELLINGTON ARCH AT CONSTITUTION HILL**

This beautiful triumphal arch by Decimus Burton stands in the fashionable West End. The bronze group, Peace in Her Quadriga, at the top, is by the sculptor, Adrian Jones.

Both photos, British Railways

**TIMBERED HOUSES OF ELIZABETHAN DAYS IN HIGH HOLBORN**

Opposite Gray's Inn Road is Staple Inn, with a fine gabled and timbered façade, restored in 1886. The striped appearance and many-paned windows mark the Tudor style unmistakably.

FELTON & BROWNE

**TOWER BRIDGE** is just east of the Tower of London (on the left here). Though the bridge looks almost medieval, actually it was built between 1886 and 1894. Ocean-going vessels berth in the Thames River below the bridge, where fifty-five miles of docks begin. For ships going farther upriver, the roadway between the great supporting towers of the bridge divides in two and each half is lifted up much as a drawbridge was drawn up above the moat of an ancient castle. Within the towers there are elevators by which the span across the top can be reached.

MC LEISH

**THE EMBANKMENT** that runs along the left bank of the Thames from Westminster Bridge to Blackfriars is especially beautiful in the evening light. Here we see, at the western end of this tree-bordered way, a silhouette of the Houses of Parliament and their famous clock tower. This area was damaged by Nazi raiders.

began to build this palace-prison-fortress as his stronghold. It grew gradually as age succeeded age. There was also a palace at Westminster, where the Houses of Parliament now stand, and the kings of England lived at either. But it is as a prison and not as a palace that the Tower is remembered, and the groans of those who sighed out their lives within four close walls, or went forth only to be beheaded on Tower Hill, are registered in the painfully-cut scrawls on its dark walls.

North and east of this part of the river lies the East End, a strange and squalid district, less known to some Londoners than are many foreign countries. Rows and rows of brown brick houses, with tiny back yards crammed with rubbish, form rows and rows of mean streets. The main thoroughfares, however, are wide and well built.

Sunday mornings are the liveliest times of all in some of these side streets. Middlesex Street, once called Petticoat Lane, and Wentworth Street running from it, are lined with stalls at which are sold all kinds of things, not only old clothes, but white mice, dogs and birds. Cats' meat and billowy embroidery are side by side; rusty old iron, which looks as if it could be of no use to anyone, lies on a barrow beside another hung with festoons of grapes. The familiar costers of the London streets are seen at their best upon Bank Holidays, but nowadays we rarely see them in their one-time customary gala dress covered with pearl buttons.

The City of London is a great financial center. Transactions involving millions of pounds go on in its narrow streets and around the open space enclosed by the Bank of England, the Royal Exchange and the Mansion House. Near by is the Guildhall, the City government building gutted by German bombs in 1940. Hundreds of banks and insurance offices, and the headquarters of the largest mercantile firms are found here close together. Into this square mile thousands of men and women pour every day from the great railway station, north and south and east and west. When evening frees

BRITISH INFORMATION SERVICES

**THE CLASSIC BUILDING OF THE WORLD-FAMOUS BRITISH MUSEUM**

Scholars from all over the globe pass through the Ionic columns to study the treasures amassed in this vast structure—the fabulous Elgin Marbles from Greece, rare manuscripts, millions of printed books. The museum is in the Bloomsbury section of London, where many famous literary figures, such as Virginia Woolf, have lived. London University is nearby.

© Underwood & Underwood

**HOUSES OF PARLIAMENT SEEN FROM ACROSS LONDON'S RIVER**

The beautiful building in which Britain's laws are made stands on the left bank of the Thames, in Westminster. The great tower at its southern end is called the Victoria Tower; the clock is called Big Ben. To the right of this photograph we can see a bit of Westminster Bridge; to the left appear the low twin towers of Westminster Abbey.

British Combine Photos, Ltd.

**SUBWAYS SERVE LONDON AS AIR-RAID SHELTERS**

Far underground, these subway stations made very handy shelters for Londoners during the aerial warfare of World War II. During the worst of the raids over London many families made these shelters a "second home," returning to them nightly to avoid the incessant bombing. The sturdy, cheerful faces are typical of England's courage.

**BUCKINGHAM PALACE, WHERE THE KING LIVES, FROM THE AIR**

Buckingham Palace is nearly surrounded by green and open spaces. From the Victoria Memorial, before the palace, the wide Mall, seen on the right, runs for a short way between the Green Park and St. James' Park, a corner of which we see in the right foreground. Separated from the Green Park by Constitution Hill are forty acres of royal garden.

them, back they go again. Then, except for a few cats and pigeons, policemen and night-watchmen, the place seems deserted.

The City, from just west of the Tower to just east of Temple Bar, was swept bare by the Great Fire in 1666, and few relics of earlier times survive. Some fragments are in those churches not wholly pulled down before being rebuilt; and, until recently, there was that priceless gem of medieval architecture Crosby Hall, which was carried off bodily to Chelsea and re-erected there.

London Bridge, with its long low lines, carries no suggestion of that older bridge which once stood here, with houses hanging out over the water, lining it like a continuous street, except for certain spaces here and there, where people could go to escape being run over by the traffic. Only from these could the river be seen. This was for very many years the only bridge.

It is an odd fact that the fashionable quarter has always moved westward. In Thames Street to-day, the noise of ponderous vans and the hoarse shouts of the draymen echo in the narrow street as in a ravine. Yet this was once the stronghold of the aristocracy. At Billingsgate, now the fish-market, lived the earls of Arundel; near by in the (present) Herald's College dwelt the proud earl of Derby. Where Blackfriars Station stands was Baynard's Castle, many times a royal palace. Hence knights went riding up Knightrider Street.

We pass on to the Strand, now a great business thoroughfare, with shops and the overflow of newspaper offices from Fleet Street, with theatres and hotels, and two dignified churches, St. Mary-le-Strand and St. Clement Danes. Here we shall find Somerset House, built on the site of the palace erected by the proud Protector Somerset in 1549-52. It is now the General Register Office for the nation, and the Board of Inland Revenue.

York, Durham, Exeter and Northumberland Houses all had here their gardens

UNDER THE TREES OF ROTTEN ROW, HYDE PARK'S RIDING TRACK

In west London, two great parks are separated only by a low fence. They are Kensington Gardens, the playground of London children, and Hyde Park. Hyde Park is crossed by many carriage drives and wide pathways. There is also here the famous Rotten Row. Its curious name perhaps comes from the French "Route du Roi"—the King's Way.

sloping to the river, and "stairs to take water at." With Charing Cross, technical centre of Greater London, we come into a new atmosphere. Around Whitehall are the Government offices, with the Foreign, Colonial, India and Home offices grouped around one quadrangle. Off Whitehall is Downing Street, in which is the queer, unpretentious home of the Prime Ministers.

### *Vast Storehouse of Treasures*

North of Trafalgar Square, with its towering Nelson Column, its bronze lions and playing fountains, is the National Gallery. Close by is St. Martin's Church, so reminiscently named St.-Martin's-in-the-Fields. Farther east, north of the Strand, we find Covent Garden, with its fruit and vegetable and flower market, busy in the early morning while most of us sleep. There is an idea of moving the market northward where it would have more room. The great markets at Smithfield and Billingsgate seem to do well enough away from the centre.

Farther north is the British Museum, a vast storehouse of treasures. The departments of art and science are at South Kensington, but the Museum, with its immense pillared portico, stands as an emblem of true learning. Buckingham Palace, west of Charing Cross, looks out upon the fine memorial to Queen Victoria, and the long vista ending in the Admiralty Arch.

The parks are a great feature in London life. St. James' Park and the Green Park lie outside Buckingham Palace. Hyde Park and Kensington Gardens are also side by side, and can show their palace, too, in Kensington Palace where Queen Victoria was born and brought up. With these takes rank Regent's Park, about two-thirds the size of both together.

### *Playgrounds and Pleasaunces*

Across the river is Battersea Park, truly democratic, forming the playing fields of hundreds of children. There are also Brockwell and Dulwich and Southwark parks. Farther out westward are Kew and Richmond. Kew is like the private garden of a great nobleman, and Richmond, with its coverts and its herds of deer, its long sweeps of undulating green and its glimpses of blue water, is unsurpassed in its wildness and beauty by any public land so near to a great city. In the northeast is Victoria Park; there are open spaces at Stoke Newington and Finsbury, and the heights of Hampstead are a playground known to thousands.

From Hyde Park Corner begins the fashionable residential district of the London of to-day, extending far beyond Chelsea and into Kensington and northward to Bayswater.

### *The Londoner at Home*

The real Londoners, however, are those who live in the city or its inner suburbs all the year round, with a brief holiday in the summer. The crowds which throng the Oval and Lord's at the great county cricket matches are mainly composed of them. They go to see the football matches at Twickenham or Stamford Bridge in their countless thousands. They throng Hampstead Heath on a Bank Holiday, and cram the river steamers to the utmost limit of capacity. On a week-day they struggle for places in crowded omnibuses or Tube trains. They know and love their London. They see the King in his glass coach and royal robes going to open Parliament. They are at the Law Courts when the Lord Chief Justice strides across in full-bottomed wig and robes. How they manage to do it no one knows, for they are a sober, working crowd. But not a street scene is staged in London, from the holding-up of a car to the Lord Mayor's Show, at which crowds of these Londoners do not manage to be present. Besides these rarer sights, they enjoy the sights on view every day, loitering by the magnificent displays in the great shop windows of Oxford or Regent streets; they throng the cheaper seats of theatres and music halls; they crowd into the picture palaces—some lordly buildings, others but gaudy halls—which have sprung up in almost every main street of Central London and its suburbs.

# LAND OF THE CYMRY

## *A Look at Wales and the Welsh*

**The people known to the English as the Welsh call themselves Cymry, and they are descended from one of the main groups of the Celtic race that inhabited Britain. The Welsh language has been spoken in Great Britain for more than two thousand years, and seven-tenths of the people of Wales speak Welsh. Some of them are unable to understand English. Wales is a very beautiful country, and only in Glamorgan and a small part of Carmarthen shall we find the countryside disfigured by mines, factories and smelting works. The Principality is still quite distinct from England, and in certain districts an Englishman may easily imagine himself in a foreign land.**

IN the ancient town of Carnarvon on a certain day more than six centuries ago, according to the accepted story, a new-born baby was placed on a shield and presented by his father, King Edward I, to the assembled Welsh chieftains. The two grandsons of Llewelyn the Great, the overlord of Wales, had recently been killed by the English, and in them had perished the last of the great Welsh princes. The chieftains demanded of the English conqueror a Welsh prince as his representative, and in reply to this demand Edward I presented them with this baby, as "a Prince who was born in Wales and could speak no English."

When that baby, the future Edward II, was nearly seventeen, he was created "Prince of Wales" by his father. Since then the eldest son of the English sovereign has been invested with the title of Prince of Wales. One month after his own coronation, King George V solemnly invested his oldest son, Edward, with this title, the ceremony, for the first time in history, taking place in Carnarvon Castle in a Welsh assembly. It was a time of great rejoicing, for the Welsh, though they differ very greatly from the people of England, are among the most loyal of the king's subjects.

This difference is due partly to ancestry and partly to the nature of the country, which has enabled the people to develop in their own way. The Welsh are usually spoken of as Celts, but there were people in Wales before the Celts. As, one after another, different tribes poured into Britain, they drove the older inhabitants ever westward. In the wild country of the west, and particularly in the mountain fastnesses of Wales, these remnants of a conquered people found a home.

One of the earliest races was that known as the "Iberian," a people of Southern Europe, dark-haired and small of stature. They used stone weapons, and it is probable that they built the stone circles that we may see on the hills of Wales.

Later, the Celts arrived, and of them there were two distinct types—the Goidels, big and rather fair, and, arriving centuries afterward, the smaller, darker Brythons. The latter settled chiefly in Wales, and from their tongue comes the Welsh language. Since then Wales has had many invaders—Romans, Anglo-Normans, Scandinavians and Irish—but the Welsh of to-day appear to be mainly a mixture of Iberian and Brython—a dark-haired race of medium stature, sturdy, independent and gifted.

They have their own language and literature and are very proud of their beautiful country, for Wales unites the romantic mountain scenery of Scotland with the delightful countryside of England. Snowdon is higher than any English mountain, and the Severn, the largest river in Britain, rises on the slopes of Plynlymmon.

Unfortunately, Welsh literature is not known in England as well as it deserves to be, for the simple reason that it is written in Welsh, which few English ever master. In Wales almost everyone can talk English as well as Welsh, though there are still a few out-of-the-way places where English is not understood.

The Welsh language looks peculiar to us in that it seems to have so many consonants and so few vowels, especially in place names. For example, Llanfairpwllgwyngyll, and Clwyd are perfectly good Welsh words; and there are many others as strange to those who know only English.

The Brythons used the word "ap," meaning "son of," in their names, and thus we get such Welsh names as "Pryce," which stands for "Ap-Rhys," son of Rhys; sometimes the "p" becomes a "b," which accounts for such names as "Bowen," son of Owen, and "Bevan," son of Evan. When Henry VIII was king he decreed that all Welshmen should take surnames. Each man took his father's name—thus Thomas ap Evan became Thomas Evans, which accounts for so many Welsh surnames being also Christian names.

The Welsh language is very soft and musical, and musical ability seems to be the birthright of the people. Many of them have beautiful voices. A Welsh village on a Sunday morning appears to be deserted, for everyone goes to church or chapel, and everyone sings there. In castle or cottage throughout the Principality we may hear voices raised in song, frequently to the haunting accompaniment of the harp.

Long before the time of Christ, the Welsh had their Druids, who were priests and teachers, and their bards, who were poets and minstrels. At their great national gatherings the two were always present. Druidism was suppressed by the Romans, but officials called Druids, and dressed like the Druids of old in flowing, white garments, preside over the bardic congress known as the Eisteddfod, which is held every year in some part of the country.

The bards are dressed in flowing robes at this festival, which lasts some days, and to it come the people in their thousands from all over Wales, from town and village and mountain farm, to take part in the various musical and literary competitions and to keep alive the national spirit. In bygone days every household of any importance had its own bard, whose songs

BRITISH INFORMATION SERVICES

**STRANGE PARTNERS—A FROWNING CASTLE AND A RAILROAD BRIDGE**

Conway Castle is a mile in circumference and is girdled with twenty-one round towers. The span belongs to the early days of railway-bridge building and is made of wrought iron.

STEEPLE HATS—ON A ROAD NEAR LLANBERIS, NORTH WALES

The quaint national costume is worn only on fete days, and these girls seem to be enjoying the occasion. Llanberis is a little highland town on Padarn Lake, not far from Mount Snowdon.

PHOTOS, UNDERWOOD & UNDERWOOD

BIRD'S-EYE VIEW OF LLANDUDNO, RESORT ON COLWYN BAY

Its situation on a peninsula, sheltered by headlands, gives Llandudno many fine beaches. Another attraction for visitors is this pier, a half mile long. A side-wheeler is docked at the end.

BRITISH INFORMATION SERVICES

**HISTORIC CASTLE OF THE "MEN OF HARLECH" IN MERIONETH**

Dating from the reign of Edward I, Harlech Castle is a fine example of thirteenth-century fortification. Its defense against the Yorkist siege in 1468 inspired the Welsh national song.

UNDERWOOD & UNDERWOOD

**TALYLLYN LAKE AT THE FOOT OF CADER IDRIS MOUNTAINS**

Reflecting the peaceful and picturesque character of the Welsh countryside is Lake Talyllyn. It lies just east of the quaint little village of Talyllyn, an idyllic vacation spot in Merioneth.

BRITISH INFORMATION SERVICES

CARNARVON CASTLE PROVIDES THE BACKDROP FOR AN EISTEDDFOD

The eisteddfod is a festival of music and poetry at which the costume of the ancient Druids is worn. They originated the custom; and the musical Welsh people revived it in the 1800's.

and chants served to while away many a long winter evening.

The March of the Men of Harlech was the song used to incite the chiefs to defend Harlech Castle when the Lancastrian Queen Margaret of Anjou, with her young son, took refuge there from the Yorkists after the battle of Northampton. Harlech is one of the six great castles that Edward I built to keep the newly conquered land in order. It is necessary to inspect the massive castle at Carnarvon in order to realize what tremendously strong places these fortresses were; it seems impossible they could ever be stormed. One part of Carnarvon Castle can only be entered by people in single file, and there is a secret way of escape to the waterside.

### *Flowers on Old Walls*

Conway, on the coast farther east, is another of these castles. The town of Conway, which is full of charming houses, is shaped like a harp. It is possible to walk round the city walls, where in summer velvety antirrhinums, of every shade of yellow, red and pink, grow wild in the cracks and crannies, and look out over the blue sea to the Great Orme's Head jutting out northward. Pearl fisheries have been in existence at Conway from the days of the Romans.

Away to the west lies the beautiful island of Anglesey, or Mona. This was the last stronghold in which the Druids held out against the Romans. The Romans built camps and roads, and many Roman coins and ornaments have been dug up in various parts. Copper is found near Amlwch. It is often called affectionately "the mother of Wales," for so fertile is its soil that it used to be said that the island could produce enough corn to provide food for the whole country.

Formerly herds of goats roamed wild in the higher pastures of the Welsh mountains, but these have almost entirely disappeared and have given place to flocks of little, black-faced sheep whose flesh provides the celebrated Welsh mutton. Their wool supplies one of the big industries of Wales and is either knitted by the housewives—for in Wales everyone knits—or is sent to the factories to be made into the well-known "Welsh flannel." It is said that this flannel industry was introduced by Flemish weavers who settled in Norman times in south Pembroke, and whose descendants form a distinct colony and speak not Welsh, but English.

### *Attractive Thatched Cottages*

Very pleasing are the little thatched cottages, usually of one story and either white or pink in color, which nestle in the green valleys or in sheltered spots on the hillsides. Often we may see stacks of coal-dust near by, for the thrifty Welsh cottager often makes her own fuel, of coal-dust mixed with clay. The farmhouses, too, with their grandfather clocks and their polished candlesticks gleaming in the bright light of the fire, make a comfortable home when the long day's work is done.

Unfortunately, the national costume is seldom worn except in isolated places or on gala occasions, though the cockle-women of Penclawdd wear it, except for the tall steeple hat, when they bring their cockles to Swansea market. The Welsh hat was a fashion that came originally from England.

Like the national costume, many of the quaint customs of Wales are either passing, or have already passed, away. Formerly it was customary in some districts to "bid" guests to come to a wedding and to bring presents with them. Sometimes a friend of the young couple, who would be known as the "bidder," took charge of this part of the business and delivered the "bidding" by word of mouth to the desired guests. But the bidder has now passed away.

### *Old Customs Dying Out*

So also has the custom by which, on the day of a funeral, the poor of the neighborhood assembled to receive food, which, as the procession left the house, was passed to them over the coffin by the women of the family. Not even in Cardiganshire, where old customs have lingered longest, are such ceremonies still to be witnessed; but it is still the custom in

BIS

**A MODERN TOOL IN THE SLATE QUARRIES OF WALES**

Beneath the shadow of Mount Snowdon, North Wales, are the biggest slate quarries in the world. The slate is shipped to all parts of the British Commonwealth. Here a hole is being drilled in the rock face of a quarry for blasting. The process requires considerable skill, as the slate must be loosened only and not shattered to powder.

**WALES IS A LAND OF GREEN HILLS AND VALLEYS**

The mountainous Welsh landscape, seen from the lofty tip of Mt. Snowdon, the highest mountain in England and Wales, is checkered with sunlight and shadow. Snowdon, in northwestern Wales, has five peaks; the high st one towers some 3,560 feet into the sky. It can be reached by way of a mountain railway from the village of Llanberis, near the foot of Snowdon.

PHOTOS, BRITISH TRAVEL ASSOCIATION

**THE RIVER DEE SPARKLES THROUGH THE COUNTRYSIDE**

The Dee takes its melodious way through the town of Llangollen in Denbighshire County in northern Wales. This little holiday town is noted for its fine salmon fishing. The river, which rises in Bala Lake in North Wales, crosses into western England and flows through Chester, emptying into the Irish Sea. For some distance the river forms the boundary line of Wales.

BRITISH INFORMATION SERVICES

**COCKLES TAKE MUSCLES, AS THE HARDY WELSH WOMEN PROVE**

Collecting cockles is women's work in Wales, and very arduous work it is. Every day in the year, women spend from five to six hours at low tide collecting the mollusks in Carmarthen Bay. They must take great care not to be cut off from the mainland by the incoming tide. The women above are sifting the cockles from their shells which is easy after they are boiled.

some parts of the country for the coffin to be borne by relays of bearers, who sing hymns as they march.

Another custom which may still be observed, although it has begun to die out, is the holding of a service known as "Plygain." This is a carol service which takes place on Christmas morning, sometimes as early as five o'clock.

Like most mountainous countries, Wales has its share of minerals. Slate is quarried under the shadow of Snowdon, and gold is found in small quantities; it has sometimes been used to make the wedding rings of royal princesses. Copper also is mined; and visitors to Wales cannot fail to notice that some cottages have copper doorsills.

The most important mineral of Wales is coal; the extreme south of the country is virtually one vast coalfield. Some of the valleys in Glamorganshire are occupied by strings of mining villages, for the coal industry of South Wales and Monmouthshire employs more than a hundred thousand men in peak periods.

**A HUMPED, EIGHTEENTH-CENTURY BRIDGE IN PONTYPRIDD**

Though a modern bridge for wheeled traffic has been built beside it, the old bridge of steps is cherished because it gave the town its present name. "Pont" means bridge. Pontypridd is eleven miles north of Cardiff; and the River Taff, which flows beneath these bridges, is a branch of the Severn River which divides Wales from England on the south.

Both photos, British Information Services

**ON THE PROMENADE AT ABERYSTWYTH, ON CARDIGAN BAY**

Townspeople and visitors bask in the sun by the sparkling bay that scoops out the west coast of Wales. Aberystwyth is a favorite seaside resort of the Welsh people, and it is also the educational center of the country. On the right are the buildings of one of the four colleges of the University of Wales; and near by is the National Library of Wales.

The scenery of South Wales, except that of the Gower coast, is less imposing than that of North Wales, but here lies the real wealth of the Principality, and Cardiff might well be termed the capital of Wales. In this city are the University, the National Museum of Wales and other institutions which make it the virtual heart of this wonderful land, which is, as yet, without a capital, though there are several aspirants to this honor.

### *The Importance of Coal*

It is coal that has made Cardiff the biggest and most important town and port in Wales. As far back as Edward II's time it was a shipping and trading town, but today the ships go out laden with coal and with the produce of those factories that the presence of much coal has made possible. Steel, iron, tin, copper, lead and zinc are all worked in this section.

In addition to its many factories, Cardiff, like Merthyr Tydfil, Aberdare, Swansea and many more towns of South Wales, has numerous smelting works. Over some of these industrial towns there hangs always a dense cloud of smoke from the furnaces. A famous traveler, coming by night to a part of this district during the middle of the last century, noticed what appeared to be glowing masses of hot lava on the hillsides. What he saw was really immense quantities of dross—waste from the smelting works—thrown out in disfiguring masses on to this naturally beautiful countryside.

Such drawbacks as these must be accepted for the sake of the prosperity that industrial life brings. Until comparatively recent times the poor, especially those of the countryside, were very poor. Less than a hundred years ago a small farmer might have been found dining on half a salt herring, some potatoes and buttermilk, and a schoolmaster reported that the food which the children brought to school for their midday meal usually consisted of barley bread, buttermilk and a red herring which was shared between two or three of them. Living thus on poor fare and enduring the hard winters of a mountainous country are, perhaps, the reasons why the Welsh developed into such an industrious and hardy people.

For several years before World War II broke out, conditions in the coal industry were bad. But this changed as coal became so vital in the manufacture of war materials. After the war, the newly elected Labor Government of Britain brought about the nationalization of coal and carried on a vigorous campaign for greater efficiency and higher production in the mines. Farming, too, improved in step with industry as scientific methods increased the yield of the land.

In addition to the program of nationalization, the Government adopted its elaborate "cradle to grave" social security system. It includes insurance against unemployment, illness and other hazards of life, pensions for the aged and disabled, and free medical and dental care.

Improvements in education moved ahead with the increase of security in Wales. Scholarships to deserving students, such as former service men and women, added to college and university enrollments. Adult education—the expenses shared by government and industry—also helped brighten the outlook for Wales and all Britain.

### *The Patron Saint of Wales*

The patron saint of Wales is St. David and the national emblem is the leek. The name "Welsh" is supposed to come from an old Anglo-Saxon word "Waelisc," meaning "foreign," and is the name the Saxons gave to the older inhabitants of Britain as they drove them back to the mountains of the west. In bygone days Wales and the Welsh suffered much from the newcomers, but history shows how they were compensated for the way in which Edward I tricked the Welsh by giving them an English baby for their prince, by the fact that the Welsh, two centuries later, gave England a Welsh king.

The Welsh are proud of their customs, their history and their misty land. Though they have sometimes resented English rule, they do not forget that Welsh blood mingles with English in the veins of British kings. The grandfather of Henry VII

BRITISH TRAVEL ASSOCIATION

**MAKING HAY WHILE THE SUN SHINES**

Harvest time has come to the peaceful farmlands of Merionethshire, one of the twelve counties of Wales, situated in the northern part of the country. Farming is not one of the major occupations in Wales, for steep slopes make the countryside more suitable for dairying and the raising of livestock. There is, however, some thin but arable soil in the valleys.

was Owen Tudor, a wealthy Welsh country man. Henry was the father of Henry VIII, and of Margaret, the wife of James IV of Scotland. From her are descended the Stuart kings, and the present royal house of Great Britain. So you see the Welsh have given a whole line of kings to their larger neighbors.

---

## *WALES: FACTS AND FIGURES*

*THE COUNTRY*

Forms a peninsula on the west coast of England. It is bounded on the east by England, on the south by the Bristol Channel, on the west by St. George's Channel and on the north by the Irish Sea. The total area, comprising 12 counties is 7,466 square miles and the population is 2,172,339.

*GOVERNMENT*

For purposes of government Wales is associated with England, and is subject in local administration to similar conditions. There are separate organizations to deal with health and education. There are 12 counties and 3 county boroughs.

*COMMERCE AND INDUSTRIES*

Commercial and industrial activity is located chiefly in South Wales and the district around Wrexham. The shipping industry of Cardiff and Swansea and the anthracite coal deposits in South Wales are the chief sources of wealth. Slate quarries are numerous. Other minerals include limestone, iron, copper, tin and lead. A large portion of Wales is pasture and grazing land. Sheep are by far the most numerous of the livestock, which is among the finest in the world.

*COMMUNICATIONS*

Under the Railways Act of 1921, the important docks at Cardiff, Barry, Port Talbot and Penarth and the railway companies associated with them were incorporated with the Great Western Railway. Both the docks and railway were nationalized under the Transport Act of 1947.

*RELIGION AND EDUCATION*

The Church of England in Wales and Monmouthshire were disestablished in 1920 under the Welsh Church Acts of 1914 and 1919, and Wales was created a separate Archbishopric Education is compulsory between the ages of 5 and 15 years. In 1903 the University of Wales was founded. It has 4 colleges (at Cardiff, Aberystwyth, Bangor and Swansea).

*CHIEF TOWNS*

Cardiff, population, 243,627; Swansea, 160,-832; Rhondda, 111,357; Merthyr Tydfil, 61,093 (preliminary figures, 1951 census).

# BONNIE SCOTLAND

## *Rich Lowlands and Romantic Highlands*

Scotland contains some of the finest scenery in the British Isles. The heather hills of the north are more beautiful in their ever-changing colors than any other mountain scenery in Europe, though lacking the austere grandeur of the Alps. The wild beauty of the Highlands forms a striking contrast to the peaceful charm of quiet lakes and Lowland valleys. The English Lake District can vie with parts of Scotland, but Loch Lomond is unique and the landscape of the famous Trossachs is unsurpassed. The beauty of Scottish scenery is only equaled by the ugliness of many of the small towns and villages; but, in spite of smoky skies, Glasgow is a splendid city, and Edinburgh one of the most delightful in the British Isles.

SCOTLAND is famous for its scenery, its ships and the independent spirit of its people. It is today a part of Great Britain, but once it was a separate kingdom and very hostile to England, and still retains some distinctive characteristics. Many tourists come to enjoy the varied charm of its mountains, glens, lakes, rivers, moors and valleys. The picturesque dress and warlike customs of the Highland clans have given the northern section an atmosphere of romance, while the Lowlanders combine sturdy thrift with a sharp sense of humor. The Scots are very industrious; they have made the valley of the Clyde famous as a great shipbuilding center, while Scottish homespun tweeds and plaids are known the world over for their durability and beauty. The fisheries of Scotland help to supply the markets of Great Britain, and great quantities of cured fish are exported. Yet for years the country was poor, and hampered by lack of resources. The tenacity, careful ability and hardworking independence of Scotsmen have developed a land where natural advantages are less plentiful than scenic beauty.

Who are the Scots? That is a question which has not been completely answered. In the sixth century invaders from Ireland seized the western Highlands. They were called Scots, and from them the land took its name, but the greater part of the Highlands was already occupied by the Picts, large-boned, red-haired barbarians about whose origin authorities disagree. In the south were yellow-haired Angles, sprung from the invaders of England, and small dark-skinned Welshmen. Eventually these four peoples merged together and were all called Scots, but the fusion required centuries.

A physical map of Scotland shows the country divided into three sections. Draw a slanting line from Aberdeen in the northeast to the Firth of Clyde on the west, and this will roughly mark off the northern Highlands. Southward toward the English border are the rolling moors or Uplands. Between them and the Highland hills lie the Lowlands, the one fertile stretch of country, for which all the barbaric tribes fought. The Romans had tried to add this rich, low-lying territory to their province of Britain. They built two walls, one of turf and earth across the Lowlands from Firth of Clyde to Firth of Forth, and the other, a splendid piece of engineering, from Solway to Wallsend. When they could not hold the northern rampart, they retreated to the Border wall and from it defended Britain against the raids of the northern barbarians. Between the two walls lay the debatable ground to which, for centuries after the Romans left, Scots and English laid claim.

The kings of England tried time after time to conquer the Scots, and there were years of warfare during which Sir William Wallace, King Robert Bruce, the Douglases and others strove to make and keep Scotland independent. Still there was constant trouble on the Border, until the two kingdoms were joined under one king, James VI of Scotland, who became

MC LEISH

**LOCH LOMOND,** its placid surface starred with green islands, is encircled by wild, rugged country and lofty mountains. At one time it would not have been safe for a farmer to allow his black-faced sheep to graze on this sunny hillside near Luss, since round the shores of the loch and on some of its islands lived unruly Highland chieftains and their robber followers. Nowadays, however, all that is changed, and pleasure boats cruise on the clear waters of Loch Lomond and bring crowds of tourists to the hotels and inns throughout the district.

INGLIS

**THE PIPER** can always stir the Scottish heart whether he plays a battle song, a dance tune, a lament for the dead or a love song. His kilt, the plaid over his shoulder and the ribbons on his bagpipes are all of the tartan distinguishing his clan or regiment. For every-day wear he may have a different but equally distinctive tartan.

McLeish

**MIST-CROWNED BEN VENUE MIRRORED IN LOVELY LOCH ACHRAY**

All the lochs of the Trossachs are beautiful, but none can afford a more exquisite picture than this view of Loch Achray, with its calm, silver water and dark, tree-grown island. Beyond it looms the huge, irregular, rocky shape of Ben Venue, which is almost 2,400 feet high, with the mists of early morning writhing about the rugged crags and veiling its summit.

BRITISH INFORMATION SERVICES

BRITISH TRAVEL ASSOCIATION

SCOTTISH DANCERS PROUDLY SHOW THEIR SKILL

The sword dance is a traditional dance of the Scottish Highlander and is performed to the music of the bagpipe. The dancers must possess the greatest skill and agility, for, as they perform the various movements of the dance, they must not allow their feet to touch the crossed swords or scabbards around which they dance. Each dancer wears the tartan of his clan.

James I of England. The son of the Scottish Queen, Mary Stuart, he was a descendant of Henry VII of England. On the death of Queen Elizabeth, he became king of England, after he had been king of Scotland for many years. It was not until the eighteenth century, however, that the two kingdoms were really made one by the Act of Union. Even after that the fierce loyalty of the Scots to the family of the Stuart kings caused terrible bloodshed, for they supported first James, the Old Pretender, and later, Bonnie Prince Charlie, both of whom tried to recover the throne of their ancestors.

The beauty of Scotland lies in its mountains and forests, its wide moors and narrow lakes, the largest of which is Loch Lomond, twenty-two miles in length. It has been said of northwestern Scotland that the "sea is all islands and the land all lakes," and a map proves the truth of this. The myriad islands off the coast are barren and rocky, but often picturesquely beautiful. Hundreds of people visit Arran for its mountains, Mull for its precipitous cliffs and Skye for its grand scenery. Some go farther out to that great chain of islands, the Outer Hebrides, which lie in the Atlantic like a huge kite with a tail to it, across the rough channel called the Minch.

One island only three miles and a half long claims attention more than all the rest. This is Iona, where Scottish Christianity was born. The great apostle Columba came here from Ireland and made Iona his home. Thence he wandered far and wide over the country to bring the light of the Gospel to the scattered people, who, in those long-ago days were as yet quite wild and barbarous.

NICHOLLS

**THE PURPLE HEATHER** that covers the hillside with its wealth of blossom grows thickly on the roadsides, the moors and mountains of Scotland, making even the most barren parts of the country beautiful. This country girl hopes to find a sprig of pure white heather, to which superstition attributes the power of bringing good fortune to the finder

**IN THE TROSSACHS** are many wooded glens where all is peaceful in the leafy shade. Ben Venue's barren slopes enhance by contrast the rich loveliness of the glen. The Trossachs district, between Loch Katrine and Loch Achray, is one of the most beautiful in Scotland, and is famous as the scene of Sir Walter Scott's poem, The Lady of the Lake.

### *Clansmen of the Hills*

The Highlands remained wild and uncivilized longer than any other part of Scotland. The Highlanders lived in tribes, or clans; they spoke only Gaelic, and were different in many ways from the English-speaking Lowlanders. Every clansman was intensely loyal to his chieftain, and ready at a moment's notice to fight for him against anyone. Now that roads and railways make the Highlands accessible, the old dress and customs have largely disappeared. Yet the traditional kilt—a skirt of knee length worn in place of trousers or breeches by the men of Scotland—remains as part of the uniform of various Scottish regiments. The distinctive, colorful tartan plaids originated as marks of Scotland's many clans in the sixteenth or seventeenth century.

Let us visit a Highland home far back in the hills, or on one of the islands. We shall find it built either of irregular stones or of mud smeared over and whitewashed. It will be thatched, and the walls will be very thick, so that the narrow deep-set windows give little light. These low cottages or shielings are all much on the same pattern, consisting as a rule of two rooms. There is usually a great inglenook like a cavern, where a peat fire is smoldering with a huge iron caldron swinging above it on a chain.

### *Where English Is a Foreign Tongue*

The old lady sitting by her spinning-wheel will wear a frilled cap surrounding her brown, wrinkled face, and she will have a shawl of good homespun across her shoulders, while her skirts will be large and very full. The wool that she is constantly spinning may be used to make knitted garments, or it may be woven into the stout cloths known as tweeds. Scottish tweeds wear practically forever and smell always of peat, amid the smoke of which the wool was spun and carded.

Some of the older people in the Highlands speak nothing but Gaelic, so that although the mistress of the house may say politely "Have you the Gaelic?" she will probably have to wait until the grandchildren come home from school to interpret for her. They speak English very correctly and slowly, like a foreign language carefully learned, which indeed it is.

### *What the Crofter Has to Eat*

Peasants living in these cottages are called "crofters," because they try to get a living from the poor soil by cultivating a small croft or plot of land. Oatmeal, or porridge, used to be the staple fare of Scotland. It is still very important, as white bread is a luxury to those who live in the wild parts. But whereas the necessities of life used to be "peat and porridge," they are now, in many sections, "coal and bacon." Well-to-do people eat a variety of fish, meats and vegetables. The fare of the poorest peasants includes porridge, brose, potatoes, turnips, oatcakes, barley scones, wheaten flour scones, sowans, butter and cheese. Scones are delicious wedge-shaped cakes baked on a griddle. Sowans is made from water in which husks of oats have been soaked; when poured off and boiled, it thickens, as some floury matter has been soaked out from the husks. An Englishman who once saw this done came home to tell of a miracle: "The woman poured some dirty water into a pan and boiled it, and it became a delicious pudding." Brose is made by pouring hot water on raw oatmeal. The crofters lead a hard life, and many of them have emigrated. Others make a living by acting as gamekeepers, or as guides to tourists. Hotels flourish throughout the Highlands, and hunters flock north every season to shoot deer and grouse and to fish for salmon.

But once a year colorful gatherings at Braemar, at Oban or Aboyne renew the spirit of the old days. Then every clansman appears in his tartan, kilt and bonnet. Athletic contests such as shot-putting are held, dancers show their skill in the Highland fling or sword-dance, and the clans march past to the tune of the pipes. Those unaccustomed to the bagpipes are at first startled by the curious skirling wail they produce. The music is fierce and plaintive, like that of no other

BRITISH INFORMATION SERVICES

**THE "OLD LOOK" IN A SCOTTISH HAMLET**

The ancient village of Culcross in Fifeshire, on the eastern coast of Scotland, still wears its centuries-old look. Mercat Cross, on the left, was erected in 1588; and the tall, thin building on the right—"The Study"—was built in the early seventeenth century. Between these two, in the distance, can be seen the quaint tower of the Tollbooth, built in 1626.

instrument, and whatever else a Scotsman may forget about his native land, the sound of the pipes will take his mind back to the days of his childhood.

In the heart of the Highlands, up near the Moray Firth, is Inverness. Here are sold some of the fine homespun tweeds and woolens. The country around is bleak, good for little besides grazing ground and game preserves. On Culloden Moor above the town Bonnie Prince Charlie was finally defeated in his attempt to regain the British crown. For weeks afterward he wandered through the wild northern country, sheltered by the loyal Highlanders, until he managed to escape to France. The whole Highland district is cut in two by the Caledonian Canal, which joins three long narrow lochs between Inverness and the west coast. It is sixty miles long and saves fishing vessels a four-hundred-mile journey around the dangerous northern coast. At its western end rises Ben Nevis, the highest mountain in the British Isles. Its hummocky crest is 4,406 feet above Loch Linnhe. From here the Grampian Mountains stretch away to the east, clear across the country. When the heather is in bloom even the barren hills become lovely. But the most famous beauty spot in the Highlands is the Trossachs country, where three beautiful lakes, Loch Katrine, Loch Achray and Loch Vennachar, are joined together by a stream. Between the first two lies a wooded glen called the Trossachs, with the bare mountain of Ben Venue towering above. This region is visited not only for its scenery but because it is the scene of Sir Walter Scott's famous poem, The Lady of the Lake.

Aberdeen, standing on the great eastern shoulder of Scotland, is a centre of the fishing industry. It has an ancient cathedral and is built almost entirely of gray granite, quarried in the neighborhood. In the herring season, which is in early summer, hundreds of girls come to the town

NIMMO

**A COTTAGE HOME** in Scotland is usually remarkable for its comfort and neatness. The hard-working, thrifty countryfolk can afford to have good furniture and to keep a big fire burning. Many, like this family of Loch Leven-side in Argyllshire, have spinning-wheels and chairs that have been handed down from generation to generation. The Scottish peasantry has long been known as the best educated in the world; we may find, in a remote country village, a ploughboy studying to enter the ministry, or a laborer who reads Latin.

**IN PEEBLESHIRE** the steep valley-sides, watered by the many small tributaries of the Tweed, are planted with oats, rye and barley although the stony ground makes hard ploughing. The rolling, grass-covered hills of this Lowland county afford good grazing for sheep.

REID

**HIGHLAND CATTLE**, which roam among the western mountains, in a half-wild condition, are akin to the wild oxen that used to live in Scotland long ago. They are hardy, fierce-looking little creatures with shaggy red hair, and are much smaller than ordinary bulls and cows.

from inland and the north, to gut and salt the herring. The work is hard and anyone not used to it would bungle it sadly; but the same girls, with shawls thrown over their heads and rough clogs for footwear, go from port to port down the coast, year by year, and work with lightning speed. The Aberdeen fish market is a sight worth seeing when boats come in from Iceland and the North Sea to land a big catch of halibut or cod on the stone quays. Fishing is the greatest single industry of the Highland coast, where soil and pasturage are poor. Sheep, however, can often graze where crops will not grow, and the black-faced sheep of the Highlands are very hardy. There is also a special breed of Highland cattle in the west. They are sturdy animals, able to thrive on scant grazing. Aberdeenshire has its polled Angus cattle which are bred for beef and so do not furnish as much milk as the Ayrshire dairy breed.

The importance of stock-raising is apparent when we realize that only one-sixth of Scotland's land surface is arable. The ground which can be cultivated yields a variety of crops: oats, barley, wheat, rye, potatoes, turnips, beans and peas. The majority of the farms are small, cov-

COMBINE

**GIRLS PACKING FISH FOR EXPORT AT A HIGHLAND COASTAL TOWN**

At Buckie, as well as at other Scottish towns along the North Sea coast, girls and women are employed to pack a large share of the fine catches for shipment to other countries of the world. With the skill that comes from long practice, they split, clean and sort the fish. These are then covered with salt, in order to preserve them, and packed into barrels.

ering less than fifty acres. Sheep farms, of course, require more room. There are also great estates, especially in the Highlands. Many of the small farmers, throughout the country, are tenants working soil belonging to large landowners. The farmhouses are usually white, and look very attractive with the green of the fields around them.

### *Lowland Cottage Homes*

Lowland villages are likely to be drab; some are picturesque. The houses are often whitewashed, but are sometimes of slaty-looking stones. The cottages stand right on the edge of the roadway and usually there is room for a tuft of sweet william, a few marigolds or some wallflower among the stones by the door.

The Southern Uplands have many sheep, grown for their wool; whereas the Highland sheep are bred for mutton. The shepherds who tend the sheep in the famous borderland on the green hills of Cheviot are a hardy, upright set of men. They walk miles every day in charge of their flocks, with their plaids thrown across one shoulder. The plaid is a long woolen wrap of a checked or dark colored design. If the wearer is caught by wild weather it serves as a cloak, or may be used as a blanket at night. With the plaid is worn the bonnet. In winter these shepherds have little to do but go back and forth over the track between the cottage and the sheep pens, to feed and tend the flock.

### *Sheep-dogs of the Cheviots*

They do not live entirely alone in the winter months, as they always have the companionship of a dog, and a more loyal, intelligent race of dogs than the Scotch collies does not exist. They understand what their masters want, without a word being spoken. One of the chief diversions at fairs is the sheep-dog trials, when a collie will unerringly pick out a certain number of sheep from a flock and either pen them, or run them up as directed.

In some of the sheep-rearing districts the wise collie dogs come to church with their masters and slink under the pews, lying as still as mice until the end of the service. The churches are very simple, bare and unadorned. The Scots bring their religion into their daily lives, and to many people who live in remote parts the long walk to the "kirk," as they call the church, is the chief pleasure of the week. They will listen to sermons of a length that would make most congregations fidget. They have a deep interest in religious matters, and in years past their ancestors endured much persecution for the sake of their beliefs.

### *A Sturdy Independent Folk*

Robert Burns, the great Scottish poet, has drawn the character of his people better than anyone else. He shows us God-fearing, shrewd, hard-working folk, economical and frugal and most independent. The Scots have often been called mean, but in reality there are no people more generous. They will give a wayfarer food, or shelter a wandering stranger, with the greatest courtesy and kindness. But they are not extravagant in their expressions of joy or affection, and many have been called "dour" merely because they are shy and reserved.

Scottish people are exceedingly intellectual. They love learning for its own sake, and even the farm laborers are often able to discuss books and philosophy. Children frequently walk many miles to get to school, and carry with them a "piece" for the day. A "piece" is a piece of bread and butter. A "jam piece" is a treat. Young men whose parents could not afford to send them to the university used to work in the fields all the summer to earn enough to keep them frugally through the winter session. Now many students receive aid from a fund which Andrew Carnegie gave to the universities in 1901. Women may attend as freely as men.

Edinburgh, Glasgow, Aberdeen and St. Andrews are the university towns of Scotland. St. Andrews is very old; its university was founded over five hundred years ago. The city is also known for its splendid golf links, which attract many visitors. Golf has been played in Scot-

MC LEISH

**GLASGOW UNIVERSITY** has a beautiful situation on a tree-covered hill overlooking the River Kelvin. Although the handsome buildings are modern, the University, founded in 1451, is the second oldest in Scotland. Many distinguished Scotsmen, such as Thomas Campbell, the poet, and Lord Kelvin, the great scientist, have been connected with it.

MC LEISH

**THE MOUND,** on which is the long, flat building of the National Art Gallery of Scotland, is a raised causeway running across the valley that divides the old and new towns of Edinburgh. From the Scott Monument, with its gargoyles and statues, we have here a fine view across the Mound to the strong old castle of Edinburgh, perched high on its steep rock.

Reid

SHEPHERD CARRYING A WEAKLING OF HIS FLOCK TO SHELTER

Sheep-rearing is an important industry in all the bleak, upland districts of Scotland, since the flocks thrive on land that is unsuitable for cultivation. This man is bringing home in his plaid a sick lamb which needs warm milk and special care. The collie dogs are the shepherd's inevitable companions; without their intelligent help many sheep would be lost land for several centuries, and is truly the national game.

The University of Edinburgh is an important educational centre. Its position in the capital of Scotland gives it prominence, and it has the right to send one member to the British Parliament. This privilege it shares with St. Andrews. The University's medical school has long had a high reputation; Charles Darwin studied there, and the great Lord Lister was for seventeen years professor of surgery. Lister's research on infection in wounds made safe operations possible.

Edinburgh is much the finest city in Scotland. It has a beautiful situation on the Firth of Forth. Trains coming in from Perth or Dundee cross the Forth on the great steel cantilever bridge which is over a mile long and stands one hundred and fifty feet above the water. The trains come into the heart of the city. Here Princes Street with its magnificent shops lies open on one side to gardens, where, among the flower-beds, rise statues of eminent men. The pinnacle of the Scott Monument towers over the greatest figure of all, that of Sir Walter Scott. Midway is the Mound, a low causeway on which stands the handsome Art Gallery. From the gardens we can look across to what is called the Old Town and see the Castle at the top of a long ridge of rock which slopes down to the Palace of Holyrood.

### *Where History Was Made*

Almost the whole of Scottish history could be written from the annals of the Castle and the Palace. Mary Queen of Scots lived at Holyrood during part of her unhappy career, and it was the scene of more than one tragic event. Other historic buildings are St. Giles' Cathedral, the Tolbooth prison and the house of John Knox. Knox was the great Scottish religious reformer; he used to preach fiery sermons from his window to crowds gathered in the street beneath. The Canongate is not a gate at all, but the most celebrated street in the Old Town. Edinburgh is a queer mixture of wealth and poverty, grandeur and misery. On the one side are fine shops, on the other tenement-houses called "lands," which used to be the fine houses of the rich.

There are factories as well. The manufacture of books and fine paper is perhaps the most important industry. Edinburgh printers and publishers have had a high reputation ever since the early days of printing. They turn out very fine work, and one specialty is the production of low-priced books.

### *World-Famous Shipyards*

The true industrial center of Scotland, however, is Glasgow. It is the second city in Great Britain, with a population of over one million; this represents about one-fifth of the people of Scotland. Glasgow owes much of its prosperity to the coal found almost at its gates and to the indispensable waterway which it has in the Clyde. Originally a shallow little stream, the river was deepened and widened until it could accommodate large vessels. When the Queen Mary was launched, in 1934, further dredging was done to accommodate the mighty liner. The Clyde is lined with enormous slips and dry docks where boats of all kinds are built and repaired. The clang of thousands of hammers striking on rivets makes a deafening racket in the ears of those who pass in the pleasure steamers from the quays at the Broomielaw. Many a huge ship now plying the Atlantic was first launched on the Clyde. Glasgow has blast furnaces within its boundaries, and great forges, boiler works, machine shops and locomotive works. It also has cotton and linen mills whose products have gained a reputation. The chemicals so necessary in many manufacturing processes are made here too; dyes and bleaching powders were early developed for the textile industries. As a port it is easily the largest in Scotland.

### *Wealth and Poverty of a Metropolis*

The great commercial city displays signs of its wealth in many fine buildings, but large sections are given over to tenements and flats. The great numbers of people employed in factories and foundries do not have very good living conditions, and the dampness of the climate

MC LEISH

**THE TOLBOOTH,** with its conical turrets and projecting clock, stands in the Canongate in the old town of Edinburgh. It is all that remains to-day of the medieval prison described by Sir Walter Scott in The Heart of Midlothian. The jail, however, occupied only the ground floor; upstairs was the court-room, which also served as the city council chamber.

MC LEIS

**EDINBURGH CASTLE,** here seen from the old town, occupies a very important place in Scottish history. In the buildings on the immediate left of the rounded battery is the hall in which, long ago, the Scots Parliament used to assemble. Here, too, are the rooms in which Queen Mary lived and here was born her son, James VI of Scotland, and James I of England

BRITISH INFORMATION SERVICES

**DOWN TO THE SEA—IN CRANS—GO HERRING FROM FRASERBURGH**

Barrels of herring to be exported cover the quay at Fraserburgh, Scotland, sixty miles from Aberdeen. The fish are sold by the cran, a barrel that contains between 750 and 800 herring.

BRITISH INFORMATION SERVICES

**EDINBURGH'S MAGNIFICENT, MILE-LONG THOROUGHFARE—PRINCES STREET—WITH ITS FAMOUS LANDMARKS**

The most picturesque section of Edinburgh, Scotland's beautiful capital, borders on Princes Street. On the south side are charmingly landscaped gardens. A monument to Sir Walter Scott appears in the foreground, and dominating the hill at the left is historic Edinburgh Castle.

MC LEISH

**HOLYROOD PALACE,** in Edinburgh, was a residence of the Scottish kings before James VI became King of Great Britain in 1603, and members of the present royal family still live in it when they visit the northern capital. The palace is chiefly associated, however, with Mary, Queen of Scots, whose rooms were in the tower on the left of the canopied main entrance. It is recorded that she loved Holyrood, and many relics of her stay are preserved. The ruined Chapel Royal is all that remains of the ancient Abbey of Holyrood.

**OLD STIRLING BRIDGE,** over the Forth, was called in medieval days the "gateway of the Highlands," and was carefully guarded against the Highlanders who adventured south in quest of plunder. When the English were trying to conquer Scotland, they captured Stirling Castle, and two miles away, at Bannockburn, they were finally defeated by King Robert Bruce.

PHILIP GENDREAU

**TRIM AND INVITING IS PORT ASKAIG ON THE ISLAND OF ISLAY**

Neat white houses make a pleasing contrast against the green backdrop of forest at Port Askaig. Islay is one of the inner Hebrides Islands, which lie off Scotland's west coast.

COMBINE

**A HYDROELECTRIC PLANT BUILT ON THE BANKS OF LOCH LOMOND**

The power station is part of a large system to provide electricity throughout Scotland. The pipes on the hillside are seven feet in diameter. They carry water from Loch Sloy.

increases the misery of life in the crowded sections.

Only twenty-five or thirty miles north of Glasgow are the wild Highlands, and the city water supply comes from Loch Katrine in the Trossachs. But south of the city and immediately around it are manufacturing towns, many of them well known. There is Paisley, once famous for its bright woven shawls, and now a centre of the cotton thread industry. The ship-yards extend to Dumbarton and Greenock. Coal and iron are mined throughout Lanarkshire and other Lowland counties.

### *Modern Industry in Ancient Towns*

Linen-making is a long-established industry, carried on in several counties. The finer grades are made at Dunfermline, a town which figures in Scottish history and is mentioned in one of the old ballads. In its ancient abbey King Robert Bruce lies buried. Dundee, on the Firth of Tay, makes coarser grades of linen but its staple industry is the manufacture of jute. Jute is an important plant fibre from which ropes, sackings, carpets and many different fabrics are made. Dundee ships bring the fibre directly from India to the docks on the Tay. The city is also known for a different and very toothsome product—marmalade.

Tartans and carpets are made at Kilmarnock and at Stirling. Stirling is a beautiful old town on the River Forth. Its strong fortress once guarded the Lowlands against the Highlands raiders, and it was called the gateway of the Highlands. A short distance from Stirling one comes to the beautiful country of the Trossachs and Loch Lomond.

### *Weaving the Fine Tweeds of Scotland*

Tweeds are manufactured in many parts of Scotland besides the Highlands. The sheep country of the south is a centre of the industry. Dumfries, near the Border, is one place where tweeds are made, but it is more renowned because Robert Burns spent the latter part of his life there. Fine woolens are made by hand in the outlying islands, and of late years these cottage industries have been much encouraged.

The great island of Lewis in the Outer Hebrides has no very high land and hardly a tree except near the one town, Stornoway. Harris, which is joined to Lewis by a tiny isthmus, was for years mainly a deer preserve. There is plenty of grass here and high hills with valleys between, in which feed droves of the tawny Highland cattle, with their wide-spreading horns a yard long. Harris tweeds are especially famous. The women spin, dye and weave the wool entirely by hand. Most of the men are fishermen. The children of the islands are thin, brown-skinned little people. They do not get enough milk, and live largely on oatmeal and potatoes.

### *Lonely Islets of the Atlantic*

These islanders are close to civilization when compared to the seventy people who used to live on St. Kilda. This is a rocky islet only three miles across, which lies forty miles out to sea and is often cut off by storms for long intervals. The islanders used to catch sea birds in nooses and use them for food. Recently the island has been deserted. All the outer islands are the homes of sea birds of many kinds, such as gulls and gannets, puffins and auks and petrels.

Off the extreme north coast of Scotland are the Orkney and Shetland Islands. The climate of these distant places is never very cold, but raging gales are common. Visitors who come in the summer hear the lark singing at midnight, for it is far enough north to be light practically all night long. Larks, indeed, are almost the only inland birds, for there are so few trees that nesting places are scarce.

Every man on the Orkneys is a fisherman, and in many of the houses big, dried fish hang from the smoky rafters overhead as if they were pieces of bacon. The people grow oats, barley and turnips on the long undulating stretches of open country. Peat is the sole fuel; we may see the women drawing home the "turfs" in wheelbarrows, or in queer boxes made of packing-cases and pulled by ropes,

REID

**SHETLAND WOMEN** do not waste a minute of the day; these two are busy knitting even while they are walking to the market at Lerwick, the capital of the far Shetland Islands that lie to the north of Scotland. The farm produce that they mean to sell is packed into panniers carried by two shaggy little ponies. The raising of these ponies is an important industry in the islands. Sheep are also reared in great numbers, and from their wool the islanders make the beautifully knitted garments that one may buy in shops all over the world.

HARDIE

**GRINDING GRAIN** in a stone handmill, laboriously turned by the long shaft that the woman holds, is very slow work. This rough and primitive method of preparing flour is still popular in Skye, the second largest island of the Inner Hebrides. The islanders are distrustful of modern changes and cling to old customs and old-fashioned implements.

On the main island there are many curious old monuments called "Picts' houses" and "standing stones," relics of a by-gone people. The chief town, Kirkwall, has a beautiful old cathedral. Kirkwall stands on the great bay or harbor of Scapa Flow, which is protected on all sides by other islands. In both World Wars the British Fleet used Scapa Flow as a strategic base.

The Shetlands are somewhat different from the Orkneys. Instead of being gathered together in a round compact group, their conformation is long and pointed, and their shores are carved and cut up by the sea into weird shapes. As in the other islands, fishing is the foremost occupation. Flocks of sheep are pastured wherever there is any chance of their getting food, even on high islands whose precipitous sides rise from the sea and form a smooth tableland. The sheep are taken over by boat and carried or swung up laboriously one by one. Shetland sheep are plucked, not sheared; the peasants believe that the wool which grows after this process is finer than that which grows after shearing. Shetland shawls are known to most people and they are made from this fine soft wool. These, with the little, rough-coated Shetland ponies, are the best-known products of the islands.

The Shetlands and the Orkneys seem very far north and remote. Yet all of Scotland lies within the latitudes which include Labrador. Even in Edinburgh the summer nights last but four or five hours. The country would be as cold as Labrador if the warm waters of the Gulf Stream did not temper the climate. The air is damp and cool, and rain comes often. When we think of Scotland, however, we do not think only of grayness and rain and bleak hills. We call to mind also the purple of the heather, the green of the wooded glens, the reds and greens and yellows of Highland tartans. We remember the bustle and activity of Glasgow, the charm of Edinburgh, and like Scotland all the more because it combines the romance of history and the romance of modern industry.

---

## *SCOTLAND: FACTS AND FIGURES*

### *THE COUNTRY*

Occupies the northern portion of the island of Great Britain, with the Atlantic Ocean on the west and north, the North Sea on the east and England on the south. Total area, including adjacent islands (186 in number), 30,405 square miles; population, 5,095,969. The islands belonging to Scotland are the Orkneys and the Shetlands on the north; the Hebrides along the west coast; those on the estuary of the Clyde—Bute, Arran and some smaller ones. The Hebrides are divided into Inner and Outer Hebrides.

### *GOVERNMENT*

As a part of the United Kingdom, general laws are made by the British Parliament in London, in both houses of which Scotland is represented, but for matters which concern the country alone there is a Secretary for Scotland. All matters conducive to health are under charge of the Scottish Board of Health. The country is divided into 33 civil counties, each with a county council.

### *COMMERCE AND INDUSTRIES*

There are valuable coal and iron fields. The existence of coal and iron deposits near the Clyde have encouraged industrial activity around Glasgow. Shipbuilding, ironworks, the manufacture of chemicals and machinery are carried on. Stirling has iron foundries. Dundee is the centre for jute, linen and hemp manufacture and marmalade, and linoleum is made at Kirkcaldy. Other manufactures are tweed cloth, carpets, shawls, silks and hosiery and paper. Fishing and stock-raising are important industries. Scotland is the original home of famous breeds of sheep and cattle.

### *COMMUNICATIONS*

Railway mileage is included with that of England. There are 184 miles of canal including the Caledonian Canal (60½ miles).

### *RELIGION AND EDUCATION*

The established church is Presbyterian. Its supreme court is the General Assembly, which consists of 1,620 members, partly clerical and partly lay. Education is compulsory up to 15 years of age, but with certain exemptions, children may leave school at 13. Aside from the regular primary and secondary education, there are continuation schools for defectives, schools for blind, deaf, reformatory and industrial schools. There are four universities—St. Andrews, Glasgow, Aberdeen and Edinburgh.

### *CHIEF TOWNS*

Edinburgh, capital, population, 466,770; Glasgow, 1,089,555; Dundee, 177,333; Aberdeen, 182,714; Paisley, 93,704.

# IRELAND NORTH AND SOUTH

## *The Land and Its People*

The moist green island just west of Wales, England and Scotland was, in 1922, divided politically into two parts, Northern Ireland and The Irish Free State. In 1937 a new constitution was adopted, by which southern Ireland (the Free State) became the sovereign independent state of Eire. The final step toward complete independence was taken late in 1948. Then the Dail (Parliament) passed a bill by which the last formal link with the British Crown and the Commonwealth was severed, and Eire became the Republic of Ireland. However, Irish citizens have citizenship rights in the United Kingdom, and Britons have the same rights in Ireland. Australia, Canada and South Africa also exchange rights of citizenship and trade with Ireland.

IRELAND (Eire in Gaelic) is a grassy plateau rimmed about with jagged low mountains along the coast. The shores are washed by the Gulf Stream, and the climate is tempered by warm winds laden with moisture. These so favor the growth of vegetation that the country has long been poetically called the Emerald Isle and its haunting charm has often been told in prose and verse.

Ireland has long been divided into four provinces, Ulster, Leinster, Connacht and Munster, and these in turn into thirty-two counties. Six counties of Ulster make up Northern Ireland, while the three remaining counties of Ulster and the other three provinces with their twenty-three counties make up the Republic of Ireland.

The earliest history of Ireland is legendary. We are told that the country was split up into a number of small kingdoms until the third century A.D., when Cormac mac Art made himself "ard-ri," which meant high king. His palace was at Tara, not far from Dublin, in County Meath. Tara was for centuries a place where warriors awaited the orders of the ard-ri and bards played their harps and chanted the praises of kings and heroes. To-day the site of Tara is a grassy mound.

The first great figure in Irish history is that of its patron saint, St. Patrick. Born about the year 389 in North Britain (though some say in Gaul), he was carried off as a slave by a band of Irish marauders. After six years of bondage, he escaped, reached Gaul, and entered the Church. He was ordained a missionary bishop and returned to Ireland where there were only a few scattered Christians. St. Patrick carried Christianity to every part of the island and the introduction of Latin as the language of the Church brought the people in contact with the learning of Europe. Schools and monasteries were founded, and flourished to such an extent that, for several centuries, they were the centres of learning and religion for all Western Europe. Missionaries were sent out not only to England (which had again become pagan after the Anglo-Saxon invasion), but also to Scotland, Germany, Switzerland, France, and even to Italy.

During the ninth and tenth centuries the country suffered from invasion by pagan Norwegians and Danes. Monasteries and colleges were burned, books destroyed and scholars dispersed. The Danes did, however, found the cities of Cork, Dublin, Waterford, Limerick and several others as forts and trading centres. Brian Boroihme, or Boru, or Boruma, King of Munster, broke the Scandinavian power at the battle of Clontarf, 1014 A.D., though he himself was killed.

In the reign of the English king, Henry II, Diarmid, King of Leinster, who had a grievance against the ard-ri, sought help from England, and Strongbow, Earl of Pembroke, took over an army to his assistance. Two years later Henry II went over to establish the English claim to all Ireland, and during Elizabeth's reign the conquest was achieved, though with much difficulty.

Under James I, the English land system was substituted for the old Irish customs

**NEAR KILLARNEY** this old bridge spans the Long Range, a stream that connects the Upper and Middle Lakes. In this wooded country, red deer come to its banks to drink, and until a few years ago, eagles nested on a precipice above. Its entire course is navigable and the round trip of five miles down its length and back is well worth taking.

NICHOLLS

**THE FRESH CHARM** of the Irish colleen has long been celebrated in song and story. Because Ireland is chiefly an agricultural country, many of its young women are from farming districts. By sharing in the hard work of the farm, as this girl is doing, they have gained sturdy good health, which adds much to their dark-haired, blue-eyed beauty.

and the great nobles of Ulster revolted. When resistance was overcome, their lands were forfeited and for the most part assigned to English and Scottish Protestants. This was the real beginning of the division between the two sections of Ireland. Many of the colonists devoted themselves to industry and the woolen and linen manufactures began to flourish.

Because James I was the son of Mary Queen of Scots, the Irish had hoped for tolerance of their religion, but were disappointed. Both Catholics and dissenters were harshly treated, and conditions were little better under Charles I. When Parliament rose against the king in England, Oliver Cromwell was sent to subdue Ireland and accomplished the task with ruthless severity. More privileges were given to the Catholics under Charles II, and under James II they were favored. Naturally they received him gladly when he was driven from England, but the Irish forces were defeated by William III at the Battle of the Boyne in 1690.

During the next hundred years life in Ireland was unhappy. English commercial jealousy discouraged manufactures and trade for all, and the Irish Parliament, composed entirely of Protestants, passed severe penal laws against the Catholics. Thousands of the best of Ireland left home, the Catholics to go to the Continent, the Protestants to America. The latter—the so-called Scotch-Irish—made ideal pioneers and many were prominent in the Revolution. Andrew Jackson, for example, was of this blood. In 1798, there was another uprising and when it was crushed, the Act of Union abolished the Irish Parliament, and gave Ireland representation in the Parliament at Westminster after January 1, 1801.

For almost 125 years afterward the story of Ireland was in large measure that of a continuous struggle for civil and religious freedom, and for separation from Great Britain. The ruling and property-owning classes differed in race, religion and language from the great mass of the people. The landlord was hated, the tenant was exploited, and there was little peace in the land. It is not surprising that poverty was almost universal. Hundreds of thousands of Irish men and women, in despair, left their homes for America, Canada, Australia, and other parts of the world where they or their children often achieved prominence in many fields.

A volume could hardly tell the long

THE IRISH REPUBLIC AND NORTHERN IRELAND

ASSOCIATED BRITISH AND IRISH RAILWAYS

**DID GIANTS WALK HERE ONCE UPON A TIME?**

The Giant's Causeway is part of a headland on the north coast of County Antrim. Its thousands of basalt columns, from 15 to 20 inches across, were formed as the earth cooled after underground volcanic disturbances. At one place the Causeway extends about 500 feet into the sea. The old fairy tales explain it as the work of giants building a causeway to Scotland.

story of the struggle. It is sufficient to say that finally, after the attempt to establish an Irish Republic, a settlement was effected in 1920 and 1922. Northern Ireland, with a population largely Protestant of English and Scottish descent, received a large measure of home rule, but chose to remain a part of the United Kingdom, and continues to send members to the British Parliament in London, though there is a local parliament in Belfast. Southern Ireland, Celtic and Catholic in the main, assumed Dominion status with a government similar to that of Canada and Australia, under the name of The Irish Free State (Saorstat Eireann in Gaelic). A constitution, adopted in 1937, restored Eire, the old name of Ireland, as the name of the state. The names of all the towns were Gaelicized, and street signs appear in both Gaelic and English. Gaelic is the national language and is taught in the schools, but English is also official. The last

© UNDERWOOD & UNDERWOOD

**ST. LAWRENCE GATE** is a twelfth-century relic of Drogheda. That Leinster seaport once had walls defended by ten gates with round towers. The one above is practically all that remains of the ancient fortifications. The town was defended against O'Neill in 1641-2, stormed by Cromwell and its garrison massacred in 1649, and surrendered to William III in 1690.

LAWRENC

**THE RUINS** of the cathedral on the Rock of Cashel in Tipperary are joined to a twelfth-century round tower built of different stone. Much of the carving and the sculptures in the cathedral is interesting and beautiful. Cormac's Chapel, also on the Rock, said to have been erected by Cormac McCarthy, is richly decorated. The Cathedral was burned in 1495.

IRISH TOURIST ASSOCIATION

**DONKEYS CARRY MEN AND MERCHANDISE ON THE ARAN ISLANDS**

Windswept and barren, the Aran Islands in the Bay of Galway are yet strangely charming. Few trees can grow on this craggy land, but ferns and rock plants flourish in the limestone crevices and around the ruins of Christian and pre-Christian architecture. These architectural remains make the islands a fruitful land of study for scholars of history and religion.

link with the British Crown and the Commonwealth was cut late in 1948, when the Dail (Parliament) in Dublin passed a bill creating the Republic of Ireland. Only citizenship rights of Irish people in the United Kingdom, and of Britons in Ireland, are retained.

Traveling inland by one of the winding roads, between stone walls covered with creepers, one finds small fields in which graze cattle, sheep and goats, horses and donkeys. Here and there the ruins of some ancient castle speak hauntingly of the past. Farms are generally small—more than half are under thirty acres—and in some of the "congested districts" there are many holdings of less than an acre. The typical farmhouse is a white-washed cottage of plastered stone with straw-thatched roof, and a patch of cabbages and another of potatoes near by. Always there is the smell of peat smoke,

IRISH TOURIST ASSOCIATION

**AN EXCITING MOMENT FOR THE ARAN ISLANDERS**

When the steamer from Galway calls at the bleakly beautiful Aran Islands, the islanders dress in their best clothes to welcome visitors. Many early architectural remains are to be found on the islands, which are on the west coast of Ireland at the entrance to Galway Bay. The islanders, who speak Gaelic, make their living mainly by fishing and kelp-burning.

**DUNLUCE CASTLE,** one of the most impregnable castles in all Ireland, was built by the MacHugolins (McQuillans), Norman settlers, on a basalt peninsula that juts out from the rugged coast of County Antrim, just west of the Giant's Causeway. See the limestone cliffs just beyond. A narrow arch built over a chasm to replace the ancient drawbridge forms the approach to the ruins. Held by the followers of Sorley Boy MacDonnell, who was one of Queen Elizabeth's toughest opponents, the castle was captured by Sir John Perrott in 1584.

VALENTINE

**BLARNEY CASTLE** was built in County Cork in 1446 by Cormac McCarthy. The walls are in part eighteen feet thick, and the castle played a rôle in the War of the Great Rebellion. The Blarney Stone, the kissing of which is alleged to confer upon one the gift of persuasive eloquence is beneath a high window, and people must be lowered by their feet to reach it.

for the peat bogs furnish the fuel in general use, as Ireland has little coal, and wood only in limited quantities.

Ireland is well-watered, having many lakes and rivers. These lakes, called "loughs" (pronounced "lochs"), are chiefly in the central plain and in Connacht, which is sown with lakes. Lough Neagh in the north is the largest lake in the British Isles, and there are others of considerable size. Many of these lakes have low shores and the waters are stained with peat, but others among the mountains and hills are surpassingly beautiful. The Lakes of Killarney are the best known.

The Shannon, the longest river in the British Isles, is about 250 miles long, and is navigable for steamers for more than half its course. It is connected with Dublin by canals. The Free State government began, in 1925, to develop the enormous water power of the river at

IRISH TOURIST ASSOCIATION

**MENDING THE NETS ON A SUNNY DAY IN THE ACHILL ISLANDS**

The Island of Achill is famous for the beauty of its rugged cliffs and its heather-covered moors. Fishing is the major occupation of many of the inhabitants. They well know the perils of the stormy North Atlantic. Their little boats, their nets and other gear must be kept in the best condition; and mending the nets is a constant task for the fishermen.

IRISH TOURIST ASSOCIATION

**SNUG LITTLE HOMES ON THE STORMY SHORES OF ACHILL ISLAND**

Achill Island is part of County Mayo and, with an area of 57 square miles, is the largest island off the coast of Ireland. The coastline is rugged and the surface very mountainous—some of the peaks are about 2,000 feet high. The islanders make a difficult living by fishing and farming, often supplemented by work in England and Scotland during the harvest season.

great expense. Distribution of this power throughout the country is provided for by a national network.

Owing to the warm, wet winds from the Atlantic, the land produces luxuriant grass. It is this rich mantle that has made green the national color. The national emblem, the shamrock, which Irishmen wear in their buttonholes on St. Patrick's Day, March 17, is a small plant of the clover family with a three-lobed leaf, and St. Patrick is supposed to have used it as an illustration of the Trinity.

Dublin, capital city of the Republic of Ireland, was at one time the capital of the whole island. Once a stronghold of the Scandinavian invaders, it later became the center of the Anglo-Norman colony. Both peoples have left many traces of their settlements in surnames prevailing in different parts of the country. De Lacy is an Anglo-Norman name, Doyle is Gaelic for Dane, and Swayne is a Norwegian surname. Dublin has two Protestant cathedrals (Catholic up to the time of Henry VIII) and a pro-cathedral

**COTTAGES OF DONEGAL** have their thatched roofs held firmly in position by a netting of stout ropes, which protects them against the strong Atlantic gales. A hole in the roof is all that permits the escape

is an important industry among the hills. From the wool a rough, durable homespun used for sports wear is woven; and many a housewife occupies her leisure hours at that homely craft with

VALENTINE

**A HOLY WELL** at Ardfert. Strong religious faith and firm belief in the power of prayer are characteristic of the people of Ireland. These women of Kerry are kneeling piously at a well which is a centre of devotion to one of Ireland's saints. Simple offerings in memory of the saint are placed at the well and his intercession is besought in matters spiritual. There are several of these wells in Ireland. At Downpatrick, a well is dedicated to St. Patrick. One to St. Columb lies hidden among the stones at Glencolumbkille, away in almost the westernmost tip of County Donegal.

which is Catholic. The two Protestant cathedrals are Christchurch and St. Patrick's. The former was founded by the Danes and rebuilt by Strongbow, who is buried there. Here, too, in 1487, the child-impostor, Lambert Simnel, was crowned king, afterward serving as a scullion in Henry VIII's kitchens. St. Patrick's was founded in 1190. In this cathedral, of which he was Dean, lies Jonathan Swift, author of Gulliver's Travels, and here the Prince of Wales, afterward Edward VII, was installed as a Knight of St. Patrick.

### *Trinity's Ancient Manuscripts*

The University of Dublin, better known as Trinity College, Dublin, is a Protestant institution, and dates from Queen Elizabeth's time. In the library of Trinity are many valuable manuscripts, including the Book of Kells. This is a copy of the Gospels in Latin, the work of an eighth-century scribe. For elaborate ornamentation and workmanship it has no rival. Here also is "Brian Boru's harp," which may have belonged to some bard of Brian Boru's court, for it is reputed to be more than nine hundred years old. The National University of Ireland, attended chiefly by Catholics, dates only from 1909, but its constituent colleges at Dublin, Cork and Galway are older.

Dublin has long been a center of culture and learning. From the days of Dean Swift the city has never been without important literary figures. Around the beginning of the present century, an unusual amount of literary talent appeared in and around Dublin, and more has developed since. Of the distinguished group, George Moore, G. W. Russell (Æ), W. B. Yeats, J. M. Synge, James Joyce, Lady Gregory and Lord Dunsany are the best known, though there were and are others almost or quite as important. All these wrote in English, but the city is also the center for those interested in the revival of Irish as a living tongue. There is an old saying that the "most beautiful English spoken anywhere is spoken in Dublin." The Abbey Theatre, one of the first experimental theatres, is famous.

### *Ulster and Its Manufactures*

Ulster, the northernmost of the four old provinces of Ireland, differs in almost every way from the remainder of the island. We have already said that under James I many Scotch and English settlers were introduced with the hope of making the whole of Ireland a loyal and Protestant country. This hope was not realized, but the settlements flourished and important manufactures of wool and linen sprang up. When the British Parliament forbade exports from Ireland manufactures decayed, and thousands of Ulstermen—often incorrectly called Scotch-Irish—migrated to America.

At a later day the oppressive laws which hindered manufacturing were repealed and now one-third of the world's production of linen is woven in Ulster. Shipyards were also established and are now exceedingly important. The Titanic, the Olympic and other large ships were built here. There are also such other manufactures as rope, tobacco, machinery and distilling. Belfast has the largest rope works in the world.

Six of the nine counties of Ulster make up the division known as Northern Ireland with Belfast as the capital. Manufacturing is the chief occupation, but agriculture and stock-raising are also important. Potatoes, hay, turnips and oats are the principal crops. Cattle, sheep, poultry and pigs are raised in large numbers. Some flax is raised, though more is imported from Belgium and Holland.

### *Linen Towns of Ulster*

Belfast, center of the linen trade, was chartered by King James I in 1613, but for many years was only a fortress and a small fishing village. Today the population is about 440,000. Queen's University, of Belfast, has been an independent university since 1909. Londonderry is the city next in importance. Armagh, another of the linen towns of Ulster, is built picturesquely on the side of a steep hill. One of St. Patrick's first churches is believed to have been here.

The city of Cork, the third city of Ire-

Irish Tourist Association

**FUEL FOR THE FARM COTTAGES OF IRELAND**

The island has a little coal, but even that little is of poor quality. So, for a source of fuel at home, the Irish cut turf from their great peat bogs, swampy lowlands covered with masses of partly decayed vegetation. (Ages ago the world's coal was formed from the same kind of material.) The dried peat burns well in open grates. It makes superior charcoal.

land, has many manufactures and also a famous butter market. About ten miles southeast, on an island in the harbor, is Cobh, a regular port of call for trans-Atlantic steamers. This town, first known as the Cove of Cork, was called Queenstown after a visit from Queen Victoria in 1849, but the name has again been changed. The harbor is so extensive that as many as six hundred merchant vessels have been counted in it at one time. A factory for making Ford cars has been established here.

Various cottage industries are carried on wherever the population is scattered. In many of the cottages in Donegal and Connacht woolen goods, cloth and carpets are made, and the whole family takes part in the work, the men doing the weaving, the women the spinning and dyeing. Irish homespuns are famous. Many of the women also are engaged in embroidering and lace-making.

Along the coasts and rivers there are important fisheries, but in the interior, the people for the most part raise cattle, horses and poultry. Many fine hunters are bred to sell abroad. Irish bacon is famous, and dairy products are carefully graded. Recently much more grain is being raised. Pigs and potatoes are raised all over Ireland. Raleigh introduced the potato to Ireland in 1584, and it grew so easily that it became to the Irish what rice is to the Eastern world and wheat to the Western, a staple food. On the rare occasions when the potato crop has failed, Ireland has starved. Between 1845 and 1847 there occurred a terrible potato famine; numbers of people died; then from the harbor of Cork started a stream of emigrants to America and Australia. To-

LAWRENCE

**CLIFFS OF DOON** by Ballybunion have been sculptured and cut into caves by countless tides. Bally (baile) is a word meaning town which appears in many Irish place-names. From here one may look across an arm of the sea to the estuary of the River Shannon and the hills beyond. A combination of mountain, sea and plain stamps the scenery of County Kerry.

LAWRENCE

**CARRICK-A-REDE** in County Antrim is interesting to the geologist, as well as attractive to the tourist. This swinging bridge over a chasm eighty feet deep connects a rock used as a fishing station with the mainland. The Giant's Causeway, shown in one of our black and white illustrations, is not far away, and the ruins of Dunluce Castle are also close by.

Irish Tourist Association

**TIME HAS NOT DIMMED THE TWINKLE IN HER EYES**

In certain parts of Ireland one may still see fashions of an earlier era. This beautiful old lady from County Cork is wearing the hooded cloak that is part of the traditional dress for women in certain districts of the southwest. These handsome cloaks are treasured as family heirlooms and may be handed down from mother to daughter for generations.

day Ireland has little more than half the population it had in 1845.

The land abounds in romantic castles, monasteries, ruined abbeys, round towers and other relics of the past. The round towers are usually found near churches. They were built, in the ninth century and later, as a defense against the invading Scandinavians. A watcher on one of these high towers could see the foe advancing and give the alarm which would bring the people hurrying to the tower for safety. The High Crosses which we find standing alone in various parts of Ireland serve as memorials or mark the boundary of some sanctuary.

Across Munster, from Tipperary through Limerick and Kerry to the Atlantic, runs a fertile tract known as the Golden Vale, which is given up to agriculture and dairy farming. Tipperary has always been famous for its butter and bacon. The song, It's a Long, Long Way to Tipperary, was written about 1912; it became a barrack-room song, and during World War I it was the favorite marching tune of the English-speaking troops.

The most Irish part of Ireland is Connacht, where towns are few and factories almost unknown. During the Middle Ages, when Galway city did a big trade with Spain, certain Spanish merchants settled here and intermarried with the Irish. Some of their descendants in Galway to-day are very dark and have a

Irish Tourist Association

**A FAIRY-TALE CASTLE, KYLEMORE ABBEY, IN COUNTY GALWAY**

Though the handsome structure looks as if it were much older, it actually was built as a residence late in the nineteenth century. It has one of the most romantic locations to be found anywhere in Ireland. The wooded slopes (Kylemore means great wood) of the height of Doaghrue frame its turrets; and the waters of the lovely Lough of Kylemore lap the abbey grounds.

IRISH TOURIST ASSOCIATION

**ISLAND OF FARMS AND FARMERS**

Ireland has been especially endowed by nature for agriculture. The rich, light soil and the mild, moist climate are ideal for farming. Ireland probably produces more food per acre, year in and year out, than any other country. The Irishman's love for his own bit of land has made it a country of many small farms, some no larger than garden plots.

EWING GALLOWAY

**JAUNTING BESIDE ONE OF KILLARNEY'S FAMOUS LAKES**

The Irish two-wheeled side-car can carry two pairs of passengers sitting comfortably at the sides, while the driver perches directly behind his horse. Between the side seats there is a well for luggage. No visit to the Emerald Isle is complete without a ride in a jaunting car. This scene is in County Kerry, in the southwestern part of Ireland.

TRANS WORLD AIRLINES

**STREET SCENE IN ADARE, LIMERICK, NOT FAR FROM THE SHANNON**

Most of the road signs in the Republic of Ireland are in two languages, English and Gaelic. This horse evidently knows its way home, however, without direction from its sleepy master who probably had to start out very early in the morning to bring the milk to town. Adare, shown here, is a County Limerick market town of less than a thousand population.

© Aerofilms

**AN AIRMAN'S VIEW OF BELFAST, INDUSTRIAL CAPITAL OF NORTHERN IRELAND**

Belfast is the capital of Protestant Northern Ireland. A city that dates from 1613, Belfast sprang up as the industrial center it is today in the nineteenth century. Streets are narrow, and some residential sections are miserably overcrowded. There are imposing buildings, however, such as the City Hall, which can be seen in the center of this photograph. Belfast owes its industrial prosperity chiefly to the linen industry, established in the seventeenth century and now a source of livelihood for thousands of workers. Shipbuilding, too, contributes to Belfast's importance.

BRITISH INFORMATION SERVICES

**FINE LINEN IN THE MAKING**

In the corner of a factory in Dungannon, a workman takes flax fibers from a scutching machine, which separates the woody fibers from the flax. The girls in the background are tying flax fibers into neat bundles. It will be manufactured into linen of the excellent quality that has made the name "Moygashel" a famous one in the world's linen markets.

foreign look. It is said that the people of the Claddagh, a district in Galway, are descendants of survivors from part of the Armada that was wrecked on the coast. Other reminders of Spain's influence are the Spanish family names to be found in many cities, and the Spanish style of architecture of many of Ireland's venerable buildings. Among these a notable example is Lynch's Castle in the city of Galway.

The women dressed in blue mantles, red bodices and petticoats, and tied a kerchief over the head. They had a special wedding-ring of pure gold, hand-carved, in the form of two hands holding a heart. Today the midsummer festival has become a game for the children, who light bonfires in the streets, and the picturesque dress is worn only on saints' days.

Pilgrimages are annually made to the peak of Croagh Patrick, a 2,500-foot mountain in County Mayo, to pray at the spot where, according to tradition, St. Patrick prayed that snakes should never infest the country.

Though customs, habits and dress are changing, in Connemara we may still see the women in red petticoats and the men in white flannel jackets and tam-o'-shanters. Some of the Aran Islanders wear curious calfskin shoes, known as "pampooties." A piece is cut from the skin of a recently killed calf and while it is still supple is fitted around the foot. As it hardens and dries it takes the shape of the foot. It is secured by thongs of skin passed around the ankle.

Rural Ireland is dotted with tiny farms either isolated or clustered in small districts. The whitewashed, thatched cottages often consist of just one or two rooms. Here the fire is still kindled on an open hearth. Over it, suspended from a hook, hangs an iron cooking pot, or an iron kettle for boiling water to make the cup of tea so dear to the heart of the Irishwoman. One very popular way of cooking meat is to put it in a closed pot on the hearth, cover it completely with burning peat sods and leave it for hours. Peat, cut

IRISH TOURIST ASSOCIATION

**PEOPLE'S PARK IN THE HISTORICAL PORT CITY OF LIMERICK**

Bustling Limerick is the third largest city in the Irish Republic. St. Patrick is said to have visited here. Limerick's museum in the spacious People's Park records its rich history.

and dried, takes the place of coal; this peat is obtained from the bogs, and as the bogs cover one-seventh of the surface of the country there is no scarcity of fuel.

Fairs are an essential part of Irish life. Ireland breeds fine horses, and horse fairs are held in February and September. Once a year, when the little pigs are old enough to leave their mothers, they are packed into curiously shaped carts called creels, and taken to the pig fair to be sold. Everybody goes to these fairs, for, in addition to the business of buying and selling, there are jugglers and fortune-tellers, ballad singers, fiddlers and various other attractions. Hurling, which is something like hockey, and Gaelic football are the national games, while steeplechasing may be said to be the national sport. Ireland is a good hunting country. The Royal Dublin Society's Horse Show is the social event of the year.

Formerly the dancing of jigs and reels was part of the education of every boy and girl. A dancing master would go the round of the countryside during the winter months, the boys and girls meeting each night in one house or another. Each pupil was supposed to bring a candle to the lesson, that the hostess should be spared the expense of lights. In similar fashion, until quite lately, it was customary for school children to take with them contributions of peat to keep the school fires burning.

Irish humor is celebrated. In the midst of the most gloomy happening—and the Irish have had troubles indeed—their wit still sparkles. No people are more hospitable or make a greater effort to put a stranger at ease. Even the most humble folk of Ireland seem to have been born with exquisite manners.

The Ireland of olden times was a great place for quaint taboos. A country man would tell you in solemn tones (though with a twinkle in his eye) that it was unlucky if the first person to enter a house on New Year's Day had red hair; and to meet a red-headed woman at the beginning of a journey or when starting any enterprise was to doom it. If a stranger entered a dairy when butter was being churned, he had to lend a hand at churning or the butter would not "come," that is, the cream would not turn into butter. When this happened it was said that the fairies or the "little people" had stolen the butter, for in spite of education

IRISH TOURIST ASSOCIATION

**THE RIVER LEE, ABOVE CORK HARBOR, SHELTERS SMALL SHIPPING**

The Irish say Cork Harbor, about fifteen miles below the River Lee, could hold the whole British fleet. Four miles long and two miles wide, it is a haven for countless vessels.

IRISH TOURIST ASSOCIATION

**DUBLIN'S DIVIDING LINE IS A LOVELY RIVER BANKED BY QUAYS**

Like the Seine in Paris, the Liffey divides Dublin into two nearly equal parts. Within the city twelve bridges span the languid river waters. The post office uses the ancient Gaelic name, Baile Atha Cliath. Translated into English, this means "The Town of the Hurdle Ford," indicating that there was a ford or crossing of the Liffey here at a very early date.

IRISH TOURIST ASSOCIATION

**THE COLLINSTOWN AIRPORT IS JUST FIVE MILES FROM DUBLIN**

Fierce Viking pirates "visited" Dublin in the early part of the ninth century. They came by sea in sturdy sailing craft, built a rude fortress and settled. Anglo-Normans, already living there, swarmed down from the hills and tried many times to drive their visitors out. Today's visitor to historic Dublin is welcomed at the city's modern, comfortable airport.

By Burton Holmes from Ewing Galloway

**O'CONNELL STREET, ONE OF DUBLIN'S IMPORTANT BUSINESS THOROUGHFARES**

Dublin presents a stirring scene of business activity here in O'Connell Street, with O'Connell Bridge across the Liffey River. The car, you will notice in the picture, bears the sign "Ballsbridge," and if you were a passenger, when you reached that destination you would probably find there a most interesting and varied assemblage of people from all parts of the world, gathered to view the races at one of the famous Dublin Horse and Agricultural Shows. There too you would see booths with exhibitions from foreign lands—a sort of fair or bazaar of nations.

© E. M. Newman from Publishers Photo Service

REMAINS OF MUCKROSS ABBEY, NEAR KILLARNEY

County Kerry contains many reminders of the past glories of Ireland, some of which are shown in other pictures, but none is more interesting than Muckross Abbey, beautiful even in ruins. This ancient monastic establishment was built about 1440 by Franciscan friars, and stands between two of the lakes of Killarney, the lower and the middle, or Jorc Lake. The celebrated ruins of Innisfallen are not far away and there are ruins of other monastic establishments, and of fine churches in Kerry, which some consider the most beautiful county in Ireland.

IRISH TOURIST ASSOCIATION

LOOKING DOWN ON THE ROOFTOPS OF CLONMEL, TIPPERARY

Viewed through a cloister of St. Mary's Church is the compact city with its well paved and tidy streets. Clonmel on both sides of the Suir River is in Tipperary and Waterford counties, the region noted for its farms and dairies, its scenic beauty and its historic past. The enterprising Danes founded this town, after their invasion of the British Isles.

the belief in fairies died hard. Not everyone could see them, but many were quite sure they had seen them dancing in the moonlight. One of these fairies was called the Leprechaun, a little elf who was said to sit by the wayside dressed in a green coat and red knee breeches, bending his brown face over a shoe which he was always trying to repair. But there was one sad fairy in Ireland, the Banshee, whose duty it was to give warning of death by wailing in the night.

A custom known as "wakening" the dead was once common. Friends and relations would watch the coffin all night, while at intervals refreshments were passed around and women mourners would raise a wail known as keening. This custom has almost died out.

The festival of All Hallows' Eve, October 31, is observed in most parts of Ireland, where it goes by the name of Holly Eve. Parties are given at which a kind of gruel is served in Northern Ireland and "barmbrack," a kind of dough cake, in some parts.

It used to be a common belief that the fairies were very busy on All Hallows' Eve, and no Irish child would touch a blackberry after that date, from the belief that the fairies in the course of their All Hallows' Eve wanderings had cast a blight on the fruit.

Of all the Irish customs the most beautiful is one connected with Christmas. During this time Christmas candles, as long as a human arm and nearly as thick, are on sale in the shops. In every Catholic household one of these candles is lighted on Christmas Eve and left to burn all night. In the country parts, in addition to the burning candle, the house door is left open to signify a welcome to the infant Christ.

---

## *IRELAND: FACTS AND FIGURES*

*THE WHOLE ISLAND*

Island in the Atlantic, west of Great Britain, from which it is separated by North Channel, the Irish Sea and St. George's Channel. Territorially it has long been divided into four provinces: Ulster with 9 counties; Leinster with 12; Connacht with 5; and Munster with 6. Politically it is divided into Northern Ireland and the Republic. Total area, 32,375 sq. mi.; est. pop. 4,329,587.

*NORTHERN IRELAND*

Comprising 6 of the 9 counties of Ulster is a part of the United Kingdom, but with a considerable measure of self-government. Representatives are sent to the British Parliament, but the local parliament of two houses meets in Belfast. The Cabinet is responsible to Parliament, and the Queen of Great Britain is represented by a Governor. Area, 5,237 square miles; population, 1,370,709. Capital and chief city, Belfast, 443,670. Agriculture is important and oats, flax, hay and potatoes are raised, besides considerable livestock, but the principal industries are the manufacture of linen, shipbuilding, engineering, rope-making and distilling. There are 672 miles of railway. There is no established church, but the majority is Protestant. Queen's University is at Belfast, and there are secondary, technical and elementary schools with over 250,000 students.

*REPUBLIC OF IRELAND*

Includes Leinster, Munster, Connacht and 3 counties of Ulster. Area, 26,600; population, 2,958,878. Since April 18, 1949, the Republic of Ireland has been an independent state with its own constitution and no ties with the Commonwealth of Nations. The constitution provides for a President, elected by direct vote for 7 years, a Prime Minister, in whom is vested executive power, and a legislature of two houses. Each of the 27 administrative counties and the 4 county boroughs has a County Council for local government. Agriculture and stock-raising are the principal occupations. The chief crops are hay, potatoes and other root crops, oats and barley. The exports are live cattle and other livestock, wool, meat, butter and eggs. There is a large brewing industry. Railway mileage, 2,835; telegraph wire, 21,712; telephone wire, 124,800; inland waterways, 650 miles. Over 90% of the population is Catholic, but the constitution guarantees freedom of conscience. Public education is provided in elementary and technical schools. Most secondary schools are under private control. There are two universities, the University of Dublin (Trinity College) and the National University of Ireland, with constituent colleges at Dublin, Cork and Galway. There are 4 state-aided teachers' colleges. Principal cities with population: Dublin, 521,322; Cork, 74,577; Limerick, 50,823.

# Lonely Islands of the Atlantic

## *Specks of Land Amid Watery Wastes*

**There are many thousands of islands of varying size in the great Atlantic Ocean, but so vast is this area of water that on the map most of them look little more than mere dots. When we remember that this, the second largest of our oceans, is over twenty-five million square miles in extent, we can understand how ships might sail across it in all directions without ever sighting one of these islands. Some of the islands have much significance as coaling, cable and naval stations. Because they are so isolated, the scientific problems of their origin and relations assume important proportions.**

THE dominant feature of the Atlantic basin is the presence of a submarine ridge running from the vicinity of Iceland to about 53 degrees south with a distinct interruption at the Equator. This ridge is almost exactly in the centre of the ocean and follows the S-shape of the coast. It is called the Dolphin Rise in the North Atlantic and the Challenger Ridge in the South Atlantic. The average depth over this ridge is about 1,700 fathoms, but much greater depths are found on each side. Northward the ridge widens and comes nearer the surface, joining a submarine plateau which extends across the North Atlantic. The main basin of the Atlantic is thus cut off from the Arctic basin.

Near its northern end, the rise bears the Azores Archipelago, and south of the Equator, Ascension, Tristan da Cunha and Gough Island. All of these consist of volcanic rocks.

Because the Atlantic is so far-reaching—it touches the Polar regions north and south, and the Equator is a little below its centre—we find its clusters of islands both in cool and in warm waters. There is naturally a great variation in their form and appearance. Very many are volcanic in origin—that is, they have been thrown up from the ocean depths by some convulsion of Nature in past ages—and others are made of coral. Some of the islands are well covered with vegetation and are fertile and beautiful; others are nothing but bare rock, and it is difficult to see what attraction they have for those people who dwell upon them.

With some of the larger islands, such as Iceland, Newfoundland, the Bahamas and others of the West Indian group, it is not our intention to deal, since they are described in other pages. We will confine ourselves to the less known but interesting islands which are scattered over the waters, from the Azores in the north to South Georgia at the opposite extreme. If we follow in the wake of some of the old sea-rovers who, centuries ago made daring voyages from Europe in their small vessels, we shall reach all the islands, for they were discovered during the early attempts to reach India. If we sail due westward from Portugal, we shall find the Azores lying directly in our track. This group of islands was given its name by the Portuguese seamen who discovered it in the fifteenth century. The word "azores," which means "hawks," was applied to the flocks of buzzards that were found there. The archipelago, as it is styled, really consists of the summits of a chain of submarine volcanoes. They are not generally active, fortunately for the inhabitants, only about three of them having been disturbed by eruptions or earthquakes within historical times. At one period, according to scientists, the islands were widely covered by forests, but now there are large areas of open land under cultivation on St. Michael's, the largest of the group, and on Terceira, Pico and Fayal, which are next in importance.

An interesting fact in connection with the Azores is that they play an important part as a meteorological station. They would seem to have been placed out in the Atlantic to serve as a sentinel for the

BLACK STAR

A MOUNTAIN RINGED INLET OF SÃO MIGUEL IN THE AZORES

Vacationists pause on a tour of São Miguel to take in the beauty of an Azores cove, one of many carved out by the sea from the islands' varicolored procession of volcanic mountains.

AMERICAN EXPORT LINES

**ONE WAY OF MEETING LIFE'S UPS AND DOWNS ON MADEIRA**

Many of the streets in town as well as country lanes are rugged on the island of Madeira, and the hammock-taxi offers to the weary tourist the best means of transport. Because of its mild climate, which does not vary much from season to season, the island is popular as a health resort. Funchal, the capital and a seaport, has a number of fine modern hotels.

purpose of warning Europe of storms that are brewing in the ocean. There are observatories at Ponta Delgada in St. Michael's, on the island of Flores, and at Horta, in Fayal, all under the supervision of the Portuguese government.

One of the ocean phenomena for which the observers at these stations are on the watch is the "houle." This is the name given to a remarkable wave that rises out of the sea, apparently without cause, somewhere between the Azores and Iceland. It gathers strength as it goes, and sweeps, at a speed that varies from four to twenty miles an hour, upon some coast hundreds of miles distant.

The houle does not always announce its coming by a storm or similar sign. It will arise suddenly on a calm day, when the sky is cloudless, and ships riding at anchor in open roadsteads may be flung high up on the beach and wrecked. When the warning of this treacherous wave is given, vessels at sea in the vicinity of the Azores have several good harbors in the islands to which they can flee for safety.

From 1580 to 1640 the Azores, as a part of the Portuguese kingdom, were subject to Spain. At that time the islands were a favorite stopping place for ships on their way home from the Indies, and it was off the island of Flores that the battle took place between the English ship Revenge, commanded by Sir Richard Grenville, and a fleet of fifty-three Spanish vessels. Today it is a stopping place for the great clippers that fly between the United States and Europe.

Supposing that we were not venturesome enough to sail so far into mid-ocean, but were content to make a shorter voyage from the Spanish or Portuguese coast, we might turn our vessel's head in the direction of Madeira. This beautiful, well-wooded island is one of a group of five islands, of which only two are inhabited. It is a Portuguese possession, but a curious story is told in an old chronicle which attributes its discovery to an Englishman. According to this account, a certain Robert Machin, in the year 1370, fled from England in a small boat, taking

A STURDY SHEPHERD WHO ROVES THE STEEP HILLSIDES OF MADEIRA

Only a few miles from the lush, banana-growing coast of the island one enters a region of bare uplands, good only for the pasturage of sheep. It can get very cool among these hills and the shepherd is protected against the weather with a sweater and an ear-covering cap. Instead of a crook, he carries a long, straight staff with a sharply pointed end.

PHOTOS, BLACK STAR

CAMACHA, A VILLAGE HIDDEN AWAY AMONG MADEIRA'S MOUNTAINS

Though the village seems so remote, it is only five miles from Funchal and has many visitors. They come to enjoy the sweeping grandeur of the view and also to buy wickerwork. Almost every inhabitant of the hamlet earns his living by fashioning various articles of wicker—furniture, baskets, trays—that find markets all over the world.

AMERICAN EXPORT LINES

"ORCHIDS TO YOU"

Flower vendors are on hand to greet the tourist in Madeira. Exotic orchids and fragrant gardenias are often tossed into the lap of a delighted visitor, who hastily throws back a coin from his car to the trusting salesman. The incongruous "beanie" perched on the head of the young woman at the left may be causing the mirth that both girls are trying so hard to suppress.

a lady. He intended to sail for France, but instead, he was blown out of his course and came to Madeira. Here the lady died and was buried, and Machin erected a cross to her memory. In 1420 the island was re-discovered by the Portuguese.

To most people Madeira is familiar as a popular health resort. It is a warm and sunny island which has much to attract the visitor. The loftiness of the mountains, often snow-covered, the sharpness of the ravines, the pleasing contours of the coast and the proximity of the sea afford many scenes of glorious beauty. In addition to the picturesqueness of its gorges and woods, its caves and bubbling springs, the island possesses a very fertile soil, on which coffee and tobacco flourish amid an abundance of

BLACK STAR

**A FOUR-FOOTED FREIGHT CARRIER OF THE CANARY ISLANDS**

The people of the Canary Islands make use of camels for a great variety of domestic and agricultural purposes. These strong and patient animals are especially useful in transporting the produce that is grown in the interior of the islands to the coastal ports. This camel is carrying a load of fruit in a wooden container. Mules are also used as beasts of burden.

fruit and flowers and tropical ferns. For centuries the vine has been grown on the island and Madeira wine has been famous. Sugar-cane growing has been attempted, but with limited success.

The chief town of Madeira is Funchal, and here there takes place annually a very curious celebration. On the last day of the year, shortly before midnight, the whole of the valley in which the capital lies seems to burst into flame. It is a magnificent firework display, in which the entire population joins. Colored lights gleam on all sides, rockets, Roman candles and fountains of fire flash into brilliance here and there, while an added effect is given by the illuminated boats which dart about the harbor. No one who has seen Funchal thus lit up can forget the sight.

Very near to Madeira, to the southward, are the Canary Islands, which were known to the Romans. One was called "Insula Canaria"—the isle of dogs—after a species of dog supposed to have been found there. Thus the group got its name. From the Canaries first came the little yellow bird which has been given the name of the country in which it dwelt. In its native home the canary is colored like a greenfinch.

Known to the Romans also as the "Fortunate Isles," the Canaries have had a stirring history. They have been fought for by French, Spanish, Portuguese and English. Over a hundred years ago they were created a province of Spain; later their ports were declared free; and in 1883-84 the laying of the submarine cable linked up these ocean islands with the rest of the world.

The Canaries are of volcanic origin, like the Azores and most of the other Atlantic islands. The famous peak of Teneriffe, which rises from the centre of that island, is still an active volcano. During the more recent disturbances several outlets were made some distance below the

**PROLIFIC SPECIES OF THE FICUS FAMILY ON TENERIFFE ISLAND**

The tropics and the temperate zone are both represented in the Canary Archipelago, and the flora comprises the date and banana palm, sugar-cane, coffee and orange tree, the agave and cactus, the laurel pine, heather, broom and lichen. The fig, though a specialty of Hierro, grows on the other islands. Clusters of fruit spring from the bare trunk.

SPANISH TOURIST OFFICE

**WASH DAY ON A HILL ABOVE TENERIFE IN THE CANARY ISLANDS**

The basins follow the shape of the hill by steps and are solidly built of concrete. For housewives who have no running water in their homes, such a place is a big convenience.

crater itself, and from these there often come little puffs of smoke and steam, which are lively evidence of its hidden fires.

If the Canaries were of old the "Fortunate Islands," they might very properly now be called the "Fruit Islands," for from them comes a great banana supply. The islands are also rich in other fruits, and, as in Madeira, the grapevine has been grown for centuries.

One notable feature of these islands is the large herds of goats to be seen there, and we may sometimes see an extraordinarily athletic feat performed by the men who look after them. In the gorge known as the Great Caldera of La Palma, for instance, where the rocks are very steep and dangerous, the goat-herd will jump after a troublesome goat that has got away to some crag many feet below. As he descends he will strike at the animal with his "lanza," a long wooden pole, but even then will be able to break his fall by sliding down the "lanza" the moment it touches the ground. It is said that these men are so expert in pole-jumping that they can even spring from the top of a house into the street without injuring themselves.

The people on the neighboring island of Gomera are among the world's most expert whistlers. They are able to imitate the exact qualities—tone, timbre, pitch, rhythm and so on—of spoken speech; and their whistled conversations carry for a much longer distance than even shouting would. The islanders have had this remarkable ability for centuries.

Let us sail still farther south, where the Atlantic makes a sweep round the coast of Morocco, until we come to Cape Verde, in Senegambia. Off this part of West Africa, three hundred miles out at sea, lie the islands named after the cape. They are fourteen in number. Being of the same volcanic character as the Canaries, the islands present a bare and un-

PHILIP GENDREAU

**ST. HELENA, WHERE NAPOLEON SPENT HIS LAST DAYS**

Lying twelve hundred miles from the nearest continent, Africa, this small, volcanic island in the South Atlantic must have been a dull dwelling place for an emperor. Jamestown, in a narrow ravine, is its only town and seaport. St. Helena is mountainous, and although once covered with forests, it is now largely barren, with wretchedly poor soil.

FREDERIC LEWIS

**ST. JAMES CHURCH IN JAMESTOWN, CAPITAL OF ST. HELENA**

Jamestown is the only town on the island, and more than half the population lives here. In 1658, the East India Company erected a fort here called James, named for the Duke of York, and around it the community of Jamestown grew up. It has an excellent harbor, and was an important port of call for ships sailing round Africa to the Orient, until the Suez Canal was opened.

Q. KEYNES FROM GENDREAU

**LONGWOOD, ISLAND HOME OF AN IMPERIAL EXILE**

In this simple dwelling on St. Helena, an island in the South Atlantic Ocean, Napoleon I passed the years of his exile until his death in May 1821. The house is three and a half miles southeast of Jamestown and is named for the Longwood Plains in the northeast part of the island. It was presented by Queen Victoria to the Emperor Napoleon III in 1858.

inviting appearance as viewed from the sea. This is deceptive; on landing, we find that the valleys of the interior are green and fertile. The Portuguese have introduced eucalyptus, baobab and dragon trees to replace the trees cut down for timber. A volcano, Pico do Cano, is still active on the island of Fogo (fire). Its crater, which stands within an older crater, is three miles in circumference and may be seen from a hundred miles at sea. Coffee is largely grown here; the biggest Cape Verde island, Saint Jago, has a good export trade in this berry.

Far more interesting to us, however, is the island of Ascension, that lonely rock which rises steeply from the South Atlantic, about half-way between the continents of Africa and South America. This island, so scientists say, is probably only the summit of a huge volcanic mass, and whatever animals or plants it may have possessed at one time have been completely exterminated by the lava from eruptions.

In history, Ascension has a particular connection with Napoleon. When, after Waterloo, the fallen French emperor was sent in exile to St. Helena, over eight hundred miles away to the southeast, it was feared that Ascension might be used by his friends with a view to effecting his rescue. So Great Britain occupied the island, and since then it has been one of her Atlantic possessions. Before that date, 1815, Ascension had remained uninhabited, except for a short period when Dampier, the buccaneer, and his crew lived upon it after they were shipwrecked. But the most picturesque feature of this ocean rock is the fact that for a long time it was under the control of the Admiralty. It actually figured in official books as a ship—H.M.S. Ascension—lying at anchor, so to speak, in latitude 7° 57′ S., longitude 14° 22′ W. Its commander was a naval captain, appointed by the governor of Gibraltar, and under him was a ship's company. This peculiar state of affairs came to an end in 1922, when the Admiralty handed over Ascension Island to the Colonial Office.

A LAND OF TROPICAL SUNSHINE AND GAY VACATIONS

Bermuda sunshine creates a pattern of light and shade along Hamilton's Front Street, the main business avenue of the capital city. The buildings face the bustling waterfront, busy with the constant arrival and departure of ships. Automobiles have been allowed in Bermuda since December 31, 1946, but the bicycle and the patient horse are very much a part of the scene.

CRYSTAL CAVE—AN UNDERGROUND FAIRYLAND

The magical beauty of thousands of stalactite "icicles" is reflected in the calm waters of Crystal Cave. Through the ages, water containing calcium carbonate has dripped through the roof of the cave. This constant dripping has left deposits of lime which have gradually formed the stalactite needles. Visitors are guided through the cavern on a pontoon bridge.

PHOTOS, BERMUDA NEWS BUREAU

ST. GEORGE—BERMUDA'S OLDEST SETTLEMENT

Narrow, winding streets, fringed by ancient walls and picturesque houses, are typical of the town of St. George, which was founded in the year 1612. This little town is the oldest Anglo-Saxon settlement in the Western Hemisphere to be continuously inhabited since its beginnings. Until 1815, when the government moved to Hamilton, it was the capital of Bermuda.

BERMUDA NEWS BUREAU

**A BERMUDA ROAD WITH WALLS OF CORAL**

A two-horse team steps smartly along a narrow road that has been cut through a hillock of solid coral limestone. The coral consists of both marine animal deposits and coral fragments blown and packed down by the wind.

It is a lonely rock; the population consists of the officials of the cable station and a hundred or so colored people from the Guinea coast. The naval garrison which used to be stationed here has been withdrawn. About thirty-four square miles in extent, the island has little vegetation, save grass and shrubs which have been planted by colonists. Around the coast there is enough to support a few thousand sheep. Were it not for the turtles which frequent its shores the inhabitants might fare badly. These creatures find their way to Ascension to lay their eggs, and enough are killed to keep the islanders in turtle meat.

The islands in the Gulf of Guinea, to the northeast of Ascension Island, are surprisingly different. The Portuguese possessions of Saint Thomas and Principe, touching the Equator, and the Spanish island of Fernando Po are covered with luxuriant vegetation. Fernando Po was christened Formosa, "the beautiful," by the Portuguese explorer who discovered it, and whose name it now bears. From a distance it appears to be a single mountain rising from the sea, so narrow is its coastal plain and so lush is the vegetation which covers its volcanic slopes. Torrential streams have cut deep beds down the mountainsides, forming many beautiful waterfalls and ravines. Oil-palms, tree ferns, African oak, mahogany trees and a variety of fruit trees grow in abundance. Cacao is an important export from the island of São Thomé; to-day the population is largely composed of descendants of the slaves who were brought from Africa to work on the cacao plantations in the latter half of the nineteenth century. The descendants of the original settlers control about one-eighth of the land.

St. Helena, the island which we are next visiting, is another of the extinct volcano type. It is simply a point of rock rising straight from the depths of the ocean. As it is approached there is no sign of a sloping beach or shore, and it presents, indeed, a gloomy and forbidding appearance in the outlines of its coast. Nor does a closer examination do much to dispel this impression. There is very little soil on St. Helena that is suitable for growing flowers or vegetables. Only here and there, in some of the valleys between the great chasms in the rock, can any earth be found.

In the olden days, when the East India Company's ships used to pass that way, they called at the island to obtain fresh water. Nowadays its chief point of interest is its association with Napoleon, who was kept a prisoner here from 1815 until his death six years later. "Longwood," the house which he occupied, is now visited every year by numbers of the emperor's admirers, mostly French people, of course. The house and

A QUIET STREET IN PONTA DELGADA

© Publishers Photo Service

THE LANDING PLACE ON A SUNNY AFTERNOON

Ponta Delgada is the chief port of St. Michael's island in the Azores. Since the construction of a 2,800-foot breakwater, the harbor has admitted large steamers. Pottery, cotton goods, straw hats and baskets are made and exported here. The city contains many interesting churches and monasteries; the sidewalks are of mosaic, usually of black and white.

ART NEEDLEWORK, AN IMPORTANT HOME INDUSTRY OF MADEIRA

On a terrace amidst a semitropical garden, diligent ladies ply their deft needles. They stitch the beautiful floral patterns that have made the embroidery of their islands famous.

PHOTOS, CASA DE PORTUGAL

FURNISHING THE INTRICATE PATTERNS FOR THE EMBROIDERERS

In a bright drafting room of a Portuguese textile house, careful workmen plot and trace designs that will be transferred to cloth and then embroidered in countless homes and factories.

© E. N. A.

**LADY OF THE FAIR AZORES DRESSED FOR A RIDE**

The ample cloak and hood of this lady form part of the riding-habit fashionable among the natives of St. Michael's in the Azores, ten small islands in mid-Atlantic that belong to Portugal. The people of the Azores are very energetic and enterprising, and make the most of the rich soil of their islands, keeping herds of cattle and growing much fruit.

grounds, with the tomb in which he was first buried, have been transferred to the keeping of France, so that that country holds a piece of territory in St. Helena.

Many hundreds of miles south of St. Helena are three islands, Nightingale, Inaccessible and Tristan which form the British province of Tristan da Cunha. Many desultory attempts at colonization have been made; at times the inhabitants have found seal fishing very profitable, but the islands are bleak and cold, and the penguins continue to outnumber the colonists many times. Gough Island, two hundred and twenty miles to the southeast, is much like Tristan da Cunha; the differences are caused by a greater amount of rainfall. It has no permanent population and except for an occasional fishing vessel, it is devoted entirely to the use of seals and sea birds.

For our next Atlantic islands let us sail up into the warmer region above the West Indies. Here lie the Bermudas, of whose "still vexed" waters Shakespeare wrote in The Tempest. Even so far back as the poet's day these islands had an unenviable reputation for storms.

It was during one of these hurricanes, in 1609, that Admiral Sir George Somers was shipwrecked there while on his way to Virginia. This disaster led to the settlement of the group and a Bermuda Company was formed three years later to send out colonists. On some old maps we find the name of the islands given as Somers; their more general title of Bermudas serves as a reminder of the Spanish seaman Juan Bermudez who first visited their shores early in the sixteenth century.

The Bermudas are coral islands, thus they are distinct from the others with which we are dealing. They are some three hundred and fifty in number, but the total area does not exceed twenty square miles. All round them are reefs, to a distance of thirty miles from the main group.

It is a remarkable fact that such coral-built islands should exist so far from the Equator, surrounded by living coral reefs, but they are right in the track of the Gulf Stream and so the surrounding waters are warm. The Bermudas are unique, further, in that no native people

**LANDING SUPPLIES ON THE BLEAK SHORE OF GRAHAM LAND**

Graham Land is the tip of Antarctica that reaches toward South America. It is included in the Falkland Islands dependency, a British colony, though Argentina also claims the territory. The boats are coming ashore at Hope Bay with supplies for a British expedition. Extensive surveys of the dependency have been made in recent years and permanent weather stations established.

PHOTOS, BRITISH INFORMATION SERVICES

**A WELCOMING PARTY IN FULL DRESS AT HOPE BAY**

Penguins flourish mid the ice and snow of the Antarctic mainland and islands, where few other animals could survive. But even some of the penguins move a little farther north before the dark winter closes down. Adele penguins like these, for instance, spend only the summer on the Antarctic ice. At other times they can be found on the rocky coasts of the Falklands.

BRITISH INFORMATION SERVICES

**A BULLOCK-AND-CART MAIL TRAIN**

Strange as it may seem, this quaint form of mail delivery is still the order of the day in Tristan da Cunha, a group of small islands belonging to Great Britain. The three islands, Tristan, Inaccessible and Nightingale, volcanic in origin, are located in the South Atlantic, midway between South Africa and South America. Only Tristan is inhabited and its settlers lead a rigorous life.

or traces of them were found upon the islands.

Vegetation grows rapidly and the islands are almost perpetually clad in green; the shores are fringed with mangrove; prickly pear grows in the most barren spots and sage bushes spring up wherever they are allowed. Citron, sour orange, lemon and lime trees grow wild. There are no streams or springs and the inhabitants are entirely dependent upon rain water which they catch and store in cisterns. Although a considerable share of its foodstuffs is imported, Bermuda supplies New York with onions, early potatoes, tomatoes and a variety of flowers. All of us are familiar with the "Bermuda" potato and "Bermuda" onion.

The charm of these islands is fully appreciated by the people of northeastern United States who flock to them during the winter months.

Passing the little, isolated islands of Martin Vaz and Trinidad, in the South Atlantic, we will just take a peep at the Falklands, which lie off Patagonia, the southern extremity of South America. The principal islands are the East and West, but there are hundreds of smaller ones clustering in the straits between these two. Their treeless slopes are swept continuously by winds from the west, southwest and south; the sky is almost always overcast and rain falls, either in a drizzle or showers, on about two hundred and fifty days out of the year. Nevertheless, the islands are well adapted for grazing and many cattle and sheep are bred here.

Farther south, nearing the Antarctic, are South Georgia and the bare, windswept islands of the South Shetlands and South Orkneys. All are attached to the Crown Colony of the Falkland Islands. Despite the fact that the Falklands have been in the possession of Great Britain since 1814, Chile and Argentina still claim certain dependencies.

---

## *LONELY ISLANDS OF THE ATLANTIC: FACTS AND FIGURES*

*THE AZORES (Western Islands)*

An archipelago in the North Atlantic Ocean, 830 miles off the coast of Portugal; divided into 3 groups; administered as an integral part of the Republic of Portugal. Total area is 922 square miles; estimated population, 284,755. Population of chief towns: Angra, the capital, 10,057; Ponta Delgada, 18,022. Chief exports: fruit (especially oranges), wine, cheese and coarse linens.

*MADEIRA*

A group of islands in the North Atlantic about 360 miles from the coast of Africa. Administered as an integral part of the Republic of Portugal. Total area, 314 square miles; population, 269,179. Chief exports: sugar, fruit and particularly wine and embroidery for which the islands are noted. Funchal, the chief town, population, 54,033.

*CAPE VERDE ISLANDS*

An archipelago belonging to Portugal about 300 miles off the west coast of Africa in the North Atlantic Ocean; administered by a Governor. Total area, 1,557 square miles; population, 147,097. Chief products are castor-oil, coffee, mustard, oranges and brandy. There are 109 primary schools. Praia is the capital of the islands.

*SÃO THOME (ST. THOMAS) AND PRINCIPE*

Two islands in the Gulf of Guinea about 125 miles off the west coast of Africa. Portuguese province administered by a Governor. Total area, 372 square miles; population 60,159. Chief products of the islands are cacao and coffee.

*BERMUDA*

British colony in the North Atlantic Ocean about 580 miles east of the United States. Administered by a Governor assisted by an Executive Council, an appointed Legislative Council and an elected House of Assembly. Consists of 20 inhabited islands and numerous uninhabited islets; area, 20 square miles; estimated population, 37,254. Chief products are fruits and vegetables. Excellent telephone and telegraph communication. Education government-aided. Population of Hamilton, chief town, 2,978.

*FALKLAND ISLANDS AND DEPENDENCIES*

British Crown Colony in South Atlantic 300 miles east of Magellan Strait. Area of Falkland Islands, 4,618 square miles; population, 2,231. Dependencies are South Georgia, South Shetlands, South Orkneys, Sandwich Group and Graham Land. Sheep-farming and whaling are carried on.

*British possessions* in the South Atlantic include the island of St. Helena, 1,200 miles off the west coast of Africa (area, 47 square miles; population, 4,748; Ascension Island, 700 miles northwest of St. Helena; Tristan da Cunha, a small group of islands halfway between the Cape of Good Hope and South America.

*CANARY ISLANDS*

An archipelago in the Atlantic Ocean about 60 miles west of the African coast. Considered as part of Spain for administrative purposes. Total area, 2,807 square miles; population, 818,326. Bananas, tomatoes, potatoes, sugar and wine are exported. Schools are numerous. Population of Santa Cruz, capital, 103,446.

*FERNANDO PO*

Spanish island in the Gulf of Guinea about 20 miles from African coast. Under a Governor-General. Area about 800 square miles; population, 33,980. Santa Isabel, capital, has a population of 15,064.

**MYRIAD SEABIRDS ON WHAT WAS ONCE H.M.S. ASCENSION**

Ascension Island, whose total area is only thirty-eight square miles, lies in the South Atlantic, and has been a British possession since 1815. It abounds in wild life—rabbits, wild goats and birds. Those that we see here are known as "wideawakes," a sea bird which frequents the island in great numbers. The eggs of this bird are collected and eaten.

# FOLK OF A WATER-LOGGED COUNTRY

## *The Netherlands and Its Fight with the Sea*

The Netherlands, better known as Holland, has been a fighting country for several centuries—and a marvelous fight this has been with its foe, the sea! Endowed with ingenuity and stubborn resolution, the men of Holland have not only resisted the sea's encroachments on their low-lying land; they have even, in places, pushed the land forward, so that now grass grows and cattle graze on acres that were once salt water. Yet the sea has had its innings, too.

"GOD made the sea; we made the shore," runs an old Dutch proverb, and it is at least more applicable to the Netherlands than to any other country in the world. For it is certain that were it not for the dykes on the seaboard and along the banks of rivers there would be very little of the country left to-day. The sea would have found an easy prey in a land that lies actually below its level; and the rivers, whose beds are continually being raised by the deposits of mud, would quickly complete the ruin made by the sea if there were not the wonderful system of canals.

Dykes and canals, windmills and "polders,"—on these four man-made devices largely depend the safety and prosperity of the country. There are hundreds of miles of dykes and canals, and thousands of acres of polders and many windmills.

We cannot set foot in the Netherlands without at once becoming aware of the dykes. Approaching the island of Walcheren by sea, we see one of the finest of these embankments, Westkapelle, stretching along the west coast of the island. This dyke rises nearly 25 feet above the sea level at low tide and is over two miles long—shorter than the famous Petten dyke near Alkmaar, but its rival in strength, massiveness and age, for it dates back to the fifteenth century.

There are dozens of similar, though smaller, dykes. They are all made of mud and sand, strengthened by wooden pillars driven many feet into the soil and "reinforced" in a variety of ways. In some cases huge blocks of granite are embedded between the lines of supports.

On many dykes trees have been planted at the summit or on the sloping sides, and their roots, gradually spreading and intertwining with each other, have formed a wooden network that helps to keep the soil together. Often the surface is protected by twigs of willow interwoven and filled in with layers of clay so as to form a complete and solid carpet; or else the seed of wild grasses has been sown, or ordinary turf laid with the same object. Dutchmen may have made the dykes, but there is nothing more remarkable than the ingenuity with which they have used the growths of Nature to make them firm.

Though the main duty of the dykes is to defend the land against invasion or violent assault by sea and river, they serve other useful purposes. Highways are sometimes laid along them, and houses are built upon them. They provide good foundations for the houses, and that is an important consideration in a country where, owing to the marshy soil, it is difficult to dig deep enough to make sure of a solid foundation.

The Dutch canals are broader than those of most countries, though they vary a good deal in this respect. While they act as drains for removing water and are used as enclosures for property, much as fences and walls and hedges are employed elsewhere, their main use is as highways for traffic. There are canals running through practically every town and village in the north and west of the country. Their banks are usually lined with shady and pleasant trees. Their only drawbacks are the mosquitoes that they attract in hot weather, and their tendency to smell rather unpleasantly.

MC LEISH

**THE ISLAND OF URK** was formerly near the centre of the Zuider Zee, and the chief occupation was fishing. Since the great dyke was finished across the entrance to the Zuider Zee it has become Lake Yssel, or Ijssel, a body of fresh water, and when the North East polder (See page 180) is completed, Urk will be a small part of a much larger island. Unless fresh-water fishing develops, the inhabitants must turn their attention to the land. About a thousand fishing boats formerly were occupied on the Zuider Zee which was, however, too shallow to be useful for navigation.

NICHOLLS

**DUTCH FISHERMEN,** like those of other countries, spend much time loitering about the piers and jetties, gossiping, looking at the boats and gazing into the water. But we must not, therefore, think them lazy, because these same men who stand here looking so idle, though picturesque, often spent the night upon their fishing smacks. When the work of reclaiming a large part of the Zuider Zee is completed Volendam will be only a port on a canal. Notice the baggy breeches and the lambskin caps of these men. Such costumes will probably soon be no longer seen.

THE NETHERLANDS WITH ITS POLDERS

The third notable feature of Holland is the polders. The term is derived from "poel," a word meaning pool, and signifies either a morass or an actual lake which has been reclaimed by draining. The making of polders was naturally begun after the dykes had been constructed; the Hollander having made his territory safe against the sea, proceeded to convert the water-logged parts into cultivable land. It was necessary to pump out the water by mechanical means, and, having done so, to transfer it to the nearest main canal that could carry it to the coast. Windmills supplied the power for pumping.

The windmill has always been a distinctive feature of the Dutch landscape, and to-day they are still to be seen performing useful duties in the agricultural industries. They saw wood, help to make paper and chop tobacco, but they are no longer used for grinding corn or for the making of polders.

In this drainage work, the first thing that the old-time Dutch engineer had to consider, before beginning to get the water out, was the problem of preventing new water from coming in and so spoiling his labors or making them more difficult. So he built a dyke around the selected polder.

The present way of making low-level polders, like the well known Schermer polder in North Holland, is to construct not one dyke round the enclosure, but a series, each on a different level, one within the other. On the outer side of each dyke is a canal dividing it from the next. These canals form an ascending series of levels, into the lowest of which is pumped the water from the polder, whence it is gradu-

McLeish

**QUAINT OLD DRAWBRIDGE INTO AMSTERDAM'S JEWISH QUARTER**

Amsterdam, the largest city of the Netherlands, is often called a "Venice of the North," for it is cut up into ninety islands connected with each other by over 300 bridges. In olden times, some of these canals were part of the fortifications, as this one may have been. In the house shown on the extreme right lived the famous painter, Rembrandt.

NICHOLLS

**UNDER THE CAPSTAN** in the village, formerly occupied chiefly in fishing, is an old seat, on which, on a sunny afternoon, it is pleasant to linger for a chat. When a Dutch girl becomes engaged she wears a plain gold ring on the third finger of her left hand and when she marries the same ring is her wedding ring, but she changes it to her right hand.

MC LEISH

**THE TOY BOAT** that this boy so proudly shows to his grandfather is a model of his father's fishing smack, from which his father was accustomed to fish, on what was once the Zuider Zee. A lambskin cap, like that worn by the old man, a short, double-breasted coat, well-patched trousers and wooden shoes make up the usual costume of the Dutch fisherman.

ally transferred to the highest level of all. This last canal conducts it into a main channel, which carries it away. Although the canals are separate, there is communication between them by means of which water can be discharged to a lower canal for irrigation or other purposes.

### *When the North Sea Broke Through*

By the polder system the Dutch have reclaimed thousands of acres of land that would otherwise have been not merely useless but unsanitary. Polders add enormously to the country's powers of production and, incidentally, to the space near the towns available for houses. Indeed, some polders have been so completely built upon that the stranger would not guess that there had been a polder there at all. Reclamation still goes on.

Until the thirteenth century, the Zuider Zee was more or less dry land, though below sea level. A series of mighty storms broke through the higher land connecting North Holland with Friesland, and the countryside became a shallow sea, of little use except to fishermen.

In 1918 the Government approved a plan for draining and cultivating four polders and for building a dyke across the Zuider Zee. The dyke was completed in 1932, two years after the first polder, Wieringermeer (North West Polder), had been drained. Based on the success of Wieringermeer, a dyke around North East Polder was soon started. By 1942, this second polder was drained and farmers worked its rich new soil. At the end of World War II, German forces destroyed the dyke around Wieringermeer; tons of water flooded its farms and towns. After the war the wall was repaired and the polder was once again fit for farming. Cultivation of North East Polder has gone on steadily and work on a dyke to enclose the southern polders was begun in 1950.

Over the greater part of the Netherlands the soil is peat, and this fact adds enormously to the difficulties of house building. Amsterdam itself, the most important of the cities, stands on the site of a treacherous morass, and is entirely built upon piles.

### *Continuous Repairs Necessary*

Amsterdam also illustrates the manner in which the canal system is constantly changing. In recent years some of its waterways have silted up and even dried up. Dredgers are always at work and the engineers always on duty to meet this or that difficulty as it arises. Indeed, we might almost say that the construction and repairing of dykes and canals and the making of polders are the staple industries of the Netherlands. In no other country is the engineering profession more important, and the high reputation of the Dutch engineers is known all over the world.

We think of the Netherlands as a rather depressingly flat country. Certainly North Holland, Friesland and Groningen answer to this description, as the only breaks in the monotonous landscape are the extensive sand dunes thrown up by the sea and wind, and the dykes that have been built. But north of Arnhem, in the southeast province of Gelderland, there is a "Dutch Switzerland" that has quite big hills. There are no great snow-capped mountains, but modest heights, with their sides covered by woods, and wide heaths where there are springs and cascades. Still, most of the country is low-lying and flat.

The unceasing struggle on the part of its inhabitants against the forces of Nature has produced a courageous and, in some ways, an amazingly interesting race. But whence came these Dutchmen?

### *The Early Inhabitants*

Prehistoric remains in Friesland and Drenthe show that the early inhabitants were apparently akin to the early inhabitants of Gaul and Britain, and that they were there when the earliest Germanic settlers arrived. Dutch history begins, however, with the invasion of the north by the Frisians and the forming of a Frieslander state that at one time spread as far south as the Belgian town of Bruges. Among the islanders of Urk and Marken we still find types that suggest the ancient race that was in the Netherlands when the first invaders came.

READY FOR SHIPPING—THE VERY ESSENCE OF SPRING

The Netherlands has many charms, and one of the greatest of these is its profusion of beautiful flowers. The raising of flowers and of bulbs for export is one of the country's greatest industries; more than thirty million dollars' worth of bulbs are exported each year. The narcissus bulbs in these baskets will brighten many a garden in lands far from Holland.

PHOTOS, STANDARD OIL CO. (N. J.)

THE SHADOWS ARE GROWING LONG—BUT THE HAY IS IN

Holland's mild climate and fertile soil make the lot of the Dutch farmer a happy one. He raises sugar-beets, flax, legumes, potatoes and many other crops. The little country exports a large surplus of its agricultural products and does a thriving trade in nursery plants and seeds. South of The Hague, in the Westland, many plants are grown under glass.

NICHOLLS

**DUTCH HOMES** have been made known to us by the beautiful pictures of the old Dutch painters. Patterned tiles in blue and white, dishes of delftware on shelves around the walls, highly polished copper and brass, straight-backed chairs and a flagged floor with a rush mat or two—these are still to be seen in some comfortable village homes.

MC LEISH

**WOMEN OF VOLENDAM** are as proud of their costume as they are of their spotlessly clean homes. They wear "winged" lace caps indoors and out, but their wooden shoes, or "klompen," are left outside. Volendam is one of the few places left where one may see these quaint costumes, for in most parts the young people are discarding them for ordinary clothes.

© Ewing Galloway

IN THE MARKET PLACE OF ALKMAAR ROUND DUTCH CHEESES LIE IN HEAPS LIKE GREAT RED CANNON BALLS

On the North Holland Canal, 20 miles by railway northwest of Amsterdam, lies Alkmaar, the chief market for cheese in North Holland. On market days many tons of cheeses are laid out in piles in the square before the town Weigh House, while the adjoining streets are full of the wagons of the neighboring peasantry who sell their produce to commission merchants and retailers. The greater portion of the milk in North Holland is reserved for the making of butter and cheese. The home industry, however, has declined and much cheese is now factory made.

### *Under Spanish Rule*

The Frisians were quite a separate race and resisted the Romans, but finally were subdued by Charlemagne, the great king of the Franks. In the Middle Ages we find the territory now comprising Holland and Belgium divided into feudal states, a considerable number of which passed in the fifteenth century into the hands of the Duke of Burgundy. Intermarriage between the Burgundy family and the Austrian and Spanish royal families brought these three countries under the rule of one monarch, who afterward became the Emperor, Charles V.

The Netherlands did not suffer terribly under Charles V, but during the reign of his son, Philip II, the country passed through the worst period of its history. Because the people offered armed resistance to his demand for heavy taxes, and because their Protestant religion was objectionable to his zealous Catholicism, Philip II established the terrible Inquisition. Many of the inhabitants were sentenced to death and it is said that there was not a family that did not suffer the loss of one or more of its members. Although many attempts were made to resist the Spaniards it was not until 1581, under the leadership of William the Silent, Prince of Orange, that they were able to renounce the Spanish authority and to declare their independence.

### *The "Golden Age" of the Netherlands*

The people were now free to turn their attention to other things than fighting and so their brave seamen were sent out to establish colonies in all parts of the world. As a commercial and colonizing power the Dutch had no rival at this time and, indeed, this period might well be termed the "Golden Age" for this little land became famous also for its literature, art and science.

There followed, however, wars with the English, their rivals on the sea, and with Austria. Then came Napoleon, who made the Netherlands a French province. His defeat at Waterloo and the subsequent Congress of Vienna resulted in all the Netherlands becoming one state. This did not at all suit the southern provinces, so in 1830 they revolted and became a separate state that took the name of Belgium. The Dutch have since then been building up their little country most successfully and improving it in all ways. A peace-loving people, they remained neutral during World War I but had no such choice in World War II.

### *Characteristics of the People*

We generally think of the modern Dutch folk as being somewhat dull and silent, slow to make up their minds, but amazingly obstinate when they have done so, and rather inclined in business to give too little and ask too much. These characteristics, however, are to be found chiefly in the north of the Netherlands, though even here the silent, contemplative Dutchman with his pipe and his glass of "schnapps" is not so common as he was. The native of Brabant in the south is a much more hasty and talkative person. So far as shrewdness in business is concerned, we are reminded of an old story that is worth retelling because it illustrates what is still the Dutch point of view. It concerns a British monarch, George II. He was staying in the town of Helvoet, and one day he stopped a pretty Dutch dairymaid and asked her what she had in her basket. "Eggs, mynheer," said she. "And what is the price?" "A ducat apiece, mynheer." The king exclaimed: "Are eggs so scarce then in Holland?" "No, mynheer," was the answer, "but kings are."

The young lady was probably a good deal smarter in her speech than most of the menfolk. The moral of the story is, however, that in business dealings the Dutch are specially inclined to take advantage of any chance that may help them to drive a good bargain. The reason is fairly obvious. They have had to fight so hard and to use their wits so strenuously for the preservation of their land and the bare necessities of existence, that the habit of looking after their own interests to an exceptional extent has gradually become part of their nature.

**VOLENDAM,** a dyke-protected town, is on the western shore of what was formerly called the Zuider Zee. Though only a little fishing village, it is popular with artists and holiday-makers from other lands, for it is one of the few places where we can still see the quaint Dutch costumes. When the reclamation project is completed, the village will front upon a canal.

MC LEISH

**PROUD SENTINEL OF THE LOW COUNTRIES,** the windmill holds head and arms into the "eye of the wind" and turns the pumps that drain the low polders or sets in motion the stones that grind the grain of the village. Holland has about 1,750 mills. And though time and ruthless invaders have taken a heavy toll, 1,300 are still in use.

### *Importance of Dutch Women*

As regards the Dutch woman, she has always taken a very important place in Dutch national life. A visitor to the Netherlands wrote: "To be master of his own house is an idea which seems never to have occurred to the mind of a genuine Dutchman; nor did he ever commence any undertaking, whether public or private, without first consulting the partner of his cares."

The shipping trade is the backbone of the two chief commercial cities, Amsterdam and Rotterdam, and agriculture and fishing are the main occupations of the rest of the country.

The black and white cows of Friesland are famous, and the trade in cheese, of which Alkmaar and Edam are the great centres, is world-wide. One of our illustrations is a picture of the Weigh House and cheese mart at Alkmaar, which is held every Friday in the season. A day or two before, countless cheeses are brought to Alkmaar by rail, road and canal, and stacked, covered by tarpaulins, in the huge open space until the opening of the market. This takes place at 10 o'clock on Friday morning, and all day long stolid-looking Dutchmen stand about the piles of cheeses, tasting with a scoop, bargaining about the price and watching while the purchases are duly weighed. There are dozens of Weigh Houses in Holland, many of which are very old. But to-day none does harder work than that of Alkmaar.

### *Acres and Acres of Tulips*

Almost as well known an industry as cheese-making is the growing of tulips and hyacinths. This is centred around Haarlem, where a "Tulip Sunday" is observed—about the third week in April—when as many people as can get there journey to the famous old town.

Anybody traveling by the railway from Leiden to Haarlem can get an excellent view of the acres upon acres of rectangular beds covered with gorgeous blossoms, and can smell the delicious scent they give to the air. The Dutchman, however, does not grow flowers chiefly because he enjoys their beauty or scent, but as a hard, though fairly profitable business.

The towns and villages around the Zuider Zee, until the great dyke was built (see map), were dependent upon the fisheries and their boats ventured far into the North Sea, even close to the English coast. In the inland towns the distilleries for the production of gin and similar spirits form a thriving industry. Amsterdam boasts its own particular industry—diamond-cutting. One district in the city, close to the Jewish quarter, is entirely devoted to this trade.

There are not many "idle rich" in the Netherlands. Neither the large, busy cities nor the villages provide them with the kind of amusement for which they are supposed to live. If anywhere, they are to be found at The Hague, which, besides being the seat of the Court, is also the least Dutch of the Dutch towns, or at Arnhem, which has maintained its medieval reputation as the gayest of the cities of Gelderland.

### *The Persistent and Methodical Dutch*

Your real Dutchman is orderly in all things. In planning his house or his garden he prefers straight lines to curved ones. That may be a fault in him; and the strictly practical outlook of the modern Dutchman has often been contrasted with the artistic spirit that made the Netherlands in the seventeenth century famous among the cultured nations. The chief masters in portraiture are Frans Hals and Rembrandt. The latter was equally great in landscape painting. Many of the modern Dutch artists, however, have worthily continued the country's artistic traditions.

Whatever defects he may have in any respect are largely compensated by his passion for cleanliness, which is famous throughout the world. The Dutch towns, especially the smaller ones, are kept spotlessly clean.

The village of Broek, in the Waterland of North Holland, has long been supposed to lead all the others in this matter. At one time it was said that in Broek men

© E. N. A.

**ARNHEM, IN GELDERLAND,** lies in a wooded and slightly hilly country, the beauty of which has long attracted many people. This avenue of lofty beeches was mowed down in the tank drive on Arnhem during World War II. About the people of this province there runs a proverb, "Great in courage, poor in goods, sword in hand, such is the motto of Gelderland."

McLeish

**ZEALAND MILKMAID GOES HER MORNING ROUNDS**

Dogs are not kept simply as pets by Dutch tradespeople. They must work for their keep between the shafts of their master's cart delivering tradesmen's goods from house to house or bringing in the vegetables from the market gardens to the groceries. In Belgium and France as well dogs are employed where in this country horses or automobiles would be used.

were forbidden to smoke except with a covered pipe bowl, so that the ash might not be scattered; and that cows were not allowed to pass through the village, but had to be conducted round the outskirts. Boys were paid, so runs the legend, to blow the dust out of cracks in the pavement four times an hour, and it was an unwritten law that if a villager, from his window, saw a leaf fall, he should come out, pick it up and drop it into the canal.

Yet whatever may have been the special virtues of Broek, that very pleasant little village is to-day no more spick-and-span than many dozens of similar ones. It does indeed struggle hard to maintain its position. At one of its farms we may still see the cows' tails tied up to a beam in the stable roof, so that the animals may not soil the glossiness of their flanks by swishing them! Whether the cows like it does not seem to matter. But plenty of other places have their own customs of cleanliness. The solitary spot in the country where this truly Dutch tradition is not observed is the foreign quarter of Amsterdam, where there is a complete indifference to soap and water.

It has been said that a Dutch housewife's idea of happiness in a future world is to have a dwelling on the Dutch model, in which she may rub and scrub and polish throughout eternity. Even in the barges on the canals the same passion prevails. A detachable washing tray can be seen on every bulwark. It would be strange perhaps if this were not so, for the barge is as important to Dutch national life as the house itself, and the woman whose home it is, is as anxious to keep it beautifully clean and tidy as if it were a palace.

Dutch churches are swept and cleaned with quite as much care as Dutch homes. In other respects, perhaps, the majority of these churches are a little dull and disappointing to the visitor. What strikes us most is their bare expanse of whitewashed wall and the absence of decorations or paintings of the sort to which the traveler is accustomed in other parts of Europe. The Netherlands is essentially a stronghold of the Protestant religion and the thoroughness with which its inhabitants did away with every sign of Papal rule can easily be explained.

The southern provinces of Brabant and

Limburg have large numbers of Roman Catholics, but otherwise the only notable exception to the Protestant communities of the country is the fishing village of Volendam. Several of the older churches elsewhere still contain carvings and tombs of historical interest; but the typical Dutch church is the small, unpretentious building of brick and stone, with its white-washed walls, plain pulpit and plainer pews.

It is in the Dutch houses that we see the Dutchman's effort to make up for the natural dullness of the country. In this

Nicholls

**OLD PEASANT COUPLE FROM OUDE BEIJERLAND, SOUTH HOLLAND**

Much of South Holland is "polder" land, or land reclaimed from the sea by dykes, or often a series of them. On its fertile soil cereals, flax and beetroot are grown. South of the island of Beijerland, in the north of which dwells this homely but good-hearted couple, is the Hollandsch Diep, an arm of the sea formed during a great flood in 1421.

© EWING GALLOWAY

**GREAT SAND DUNES** are Zoutlande's only protection against the North Sea, for this little Zealand village on the island of Walcheren lies below sea level. Fortunately the dunes here are natural, but, needless to say, the people who live behind them quickly repair them if storm or strong wind lessen their height. The coarse marram grass that grows upon the dunes binds together the loose, shifting sand. During World War II the Germans flooded this area so that the village was completely inundated. The starched caps worn by Dutch women vary greatly in shape.

MC LEISH

**MIDDELBURG,** the capital of Zealand, always a pleasant spot, was at its best on fair days and market days, for then the country people from all the islands of Zealand flocked to the town in their varied costumes. Unfortunately, Middelburg itself and much of the town of Flushing was destroyed in the second World War, when Germany invaded The Netherlands

© Royal Dutch Air Service

LOOKING DOWN ON THE THRONGED HARBOR OF ROTTERDAM, THE BUSIEST SEAPORT OF THE NETHERLANDS

Rotterdam is now the second largest town in the Netherlands, but only within the last hundred years has it become very important. It stands on both banks of the River Maas—the old town on the right bank and

island of Noordereiland. We can just see an end of it in the top left-hand corner of this photograph. On May 10, 1940, German parachute troops were landed near Rotterdam and the city was bombed by air so that

**THE HAGUE: AN AIR VIEW OF A FAMOUS CITY, WHICH IS THE SEAT OF THE GOVERNMENT**

The handsome, spacious city of The Hague was once the hunting resort of the Counts of Holland, and is therefore still called in Dutch 's Graven Hage, which means "The Count's Enclosure." Although it became a large place and the political capital at the end of the sixteenth century, it was not given the privileges of a town until the nineteenth century, and so for a long time it was called "the largest village in Europe." Across the ornamental water in the foreground of this photograph is the Binnenhof, the building in which the Dutch parliament meets.

MC LEISH

**UTRECHT** is an old and interesting town that dates back to Roman times. In the thirteenth century its cathedral was built on the site of a church founded in 720 by St. Willibrord, Utrecht's first bishop. The graceful tower that we see here is separated from the rest of the cathedral, since the nave, which collapsed in 1674, has never been rebuilt.

© E. N. A

**AT HAARLEM** all that remains of the many gates which pierced the protecting walls that once surrounded the town is the dignified and many towered Spaarnewouder or Amsterdam Gate shown here. Haarlem is one of the most attractive towns in the Netherlands for in the spring it is encircled by fields of hyacinths, tulips and narcissi which it cultivates.

land of monotonously low horizons the houses, which, in the towns at any rate, are high and narrow, are built with steep gables, straight or stepped, that break the sky line. To compensate for the gray skies that brood over the Netherlands, these houses are painted in bright colors.

In Broek, the little dwellings show an amazing variety of paint, greens and reds predominating, and the painted wooden houses in a few other villages, with their red tile roofs, are similarly attractive. Colored glass is often used for the windows, and even the plain glass windows are kept so carefully polished that their gleaming brightness is a feature of the house. Nor must we forget the charming effect of the shutters checkered in blue and yellow, or in red and black or white.

The interiors of the houses vary with individual tastes, but there is generally plenty of color in them. Modern Delft ware is inferior to the older product, but it retains all its popularity in the Dutch household, whether for tiles or china. Brass and copper utensils made in the country not only appeal to the housewife's fondness for rubbing and polishing, but, properly burnished, they help to make a room sparkle with light and warmth.

Many picturesque national costumes survive. The style of dress that travelers talked about as a curiosity more than a century ago is still worn in Volendam. Women with embroidered bodices and huge, mitre-like caps, and men in their less colorful but distinctive short jackets with two rows of buttons and enormously wide trousers, are still to be seen about the Volendam quays. Other Dutch fishermen also wear the capacious trousers fastened by a band round the waist, and the use of wooden clogs for shoes is common among country and sea-faring folk.

---

## THE NETHERLANDS: FACTS AND FIGURES

### THE COUNTRY

The Netherlands (generally called Holland), in northwestern Europe, is bounded on the south by Belgium, east by Germany and north and west by the North Sea. The area, excluding water, is 12,883 square miles; including interior waters, 13,551 square miles; population is 9,884,415 (1948).

### GOVERNMENT AND CONSTITUTION

Monarchy, hereditary and constitutional. Executive power vested in Sovereign; legislative authority rests conjointly in Sovereign and parliament (called States-General) consisting of 2 chambers; Upper or First Chamber composed of 50 members elected by provincial states; members of the Second Chamber, numbering 100, are elected directly by universal suffrage. The Sovereign exercises executive authority through a Council of Ministers. There is also a State Council of 14 members. During the war a temporary government was set up in England. The Netherlands was cleared of German forces in the spring of 1945, and the legitimate government was resumed in its homeland.

### COMMERCE AND INDUSTRY

Agriculture and animal husbandry are highly intensive. Large estates prevail in provinces of Zealand, South Holland, Groningen and North Holland; small estates in North Brabant, Guelders, Limburg and Overijssel. Principal crops are rye, oats, wheat, potatoes, sugar-beets, vegetables, fruits and bulbous plants. There is a large milk output. Coal is the only important mineral. Herring and oyster-fishing important. Shipbuilding is carried on; manufacturing industries include diamond-cutting, distilling, sugar-refining, beet-sugar factories, salt works, breweries and tobacoo factories. Chief exports are fish, cheese, butter, eggs, sugar, vegetable oils and chemicals. Imports are corn, spice, coffee, manufactured goods, mineral oils, raw cotton, machinery, iron and steel.

### COMMUNICATIONS

The total length of canals and rivers is about 4,817 miles; railway, 2,080 miles. Telegraph lines are mostly state-owned; the mileage of wires for state lines is 4,473 miles; telephone wire mileage, 317,815. There is regular international airplane service.

### RELIGION AND EDUCATION

Entire freedom of religion. The royal family and a great part of the inhabitants belong to the Reformed Church. State budget contains allowances for different churches. Education compulsory between the ages of 6 and 13. Religious and sectarian instruction are separate. There are many private schools largely supported by the state; numerous technical schools, 4 famous public universities at Leiden, Utrecht, Groningen and Amsterdam, 1 technical college, 1 agricultural college and 2 private universities.

### CHIEF TOWNS

Amsterdam, capital, population, 828,286; Rotterdam, 667,226; The Hague (seat of the Court), 552,154; Utrecht, 190,494; Haarlem, 160,789; Eindhoven, 138,707; Groningen, 135,311; Tilburg, 118,318.

# LITTLE BELGIUM'S TWO STURDY RA

## *Thrifty People Who Have Made Their Country Rich*

Belgium, the most densely populated country of Europe, is a hive of industry, blessed with the twins of modern power, iron and coal, located in the wilderness of the Ardennes, where Caesar's legions trod and the legendary werewolf prowls. A convenient pathway to France, England and Germany, Belgium, the Innocent Bystander, has suffered the repeated tragedy of war. She has a rich colony in Africa. Roused by Stanley's discoveries Leopold II realized the great economic possibilities of the Congo. Out of Katanga comes the ore, pitchblende, from which comes radium and atomic fission material. Guilds are no longer existent but the guild spirit is still abroad; pride in workmanship is an ineradicable component of the Belgian character.

THE little country of Belgium is one of the best known and most interesting of the European countries. Even those of us who have not been able to travel know that its people played a heroic part in World War I and that the land was devastated during the years of German occupation. In May, 1940, the Germans invaded Belgium again. Again her beautiful medieval cities were subjected to the cruel ravages of war and some historic edifices were ruined.

Although people may know the cities and buildings of Belgium very well, it is not easy to understand or to get to know the Belgians as a people. This is because the Belgians do not make friends easily; they are a quiet and reserved race. Before a Belgian will tell you about himself with freedom, it is necessary to win his confidence and to appeal to his heart, and that is not easy when one is only staying a short time in the country.

It is because of their reserved natures that the Belgians are very often misunderstood. Until World War I they were treated by other nations with a certain amount of disdain. The war brought a great change, for it was then that the Belgians showed themselves to be a nation of heroes.

The Belgian nation is made up of two distinct races, the Flemings and the Walloons. The Flemings belong to the same Teutonic stock as the Anglo-Saxons; the Walloons are allied racially to their neighbors, the French. Formerly Walloons and Flemings were quite distinct. However, they have inter-married so much in the last few centuries and there has been such admixture of foreign blood that racial differences have tended to become far less noticeable.

The Walloons and the Flemings are much the same in general character. This explains, perhaps, why they have seldom fought with each other during the many centuries that they have been united. A strong bond between them has been a common religious faith—both peoples are Roman Catholics. They speak entirely different languages, however. The language of the Walloons is akin to French; the Flemings speak a tongue similar to that of the Germans.

The Belgian peasants are extremely hard-working and lead simple lives. Seldom are they ill, and we may see peasants of a great age still working and taking a prominent place in the life of their village. Although they work from daybreak to sunset and have few pleasures, on Sunday they put on their best clothes and go out to amuse themselves. They love to sit in a café drinking coffee or light beer or in the public gardens, where often a band may be playing.

It is entirely due to the superlati industry of the people that Belgium is of the most, if not the most, intensi cultivated country in the worl of the land is fertile, especia rivers where the rich sedim deposited, but much of Holland, has been recla sand dunes, polders

JOEL

**OF BRUGES** are like mirrors, reflecting most delightfully the old houses We stand on the Quai du Rosaire, almost in the centre of the town, for this etops we see the spires and turrets of the town hall, a Gothic build- Bruges is in west Belgium, not far from the Dutch frontier.

NICHOLLS

**"A CITY OF BRIDGES"** that is Bruges, for it has so many of them. Its name—in Flemish "Brugge"—means bridges. This is the Pont du Cheval, or Bridge of the Horse, seen from the Quai Vert. Over the houses and trees towers the famous belfry. This waterway is the River Reye, that winds across the town. Two canals connect Bruges with the North Sea

BELGIAN GOVERNMENT INFORMATION CENTER

**HIGH FASHION**

This townsman of Binche is all dressed up for the carnival, a three-day festival that comes just before Lent. Binche is in southwestern Belgium. Most of the people of this pleasant town are French-speaking Walloons.

lightful it is to drive through the countryside on the straight well-paved roads, lined with trees, and to see the small farms looking for all the world like model gardens. This is especially true in the central part and in Flanders in the western part. Almost all kinds of grain, vegetables and fruit are grown, and some of the highly cultivated varieties, such as endive and luscious, meaty grapes, are grown for export. In spite of the large agricultural production, Belgium, which is even more densely populated than China, has to get some of her food from other countries.

The mineral wealth of Belgium is great; it is almost entirely confined to the four southern provinces of Hainaut, Liége, Namur and Luxembourg. The most valuable mineral of all is coal; the Namur coal field, with an area of over 500 square miles, is particularly rich. There are great deposits of iron in the province of Liége and also in the country between the Sambre and the Meuse. Manganese is obtained in both Liége and Namur. Liége is the principal source of calamine, or zinc ore. Much of it is sent to France to be treated.

Although Belgian children, after their twelfth year, and women were formerly allowed to work in mines, social legislation has changed all that. Belgian workers now enjoy social security and modern employee benefits.

The "black diamonds" of coal, lying so temptingly close to the surface, have made a bustling, industrial center of the dreary, barren area that was once known as the "Black Country." The sand of this section is responsible for the fine quality of Belgian glass.

Belgium is renowned for its hand-made laces. Its linen and woolen goods combine effective designs with great durability.

Geographically, as well as racially, Belgium is divided into two sections. The flat country of the north and the hill country of the south are separated by the River Meuse. The river system also shares this peculiarity, for the two chief rivers flowing through Belgium, the Schelde and the Meuse, differ greatly. The sluggish Schelde may be described as the river of the lowland, while the swift-flowing Meuse, which breaks its way through the ranges of the beautiful Ardennes, may be called the river of French Belgium. Most of the famous towns of Belgium are situated on the banks of one of these important rivers.

Ghent is situated at the junction of the Schelde and Lys and is the capital of East Flanders. It is the centre of the important cotton and linen industries of Belgium. In the eighteenth century, Ghent was one of the wealthiest and most important cities in all Europe, and it still has many memorials of its past greatness. Everyone goes to see the famous old belfry which has stood there since the twelfth century, and its forty-four bells have rung out on many great historical occasions. Ghent also has a beautiful cathedral and fine law courts which are almost surrounded by water.

Brussels, which is by far the largest town in Belgium, is situated in the centre of the kingdom, on the River Senne. Chief among its ancient buildings are the beautiful Town Hall, the Cathedral of St. Gudule and the Guild Houses which date from the Middle Ages, but unlike most of the other Belgian towns, it does not contain many relics of the past. It is the capital and the centre of modern Belgium, and is a beautiful city, with interesting shops and fine streets and avenues.

Painters love the old cities and towns of Belgium, for in them is still preserved the spirit of medieval Europe. Of these fine old towns, Bruges, which is called the "Venice of the North" on account of its many waterways, is undoubtedly the most picturesque and interesting. At one time it was the great commercial and artistic centre of Northern Europe, and here great scholars and fine painters were encouraged to make their homes. Vessels

STANDARD OIL CO. (N. J.)

GOING TO WORK UNDER THEIR OWN STEAM

No traffic jams beset the Belgian worker cycling to business in the early morning. In Belgium, bicycles are an important means of transportation as well as recreation. Plainly marked bicycle paths parallel many of the main highways.

© E. N. A.

**FROM THE BELFRY** of Bruges, which is 353 feet high and houses a fine carillon of forty-seven bells, we look down over a jumble of narrow, pointed roofs to the twelfth century cathedral of St. Salvator. Bruges is a fine example of a prosperous medieval town. At the height of its prosperity, in the fourteenth century, not only trade but art prospered exceedingly.

MC LEISH

**THE LAW COURTS OF BRUSSELS** occupy a stupendous building that, standing on high ground, dominates the city. It is quite modern (the foundation stone was laid in 1866) and it has an area greater than that of St. Peter's at Rome. We are looking at it from the lofty and lovely tower of the town hall. The church is that of Notre Dame de la Chapelle.

SABENA

**WHERE NAPOLEON BONAPARTE WENT DOWN TO FINAL DEFEAT**

Cattle now graze in the green meadow where once raged the famous Battle of Waterloo. The battleground is near the small village of Waterloo in Belgium. It was here that Napoleon met disaster on June 18, 1815. In the background stands the monument of the Lion, built on the spot where the Prince of Orange, commanding the Dutch and Belgian troops, was wounded.

of all countries unloaded their rich and varied cargoes here, and often as many as one hundred and fifty stately vessels entered the dock in one day.

Every year thousands of visitors come to visit wonderful Bruges to admire its striking architecture and its priceless art treasures. In its quaint old streets peasants may be seen sitting at their doors making beautiful and valuable lace, for lace-making is one of the industries for which the city is famed.

If we are at Bruges for the first Monday after May 2, we shall be able to see the celebrated yearly procession called the procession of the "Holy Blood." This magnificent religious ceremony always attracts large numbers of pilgrims and sightseers to the ancient Flemish city. The object is to honor the Relic of the Precious Blood shed on Calvary.

The relic was given in 1148 to the Count of Flanders by his brother-in-law, Baldwin III, King of Jerusalem. The procession depicts episodes in the lives of great saints and scenes from the Old and New Testaments, then come the relic and clergy, followed by bishops and civic authorities in gorgeous robes. Some idea of the magnificence of the spectacle may be gathered from the fact that the procession lasts at least two hours and a half, and the gorgeous costumes and banners are of immense value.

© E. N. A.

**TAPERING TOWER AND FINE FAÇADE OF THE PRIDE OF BRUSSELS**

The noblest building in Brussels—some say in all of Belgium—is its town hall, which stands on the south side of the market place, or Grand' Place. It was begun in 1410, and its graceful, open spire was finished in 1454. On the summit is an unusual weather-vane—a gigantic gilded statue of St. Michael, brandishing a sword. To the right of the photograph we see some of the old Guild Houses, which are shown in color on page 212.

MC LEISH

**AROUND THE GRAND' PLACE,** the beautiful and interesting market square of Brussels, are many delightful old buildings—the Guild Houses of the ancient corporations. On the left is a corner of the town hall; next come the Mercers' Hall, the Skippers' Hall, with its gable like a ship's stern, and the Halls of the Archers, Coopers and Grease-makers.

MC LEISH

**GOTHIC ARCHITECTURE** is seen at its finest in some of the old towns of Belgium. In the centre of Louvain, an important town of the fourteenth century, stood this beautiful Gothic town hall. It escaped damage during the first World War, but in the German invasion in 1940, it is said to have been damaged to some extent.

BLACK STAR

**UNLOADING A SHIP IN THE RECONSTRUCTED PORT OF ANTWERP**

The port of Antwerp, located on the Schelde River about fifty miles from the sea, was once one of the most important harbors in the world. During World War II it was severely damaged by thousands of flying bombs, but destruction in the city itself was relatively light. Reconstruction was rapid and today Antwerp is again a busy and important shipping center.

BLACK STAR

**REAPING A HARVEST OF GOLD**

These workmen are busily harvesting a field of flax that will be transformed into the finest of Belgian linen and lace. The quality of the linen from Flanders is world-famous, and the secret lies in the river Lys. Because of some property in its water, it excels all other rivers in rotting flax. Linen thread made from flax that has been so processed is fabulously fine.

**IN THE LOW COUNTRY** of North Flanders there are long, straight canals, fringed with trim poplars and overlooked here and there by sturdy windmills. This is the canal that runs from Bruges to Damme and thence to Sluys. Sleepy little Damme used once to be the seaport of the wealthy town of Bruges, and was then an important place commercially. It stood

KNOX

at that time upon a river, the Zwyn. But early in the fifteenth century the waterway began to be filled up with silt and sand, which sounded the death-knell to the prosperity of Damme and Sluys, and even of opulent Bruges. By the nineteenth century, the river was dried up. A canal now connects these three towns with the sea, and a canal connects Bruges witn Ostend.

Donald McLeish

GHENT'S CATHEDRAL AND HER TRIBUTE TO HER ILLUSTRIOUS SONS

Ghent has many old buildings in the Flemish style, but foremost of all its public edifices is the great Cathedral of St. Bavon. Though externally plain, the great church is richly decorated within and contains the famous Adoration of the Lamb by the brothers Van Eyck, who made Ghent the centre of Flemish art and whose monument is seen on the right.

**A CITY OF ISLANDS**

This is a typical scene in Ghent showing one of the many canals that divide the city into a number of islands. About two hundred bridges, such as the one whose hand rail shows in the foreground, connect the islands. Ghent is a bustling port, connected by a deep ship canal with Terneuzen in Holland and by other canals with Zeebrugge, Bruges and Ostend in Belgium.

PHOTOS, PHILIP GENDREAU

**VACATIONERS' PARADISE**

Ostend, a seaport in the province of West Flanders, is a popular seaside resort. It is easy to reach since it is connected with much of Europe and other parts of Belgium by rail and with England by boat. Its sandy coast and excellent sea bathing attract crowds of visitors. A wide sea wall (digue) of stone and terra cotta provides a delightful water-front promenade.

SMITH, BRUSSELS

**THE BEGUINAGE STE. ELIZABETH,** which is in the southwest of Bruges, is surrounded by a moat, and all the houses, which are low and whitewashed, face toward an elm-shaded courtyard. It was founded in the thirteenth century and has a fine church that dates from 1605. The inhabitants of this little settlement were Beguines, pious women who devoted their lives to charity. They were not nuns and took no vows. These sisterhoods were founded in the twelfth century and once flourished in France, Germany, the Netherlands, and countries nearby.

SMITH, BRUSSELS

**BETWEEN CLIFF AND RIVER,** the town of Dinant stretches for nearly a mile along the right bank of the River Meuse directly south of Namur. It is a tourist centre located in the wooded, hilly part of eastern Belgium which is known as the Ardennes. Before the first World War, Dinant was a picturesque old town; but the German invaders burned it almost to the ground, leaving only 112 houses standing. After 1918 it was rebuilt, but in 1940 it was again partly destroyed by German forces. This picture was taken between the wars.

EUROPEAN

**IN A BRUGES SHOP WINDOW—EXQUISITE HANDMADE LACE**

Making beautifully patterned cobwebs of lace is still practiced by many women in Bruges. Lace-making was a flourishing industry there as early as the sixteenth century. It reached a peak in the eighteenth century, and then the art declined after the introduction of machinery. However, it is still passed on from mother to daughter in parts of modern Belgium.

PHILIP GENDREAU

**HANDS THAT HAVE NOT LOST THEIR SKILL**

A lace-maker sits in the sun outside her door in Bruges as she works out an intricate pattern. Flanders, in the western part of which Bruges is located, is noted for the quantities of fine pillow or bobbin lace that it produces. It is famous, too, for its varied and artistic designs in needle-point lace, so called because it is made with a needle rather than with a bobbin.

© E. N. A.

**THE FOREST OF THE ARDENNES,** the Belgian Highlands, has many beauties such as this to charm the eye and the imagination. This lovely spot is in the valley of the River Lesse, five miles from Dinant. A castle was built upon this rock in the thirteenth century, but it was destroyed in the sixteenth, and in 1581 this, the Château de Walzin, was erected.

In the tapestry of Belgium's history, the thirteenth and fourteenth centuries gleam with a special luster. The feudal age was dying out, and the yeast was working that was to produce the Renaissance. Belgium was extremely prosperous at this time. Trade and industry, especially the cloth industry, were at a height. Such towns as Bruges, Ghent and Ypres were governed as free cities. Many of their citizens, particularly the guild masters and the merchants, were wealthy. These men took pride in their towns and sought to make them beautiful. We can still see some of the handsome guild houses and belfries that they erected, though war has taken its toll of others.

### *The Low Countries under Spain*

The Low Countries still formed a single territory, which included both the present-day countries of Holland and Belgium. Belgium, the southern part, was then called the Spanish Netherlands. During the sixteenth century the Low Countries suffered under Spanish rule. However, the greater hardships fell on the Dutch Netherlands when its people turned to Protestantism at the time of the Reformation. The Spanish Netherlands, though it, too, was governed far from wisely, retained a certain measure of prosperity.

After the Dutch gained their independence from Spain, in 1581, they were frequently at war with the people of the Spanish Netherlands—as also were the French. In fact, Belgium was so often the battlefield of Europe during the following centuries that it was nicknamed the "cockpit of Europe."

### *Modern Belgium Is Born*

Friction between France and Belgium continued into Napoleon's day, and he invaded Belgium. After his defeat at Waterloo, in June 1815, Belgium was joined to Holland once more. This was not a satisfactory arrangement, however. In 1830 there was a revolt, and the separate kingdom of Belgium came into existence. The name "Belgium" was taken from Belgae, the name of the tribes who lived there in Julius Caesar's time.

Belgium now entered on a period of growing prosperity. In spite of its small size, the nation came to the fore in trade, in industry and in the arts. It also acquired a great overseas source of wealth when, in 1908, it obtained possession of a vast part of the Congo Basin—since called the Belgian Congo—one of the richest of African territories.

### *The First World War*

The future of the little country looked very bright when suddenly, in the summer of 1914, it was plunged into a desperate plight. German armies invaded its borders and forced their way through cities and towns, fields and woods in a drive toward Paris. The fact that the French capital did not fall was at least partly due to the resistance of the Belgian armies, who hindered the advance until French and British forces arrived. But Belgium could not be saved; and it suffered the harsh fate of occupation all during World War I.

At no time was the Western Front very far from Belgium. Destruction was enormous. Not only were treasured old buildings bombed into ruins but the land itself was almost hopelessly devastated. Yet in the years following the war, by dint of heroic effort, the Belgian people rebuilt their cities, set the wheels of industry turning and coaxed farms into thriving.

### *Triumph over Nazi Occupation*

Then the rumble of approaching war was heard again. The Belgians sought to remain neutral as they had tried to do before, but their efforts were as fruitless with Hitler as they had been with the Kaiser. Armed with tremendous air power and mechanized forces, the nazi hordes quickly engulfed Belgium in the spring of 1940; and a German occupation began that was even more bitter than that of 1914–18. It speaks volumes for the industry and hardihood of the Belgian people, however, that none of the occupied countries recovered as quickly as Belgium did after the end of World War II.

The first sight of Belgium that the visitor obtains, if he approaches it by sea,

STANDARD OIL CO. (N. J.)

**A MOVABLE BRIDGE SPANS THE DYLE AT MECHELEN IN BELGIUM**

Mechelen, or Malines, as the French call it, lies on the bank of the River Dyle. Small tributaries from the Dyle branch out through the circular city, which was once enclosed with a ring of walls. Mechelen is one of the centers of religion in Belgium. Its churches are magnificent, and in them are sculptures and paintings by such famous artists as Reubens.

PIX

**NAMUR'S FAMOUS CITADEL TOWERS ABOVE THE MEUSE**

Though Namur dates from Roman times and a Roman fort once stood on the site of today's citadel, the city has few old buildings. Because it occupies a strategic position at the junction of the Meuse and Sambre rivers, it has been besieged many times. Part of this fine, nine-arched bridge—the Pont de Jambes—was blown up in 1914 to delay the German advance.

is a long expanse of yellow sand, with low dunes at the back like baby mountains. There are no cliffs or rocks or even shingle; there are no trees, just bare sand, with moss and rushes on the higher ground. In winter this sand blows along the coast with great violence.

The industrious Belgians have fortified their low coast against the onslaughts of the sea by means of ramparts of brick and stone, which are called "digues de mer." A "digue," no matter how thick, will not last if it rests on sand alone, so a thick bed of green branches is laid down as a foundation. The finest and longest digue is that which extends from Ostend for over two miles.

Ostend is one of the finest European summer resorts and is filled with holiday-makers of all nationalities. Luxurious hotels and casinos cater to the visitors. English is understood in all the shops and hotels, which shows how popular the town is with the English-speaking people. All along the magnificent Digue are cafés and splendid hotels, and the bright sunshades and bathing costumes on the sands make the everyday scene look like that at a fair or carnival.

Some of the villages of Belgium are worth visiting. There is one called Coxyde, which lies among the dunes not far from the sea. The peasants here live by fishing but in a very curious way, for they do it on horseback. It is strange, indeed, to see the peasants, with baskets and nets fastened to long poles, riding about in the water catching fish.

Traveling in Belgium is cheap and easy, and the best way to see the country is to journey on a barge along the many canals that are to be found in the land.

The Belgians keep their canals in good order and use them as much as possible in order to save money. All day long the barges move slowly along the canals, pulled by a funny little steam tug or by horses.

Possibly because they are so industrious, Belgians relish their occasional moments of relaxation. Sports, such as bicycling, soccer and even American baseball and basketball, are popular. Belgians are expert pigeon fanciers, and they enjoy watching their feathered charges race.

The home life of the country is rich in age-old customs. When a baby is born, for example, parents send sugared candy to their friends. The box is tied up with blue ribbon if it is a boy and with pink ribbon if it is a girl. When a child is christened the godfather gives the mother and godmother a pair of gloves, and there are many other curious customs connected with the christening.

Belgian children look forward to New Year's Day, Christmas and other feast days with great eagerness, for then they have great fun. They have a custom at Christmas which is rather quaint. If a child has been very good all the year he finds a rich cake under his pillow, which is supposed to have been put there by the Archangel Gabriel and to have been made in Heaven. It is called "engels koek."

New Year's Day is a great festival in Belgium. Everyone must call on everyone, so that the door-bell is ringing all day long. In addition to these friendly calls, anyone who has performed the slightest service for a householder during the year comes to beg for a Christmas-box. The gift is usually in the form of a small sum of money; and few such "beggars" are turned away.

On November 11 comes St. Martin's Day, when the children must stand against the wall with their eyes shut. When they turn round the floor is strewn with nuts and candy, which are supposed to have been sent by St. Martin as a gift for good boys and girls.

---

## *BELGIUM: FACTS AND FIGURES*

### *THE COUNTRY*

In northwestern Europe. Bounded on the north by the Netherlands, on the east by Germany and Luxembourg, on the south and southwest by France and on the west by the North Sea. Area, 11,775 square miles, including the cantons of Eupen and Malmédy; population (1947), 8,512,195.

### *GOVERNMENT*

A constitutional, representative and hereditary monarchy. Legislative power is vested in the king, Senate and Chamber of Representatives. When the Nazis invaded Belgium in World War II, the reigning king, Leopold III, surrendered to the Germans and was imprisoned. From 1944 to 1950 Belgium was ruled by a Prince Regent, Leopold's brother Charles. In 1950, the throne passed to Leopold's son Baudouin, who reigned as Prince Royal until July 17, 1951, when he became King of the Belgians.

### *COMMERCE AND INDUSTRY*

Agriculture intensive but density of population necessitates importing foods. The chief crops are oats, rye, wheat, fodder, beets, potatoes, sugar-beets and flax. Cattle, pigs, horses and sheep are raised in considerable numbers. 18% of land surface covered by forest. Industrial activity largely due to rich coal fields. The principal manufactures are artificial silk, motor cars, glass, iron and steel, lace, linen and gloves. Diamond-cutting in Antwerp is important. The chief exports are iron and steel products, glass and glassware, diamonds, textile products (linen, cotton fabrics and rayon), rabbit skins, cement and chemical products; imports are grain, cotton, mineral oils, crude copper, automobiles, oil cake, motors and engines, tobacco and lumber.

### *COMMUNICATIONS*

Most roads are stone paved. Railway mileage, 3,121; navigable waterways (rivers and canals), 968. Length of telegraph line, 36,931 miles; telephone line, 2,170,389 miles.

### *RELIGION AND EDUCATION*

There is full religious liberty and part of income of ministers of all denominations is paid from national treasury. Majority of inhabitants are Roman Catholic. Primary schools are supported by communes. There are many private or free schools mostly under ecclesiastical care. Secondary education is provided in royal athenæums and special schools. There are 4 universities—at Brussels, Louvain, Ghent and Liége.

### *CHIEF TOWNS*

Population (1948): Brussels, capital, with suburbs, 960,740; Antwerp, 266,636; Ghent, 166,-797; Liége, 156,664; Mechlin (Malines), 60,740; Deurne, 57,362; Brugge, 52,984.

# THE BEAUTIFUL LAND OF FRANCE

## *An Industrious People and an Ancient Culture*

France is only about six hundred miles across from north to south or east to west. Yet within this small compass are wild Alpine and Pyrenees peaks, strange volcanic landscapes, wooded hills, parklike fields, rushing mountain torrents and placid rivers. From the days of the Caesars, this lovely land has played an important part in Western civilization. As the meeting place of northern and southern Europeans in ancient times, Celts, Latins, Franks and Norsemen all contributed to the formation of the French people and the flowering of a great culture—which still endures.

FRANCE has suffered greatly in our century. Although her losses in human life were not so great as during the war of 1914–18, the second World War left her almost completely ruined. Two million houses were either totally or partially wrecked, 12,000 bridges or other public works were completely destroyed, two-thirds of her rolling stock and of her merchant marine were lost, and her industrial production was cut to 40 per cent of the 1938 figures. The soil was exhausted from lack of fertilizer, and necessary farm machinery was in sad need of repair or complete replacement. Such was the state in which France found herself at the end of World War II.

However, with all the fortitude that has enabled the peoples of Western Europe to cope with calamities over hundreds of years, the French went to work to repair the damage and to heal their wounds. The road ahead was rocky, nevertheless. There was trouble in the overseas territories and an unstable political and social situation at home. What would France be by 1965 or 1975? A fourth-rate power or a first-class one taking the leadership in a united European community? No one could be certain.

The fairy godmothers were kind to France at her birth. Although the country is not large in area, it has, in every respect, balance and harmony. Its shape is almost a regular hexagon. While it is in close contact with the rest of continental Europe, it has easy access to the lands across the seas. In fact, it has windows on four bodies of water—the Mediterranean Sea, the Atlantic Ocean, the English Channel and the North Sea. The surface of France is about half mountain and half plain, and the agricultural and industrial resources are equally well balanced. The climate is mild, with little variation in temperature because France is lapped by water on almost all sides. There is a good network of waterways, spreading out from four great rivers—the Seine, the Loire, the Garonne and the Rhone.

The country is exceptionally well adapted to man's needs. This explains why so many peoples have attempted to settle there. For hundreds of years a succession of invaders from the east overran the region; and each wave mingled with those who already occupied the land. Thus one cannot say today that there is a French race. There certainly is a French nation, but its unity stems from entirely different things: from its history, its will, its culture, its ideals forged and accepted by all who call themselves French.

The history of France is nothing less than a long progression of different peoples toward a common purpose and destiny. Three outside factors also contributed to the formation of the nation—the Roman conquest, Christianity and the monarchy.

The settlement of ancient Gaul is lost in the mists of time. Twenty or thirty thousand years before the advent of Christianity, when giant elephants, rhinoceroses and hippopotamuses roamed the banks of the Seine and the Marne, very primitive men were already living in this outpost of Western Europe. Some of their weapons have been found—crude hand axes that scientists call *coups de poing*. After them came men who corresponded more to modern racial groups, some broad-headed and some long-headed. At the beginning of the twentieth century, skeletons thousands of years old were found near Monaco, on the Mediterranean coast.

A series of caves in the Dordogne Department, in southwestern France, show one of the most noteworthy stages in the development of man. At Eyzies, at Lascaux, at Font-de-Gaume, there are remarkable wall paintings of horses, mammoths, bison and even men, showing us how the inhabitants of France lived ten thousand or fifteen thousand years before Christ.

In comparatively recent times, that is, in Julius Caesar's day, France was called Gaul. As Caesar tells us in his commentaries, the Gauls were barbarians compared to the Romans. Courageous to the point of recklessness, the Gauls feared but one thing—that the sky should fall upon their heads! But they were also fickle,

MOST OF THE GREAT RIVERS OF FRANCE FLOW NORTHWEST

STANDARD OIL CO. (N. J.)

**WASH DAY AT NEMOURS, BY A PLACID STREAM**

Nemours is a village south of Paris, on the Loing River. It contains several famous old churches, one of which we see. In the foreground women are washing clothes in the river.

turbulent and undisciplined. The Roman conquest to which they finally yielded two thousand years ago brought them many new things: roads, a single language (Latin) and a single government, new ways of clearing and tilling the soil, city life, more refined ways of living—in fact, civilization. Within a few years Gaul became one of the most prosperous of the Roman provinces.

However, the Roman peace did not last and the frontiers of the Empire fell under the advance of the pagan Teutonic tribes, among them, the Franks. During the course of several centuries, their leaders overran the country. One of them, Clovis, founded the Merovingian dynasty, the first Frankish dynasty in Gaul. He established his rule over a large expanse of land. His wife was a Christian and eventually he, too, became a Christian. For the second time Rome played a decisive part in the history of the French nation. This time it was no longer the Rome of the emperors but the Rome of the popes. When Clovis was baptized at Reims in 496, Christianity was established in the west of Europe. Rome not only backed the Frankish kingdom with its worldly power, which was great, but also brought it a new civilization more humane than the Roman had been. The Church opposed slavery, freed men from the yoke of the state and introduced new ideas of brother-

FRENCH EMBASSY—INFORMATION DIVISION

**SHAPING A VASE IN THE OLD WAY**

Pottery has long been an important French industry; and quaint, charming ceramics are still turned out by skilled artisans using methods handed down from father to son.

hood and justice for all men.

The first two Frankish dynasties, the Merovingian and the Carolingian, did not have an easy time, however. The tribal leaders, or barons, fought hard among themselves and often against the king. For several centuries the Vikings from Norway and Denmark periodically sailed up the rivers of France, devastating the cities along the banks. It was only during the reign of the great Charlemagne, one of the Carolingian rulers, that there was a semblance of order. He established an empire of the West for a few years and was crowned Emperor by the Pope at Rome in the year 800.

Hugh Capet founded the third dynasty, in 987. During his reign, the royal domain was only a narrow strip of land between the Seine and Loire rivers. In 1848, when his last descendant, Louis-Philippe, was overthrown, France had reached the limits that she still has today. For nine hundred years, therefore, the history of France is also that of a family, the family of the kings of France.

The monarchy of the Capets had very humble beginnings. A number of peaceful reigns, succeeding each other without disputes, and alliances through marriage slowly brought about territorial unity. At the same time the kings gathered the reins of authority ever more firmly into their hands. The powerful vassals—the dukes and counts of Brittany, of Anjou, of Aquitaine and of Burgundy, who might have contested the kings' growing control—were kept busy with the Crusades and with the wars with England.

During the fourteenth and fifteenth centuries, England and France wore themselves out in a prolonged struggle. The kings of England, descendants of William the Conqueror, claimed land rights in France and even the crown of France. The strife lasted for a hundred years, and France was put to the fire and the sword. One of the most famous figures of this contest was the Black Prince—the Prince of Wales, son of Edward III of England. Early in the 1400's, Jeanne d'Arc, a humble peasant girl from Lorraine, was inspired to take command of the French army. She won battles, liberated cities besieged by the English, and raised the drooping spirits of the French to carry on the fight to save their country. It was through her efforts that Charles VII, who had not been sure of his rights to the throne of France, was crowned at Reims in 1422. Thanks to Jeanne d'Arc, the English were finally chased from French soil.

### *Adversity Makes Brotherhood*

Throughout the long struggle with the English, when all shared the same anguish and rejoiced in the same victories, the French little by little became aware of their national unity. At the beginning of the sixteenth century, when King Louis XI died—which marks the advent of modern times—it seemed that the French nation had come into its own.

Three of the best-known kings are Louis IX, Henri IV and Louis XIV. Louis IX (1215–70), who was later canonized as Saint Louis, is undoubtedly one of the noblest figures in history. A truly good man, he took care of the sick, built hospitals and dispensed justice himself under

TRANS WORLD AIRLINES

**FLYING FINGERS MAKE LACY COBWEBS**

Balancing easily on their heads the tall caps that are a feature of the region, these women of Pont l'Abbé, Brittany, create beautiful hand-made lace. It is sure to find a ready market.

FRENCH EMBASSY—INFORMATION DIVISION

**BY THE DOCKSIDE, BOULOGNE**

Boulogne, on the narrow Strait of Calais, is one of the fishing centers of northern France. Napoleon improved the fine natural harbor, as part of his plan to invade England.

an oak at Vincennes. Every Friday the poor were invited to his table.

Henri IV (1553–1610), a Protestant converted to Catholicism, remains to this day one of the most popular sovereigns in France. It was he who wanted all Frenchmen to have chicken in the pot every Sunday. Perhaps his greatest achievement was that he put an end to the bitter wars of religion.

One of the most glamorous reigns was that of Louis XIV (1638–1715)—the Grand Monarch. At the beginning of the eighteenth century, the French armies were everywhere victorious. The French navy was as powerful as the English navy, and French navigators were exploring far-away seas. All over France the royal authority was accepted and revered. In the arts and literature, the names of Corneille, Racine, Molière, Pascal, Mansard and Lenôtre are the shining stars of the "great century." But the end of Louis XIV's reign found France impoverished by numerous wars. Moreover, the absence of real individual liberty, the absolute power of the king and the doctrine of rule by divine right had made him almost a despot.

Discontent increased during the reigns of Louis XV and Louis XVI, who were unable to bring about much-needed reforms. The climax came with the Revolution of 1789, and three years later the First Republic was born. A young and gifted general, Napoleon Bonaparte, galvanized the nation and carried its standards to the very limits of Europe. However, with him the ideals of equality and liberty

STANDARD OIL CO. (N. J.)

**HARVEST DAY IN THE WHEAT FIELD**

The wheat is shocked and piled in a huge stack and covered. Later the threshing machine will come into the field and thresh the golden grain. The scene is at Pontoise, near Paris.

STANDARD OIL CO. (N. J.)

PINNACLES ABOVE THE HILL TOWN OF CHARTRES

At Chartres one of the great Gothic cathedrals crowns a lofty hill. The narrow streets of the old part of town twist and turn and climb sharply, making driving perilous if not impossible.

TRANS WORLD AIRLINES

**CHAMBORD'S CHATEAU WITH ITS FOREST OF TURRETS**

There are 440 rooms in the Renaissance Château of Chambord, and thirteen grand staircases. The castle was built for Francis I. It is set in a spacious formal park, enclosed by walls.

FRENCH EMBASSY—INFORMATION DIVISION

**BEAUVAIS TAPESTRY IN THE MAKING**

In the tapestry factory at Beauvais skillful hands weave colorful and complicated designs. The factory is supported by the Government and its finest products are displayed in museums.

that had arisen in 1789 went into eclipse. In 1804 he became Emperor. When the combined forces of all the sovereigns of Europe finally conquered him at Waterloo, France was left bleeding, ruined and ready to accept the restoration of the monarchy under Louis XVIII. Two more kings followed him to the throne—Charles X and then Louis-Philippe. The last was overthrown by the revolution of 1848, when the Second Republic came into existence.

In spite of everything, the country possessed such resources that it recovered rapidly. In 1851, a nephew of Napoleon I seized power and ruled as Emperor Napoleon III. Twenty years later, the Second Empire crumbled as a result of an unsuccessful war with Prussia. Then the Third Republic was proclaimed. It was more fortunate than its predecessors; it lasted until 1940. After the interval of the German occupation and the Liberation, France again became a republic, the Fourth, in 1946.

One of the foundation stones of France's stability and wealth is her agriculture. Out of 21,000,000 Frenchmen engaged in some occupation, 8,000,000 are employed in agriculture, not counting the village craftsmen and shopkeepers who also live close to the soil. Of this number, 6,000,000 are their own masters, either as landowners or farmers, and only 2,000,000 work for wages.

French farms in general are small. When one takes a walk in the French countryside or flies over it, he is always astonished to see how the land is divided. In most cases the fields are narrow strips, the color of which changes according to the seasons. This parceling is largely the result of the laws of inheritance enacted at the time of the Revolution. By these laws a landowner must divide his property equally among all his children. This has left him no other choice but to break up his domain if he has more than one child.

The result is a very inefficient means of working the land. Farms have grown smaller and smaller. If a farmer acquires a number of small plots, by inheritance or purchase, they are likely to be widely scattered. This is one reason why the French farmer complains of his lot.

However, since World War II, efforts have been made to remedy the situation. In fact, the life of the French peasant has been undergoing great changes. For one thing, co-operatives of farm equipment have been set up here and there. By 1965 or 1975, it is probable that several sections of the countryside will have been completely electrified and otherwise modernized.

The French farmer gets rich rewards from the soil. He works hard but he fares better than his Bulgarian, German, Italian or Yugoslav counterpart.

No French farm is without domestic animals, and a good part of the farmer's income stems from his livestock. Cereals, beets, potatoes, fruits and vegetables, and

TRANS WORLD AIRLINES

**MEDIEVAL CASTLE NEAR CHINON**

The castle of Langeais, near Chinon, was built in 990. Its steep roofs, conelike turrets, and small windows show its medieval origin. Here Charles VIII married Anne of Brittany in 1491.

the vine flourish on the rich soil. More rational methods of farming should make the yields even better. As it is, before the war, in 1939, the wheat crop alone had twice the value of the coal and iron ore mined in France in the same year. The wheat crop, however, is just sufficient for home consumption, for the French are great eaters of bread.

The pleasures of the table have always held a high place in France; and French cookery, famous the world over, is both a science and an art. In the tourist guides to the country, some restaurants may have two or three stars, a certain sign of their excellence.

Cassoulet of Toulouse (baked beans with salted goose), sauerkraut of Alsace, bouillabaisse (a sort of fish soup) from Marseilles, foie gras (goose-liver paste) with truffles, chicken with mushrooms, duck à l'orange, lobster à l'armoricaine (Brittany), pike croquettes, ham à la crème, snails à la bourguignonne (Burgundy), not to mention the celebrated châteaubriant (a superlative steak) with French-fried potatoes—these are the favorite dishes of the Frenchman and the delight of the visitor.

A marvelous choice of wines, unique in the world, serves as a worthy accompaniment to the regional dishes. When the Greeks landed at Marseilles several centuries before Christ, they introduced the grapevine into France. It has prospered. For two thousand years, from south of the Loire River to Paris and Alsace, the French peasant has taken the most tender care of his vineyard. In September, gay companies of grape-pickers can be seen, their heads covered with broad straw hats, picking the juicy clusters and placing them in wicker baskets. These are then loaded on carts drawn slowly by horses or oxen. At twilight, the whole company, singing the old songs and the new, takes the road back to the village that is marked by a church spire on the horizon.

STANDARD OIL CO. (N. J.)

**RELIGIOUS PROCESSION IN VILLERSEXEL**

Villersexel is a small, neat town in Haute (Upper) Saone, not far from the city of Dijon. It was the scene of a battle in the war of 1870–71. Above, a Sunday School procession of children.

BLACK STAR

**STRASBOURG'S SOARING GOTHIC CATHEDRAL**

All the lines point upward in Strasbourg's cathedral, one of the most glorious examples of the Gothic style. Above the arched doorway is a stained-glass rose window forty-two feet wide.

ANDRÉ DE DIENES

**WINTER IS NEVER FAR FROM CHAMONIX**

The valley of Chamonix is bordered on the east by the Mont Blanc range, eternally snowclad, with glaciers moving down the slopes. Chamonix is a Mecca for those who love snow sports.

School attendance up to the age of sixteen, the spread of technical education among farmers, the modernization of rural enterprises in the villages and the creation of cultural centers for the French farmers and their families should help to keep them attached to the soil. Young farm people, especially, may be less likely to pine for city life.

### *Gems of Gothic Architecture*

Between the eleventh and fourteenth centuries, a series of unique monuments sprang up all over France—the Gothic cathedrals. They are typical creations of French architectural genius, in a style of artistic expression as characteristic as the Greek temple, the Egyptian pyramid or the American skyscraper. During this late period of the Middle Ages, each city of France tried to perpetuate its name by building a temple to God surpassing in beauty, in lightness of touch and in richness the one of the neighboring town. In Amiens, in Chartres, in Reims, in Bourges, in Rouen, these magnificent

LANDAU

TINKLING COWBELLS IN THE ALPS

There is good pasture for the cows in many places high in the French Alps, though the sun glistens on snowy peaks that seem, on a clear day, very near. Most French farms are small.

STANDARD OIL CO. (N. J.)

WHO WILL BUY MY CAULIFLOWERS?

Market day in Nevers. Most French towns have a market day once a week. Farmers bring their produce to sell; and in return buy clothing, household goods, tools and other necessities.

© UNDERWOOD & UNDERWOOD

**THE DORDOGNE RIVER,** before it leaves the Auvergne Mountains, is rapid and wild. Here it flows placidly among grass and trees; later it becomes a busy highway thronged with ships. It runs for three hundred miles through southwest France to unite with the Garonne, thirteen miles from Bordeaux, and form the Gironde, an estuary on the Atlantic Coast.

KNOX

**LOMBARDY POPLARS** border the trim straight roads so typical of France, roads as different as can be from the winding, grass-fringed lanes of England. To French people, doubtless, those country roads would appear untidy in comparison to a road running straight as a dart to its destination and lined by the most regular and erect of trees.

STANDARD OIL CO. (N. J.)

**OUTSKIRTS OF SISTERON, SNUGGLED AGAINST THE MOUNTAINS**

Sisteron, on the Durance River in southeastern France, hugs its mountain (one of the Maritime Alps). The town was built in the Middle Ages and still keeps something of its medieval character.

structures soar to the skies with airy grace. The peaks of the naves reach from 98 to 164 feet high, and the spires from 377 feet (Chartres) to 465 feet (Strasbourg). Delicate openwork in some of the walls belies the actual solidity of the buildings. Inside, a glowing light streams through the stained-glass windows that pierce the large bays.

The stone itself appears to be spiritualized. Pillars, flying buttresses, groined arches, pointed arches—their lines draw the eyes up and up as if the builders had tried to reach the kingdom of heaven itself. Still these temples mysteriously remain linked to man's needs. Under their arches and their jeweled windows one has a sense of peace, of inner security.

Along with the new style in architecture, the construction of the cathedrals also brought about a marvelous rebirth of sculpture. Indeed, in the Middle Ages art was considered a means of education. Few people could read and write, but they could learn from the bas-reliefs and the statues in the cathedrals. Here, in stone, are stories from the Old and New Testaments and the lives of the saints. There

**WINE TESTERS, GEVREY-CHAMBERTIN**

The wine testers, garbed in red and gold, open the festivities with a procession to church. Silver cups, for tasting the wine, hang round their necks and adorn the leader's staff.

PHOTOS, FRENCH EMBASSY—INFORMATION DIVISION

**HARVEST IN THE COTE D'OR**

The Côte d'Or (Golden Hillside) is a department of France celebrated for its excellent and abundant wines. The prosperous vineyard above is near Beaune, in the heart of this rich region.

WAYMARK

**AN OLD BRIDGE** over the Gave de Pau takes us into Orthez, a little town of the Pyrenees whose history reaches far back into the past. In the 13th century it had a splendid court. A five-sided tower, at that time the keep of a castle, and some buildings a century older are still standing. In 1569 the town was besieged and taken by Protestant troops, and in 1814, not far from here, the Duke of Wellington with his army won a great victory over the French. Orthez stands at an important junction of roads leading over the Pyrenees Mountains and on into Spain.

© E. N. A.

**IN THE PYRENEES** there are few valleys more beautiful than the Vallée d'Ossau which runs northward from the cleft summit of the Pic du Midi d'Ossau, 9,465 feet high. The name means the Valley of the Bears, but no bears are to be found there now, only chamois, and they are becoming fewer and fewer. Once the Vallée was a self-governing commonwealth, and its people are still very independent. The women till the fields and spin with distaff and spindle, and wear quaint red hoods. The men wear clothes of brown wool that are brightened by gay sashes.

are more worldly sculptures, too, that teach man something of the other arts, the sciences and the professions. At Chartres alone there are more than two thousand sculptured figures. It would take more than a lifetime to make a detailed study of all of them. No wonder then that the cathedrals have been called the Bible of the poor.

Besides the great Gothic cathedrals and the earlier Romanesque churches, the wonderful castles of the Renaissance that adorn the banks of the Loire River remind us of the glorious past of this old land.

The French people thus have lived surrounded by masterpieces, in an atmosphere of nobility and beauty. For ten centuries, in spite of military and political reverses, France has been a creator in the realms of thought, of literature and of the arts. Indeed, France still deserves the title "mother of letters and arts" that a poet of the Renaissance bestowed upon her. Always ready to welcome exiles, she has also been open to new ideas. This helps to explain the breadth of her culture.

Among writers and philosophers, there are the names of Pascal, Montaigne, Racine, Descartes, Voltaire, Rousseau, Chateaubriand, Victor Hugo and Balzac. Among her painters are Watteau, Fragonard, Corot, Renoir and Cézanne. World-famous musical composers are Rameau, Debussy and Ravel. Her scientists include Ampère and the Curies. Their work belongs just as much to the heritage of all humanity as to that of France. The vein is not exhausted today. Claudel, Valéry, Péguy, Gide, Langevin, the Duke de Broglie, painters such as Matisse, Rouault, Utrillo, architects such as Auguste Perret or Frantz Jourdain are proof of the vitality of the recent intellectual and artistic life of France.

The average city Frenchman—Monsieur Dupont, as he is usually called—used to be represented as a little man, a bachelor, who sported a mustache, wore a derby, was a great talker, was ignorant of geography and never set foot out of his country. This portrait was never really lifelike.

Today Monsieur Dupont is a married man and a real family man as in the past. In spite of the greater ease that the law of 1945 offers for obtaining a divorce, there

RAPHO-GUILLUMETTE

**LYONS TURNS HER FACE TO THE RIVER**

Lyons (or Lyon), third largest city of France, is strategically situated on the River Saone, at the point where it joins the Rhone. Lyons is an industrial center and a railroad junction.

are very few. Of the couples who do seek a divorce, most are childless. Since World War II the French population has been increasing. The surplus of births over deaths was 324,000 in 1950 as compared to 35,000 in 1938.

that he can use at once rather than put his savings in a stocking. If he can afford it, Monsieur Dupont has a car. If not, he is contented with a velomotor or a bicycle. The old-time Sunday stroll along the boulevards has given way to a week end in

RAPHO-GUILLUMETTE

**FUN FOR THE CHILDREN IN PLACE BELLECOUR**

Place Bellecour, a spacious open square in the heart of Lyons, in olden days was a stately promenade where fashionable folk gathered. Today it is largely given over to the children.

the forests of Fontainebleau or Compiègne.

Today Monsieur Dupont, the average Frenchman, has also taken up sports. In the winter he takes a ski train to spend a week in a resort in the Alps or the Pyrenees. In the summer he goes camping, or he visits Italy, Austria or England. He is even learning foreign languages.

One of the favorite vacation spots of the French people is Provence on the Côte d'Azur—the French Riviera at the eastern end of the Mediterranean coast. Formerly it was the playground of a privileged few.

The Côte d'Azur is without rival for beauty. It is a land of contrasts, basking in dazzling sunlight. There is contrast in the contours. A few hours from Nice, the peaks of the Alps surge upward to a

Monsieur Dupont has, on the average, three children in spite of the fact that his salary is low and his apartment is apt to be small. One of the most distressing problems for young engaged couples is to find a place where they may set up their own household. In cities such as Lyons, Marseilles, Lille, Paris and Bordeaux, apartments are either not to be found or they are extremely expensive.

Monsieur Dupont no longer has a mustache, no longer wears a derby. Nor does he live any longer on a fixed income from land or stocks or bonds. Since 1930 such incomes have melted like snow in the sun. For some years France has been suffering from severe inflation, and Monsieur Dupont has lost much of his old sense of thrift. Today he prefers to buy goods

P. L. M.

**THE FOUNTAIN OF VAUCLUSE** is one of the most beautiful spots in South France. Here the River Sorgue rises in a semicircle of frowning cliffs, the entrance to which is guarded by the ruins of an ancient castle. Sometimes the little stream comes gushing out of a deep pool in a cavern, falling in cascades over the mossy stones; at other times the pool is very still and the water trickles out from holes in the rock some hundred yards below. Where you see the paper mill the house of the Italian poet Petrarch once stood. Here he meditated and wrote.

**ST. MICHEL D'AIGUILLE** is a church perched atop an isolated rock nearly three hundred feet high. It is reached by a long flight of steps. So precipitous are the sides of the rock that it is a constant source of wonder that the tenth-century builders contrived to carry up their materials. The church-crowned rock is north of Le Puy, a town in central France.

FRENCH EMBASSY—INFORMATION DIVISION

ACRES OF BLOSSOMS NEAR GRASSE

Grasse, in Provence, the southeastern region of France, is the center of the flower industry. Vast fields of fragrant blooms are grown for export, and also to be distilled into perfume.

FRENCH EMBASSY—INFORMATION DIVISION

**RICH FABRICS COME FROM LYONS**

Textiles from Lyons, especially silks and velvets, are of high quality. There have been times when more than half the citizens depended, directly or indirectly, on the silk industry.

MC LEISH

**DELIGHTFUL CHAMONIX,** one of the best known and most popular resorts in the French Alps, lies in a narrow valley beneath Europe's loftiest mountain. We do not see Mont Blanc in this picture, though on the left we can recognize the foot of the Mer de Glace, its enormous glacier. The cloud-capped peak before us is the beautiful Aiguille Verte.

NICHOLLS

**AT THE FOUNTAIN** in sleepy little Puget-Theniers, the capital of a district in Provence not far from Nice, a muleteer waters his sturdy, sure-footed steed. Sureness of foot is a valuable asset, for the little town lies in a small valley among the wild and rocky slopes of the Alpes-Maritimes. A castle in ruins gives evidence that it was once fortified.

height of six thousand feet, a paradise for skiers until the early months of summer. In this same region are the deep gorges of the Verdon River.

There is contrast along the coast, marked by limestone coves, narrow creeks and wide pebbled beaches lapped by waters of cobalt blue.

Vegetation is just as varied. In a walk of only a few miles, one may pass through scrub, pine woods, forests of hundred-year-old beeches, flowery fields, groves of palm or olive trees and thickets of spiny-leaved agaves or prickly cactus.

There are ancient towns, such as Antibes, Fréjus and Hyères, which date back to the times of the Romans. On high points little villages perch like eagles' nests, a reminder of the days when the inhabitants needed protection from the pirates of the Barbary coast. Only a stone's throw away from these quaint old towns are the modern hotels of summer resorts such as Cannes, Juanles-Pins, Sainte-Mavime and Saint-Raphaël.

### *The Sun-drenched Côte d'Azur*

The Côte d'Azur is well named. Perhaps nowhere else on earth are the blue of the sea and the sky so vivid. Color beguiles the eyes everywhere: the green of the forests, the silver-gray of the olive trees, the red of the porphyritic rock, the white of the limestone. The climate is warm in winter and is freshened in summer by the light breezes from the Mediterranean, whose waters are always cool.

Provence is the center of the flower industry. Alphonse Karr, a writer of the nineteenth century, started it. He settled on the Côte d'Azur during the reign of Napoleon III and was enraptured at the sight of all the flowers growing there. "Leave Paris," he wrote, "plant your cane in my garden, and the next day when you wake up, you will see that roses have grown on it." With the help of a friend, he began to cultivate flowers on a large scale. Then he had the idea of sending bouquets of violets to Paris by mail. This venture turned out to be a huge success.

Nowadays eight thousand horticulturists are engaged in this business, and cut flowers are sent by plane as far as the Scandinavian countries.

At Grasse, Vence, Menton, Vallauris, there are whole fields of violets, mignonettes, jasmine, orange trees, mimosa, carnations and pinks. Anyone who has ever seen these fields in bloom, saturating the air with fragrance, will never forget the experience.

In the region of Grasse the distillation of flowers dates back to the sixteenth century. It was then that Catherine de Médicis had a Florentine specialist in this delicate art settle in Grasse. Today large factories with the most modern equipment extract the perfume-yielding oils from the flowers cultivated in the region. These factories also extract essences from aromatic plants and from fruit, some of it shipped in from outside France.

In one of the most up-to-date methods of distillation, the crushed flowers are placed in contact with a petroleum compound for eight hours. When it has been saturated with perfume, the dissolvent is distilled in a vacuum. The purified residue is then treated with alcohol to produce the essence. Five hundred thousand rosebuds are necessary to yield one quart of rose essence.

Life in the great industrial centers of France is entirely different from life in Provence or in the Basque country of the Pyrenees. The miners in the coal fields of the Nord or of Saint-Etienne, the workers in the big steel mills of Lorraine and Le Creusot work hard. Their poor living conditions have been a cause of concern for many years. Before the second World War, several of the industries had begun to provide better housing for the workers. After the war some of the key industries were nationalized, and this brought about further improvement.

### *Compulsory Social Security*

The Government introduced a general and compulsory social-service system, to which both employers and employees must contribute. Its principle is simple. Each month both employers and employees must pay a certain amount (less for the workers) to a central treasury. Considerable

PHILIP GENDREAU

**ENTRANCE TO THE BASILICA, LOURDES**

The Basilica at Lourdes is built over the grotto where little Bernadette Soubirous a century ago had a vision of the Virgin Mary. Miraculous cures here are frequently reported.

AMERICAN EXPORT LINES COLLECTION

**THE STERN FORTRESS OF CHATEAU D'IF**

Francis I had this grim prison built on the tiny rocky isle of If, just outside Marseilles, in the Mediterranean. Here Dumas placed his hero, Edmond Dantès, "The Count of Monte Cristo."

STANDARD OIL CO. (N. J.)

**THE PICTURESQUE OLD HARBOR OF MARSEILLES**

Marseilles is the greatest commercial seaport of France. There is an Old Harbor, now used mostly by small boats, and a magnificently equipped New Harbor of more than three hundred acres.

STANDARD OIL CO. (N. J.)

**CATCHING THE NEWS IN PASSING**

Frenchmen are avid readers of newspapers They will call for a paper to read while sipping coffee or an aperitif at a café; and the street-corner bulletin board is well scanned.

FRENCH EMBASSY—INFORMATION DIVISION

HAND-FED CAPONS FOR TENDER MEAT

A curious custom is sometimes followed on the farms of southwest France. Capons are kept in cages, so they cannot move about, crammed with corn by hand, to insure fat, tender meat.

STANDARD OIL CO. (N. J.)

TWO-LEVEL TRAFFIC IN ST. RESTITUT

A corner in St. Restitut, in southern France, showing Italian influence in the tiled roof and plastered stones of the building. At the right, a street on a higher level.

sums of money are thus set aside. They are used to pay medical expenses, to help the unemployed, to send tubercular patients to the mountains and to provide pensions for aged workers.

A system of family allowances helps the families with many children and allows mothers to stay at home. Before, many mothers worked outside their homes to eke out the meager family income.

In spite of some flaws, the social-security system represents noteworthy social progress. Eventually, among other results, these measures, including compulsory medical care, will raise the health standards of the French people.

The French generation that came of age during the troubled years of the occupation and after has been schooled in adversity and has found it hard to make its way. That is why some young French men and women have chosen to leave their country. Since the war there has been an emigration movement, similar to that of the seventeenth and eighteenth centuries, toward Canada, South America, Africa and Australia.

After the tragic defeat of 1940 and the years of German occupation, when the life of France almost stood still, the French people realized that only by a tremendous effort could they hold their own in a world dominated by two industrial giants, the United States and the Soviet Union.

TRANS WORLD AIRLINES

**FISHERMAN'S LUCK—A DAY ON SHORE AT CANNES**

First a health resort, then a winter resort, now a year-round vacation spot, Cannes, on the Riviera, has a charm for all. Its greatest attraction is its sunny, mild weather.

**PONT DU GARD NEAR NIMES**

There are many remains of Roman occupation at Nîmes, including an amphitheater and temple. Near by are some Roman baths and part of an aqueduct, the Pont du Gard, built under Agrippa.

One step in this direction was the Monnet Plan, drawn up in 1947. It called for nothing less than to make French agriculture and industry completely modern. From the very beginning, however, the French were under no illusions as to the size of the task or that it might take years to carry out. Yet a good start has been made, in spite of the enormous expense of general rearmament and of the war in Indochina.

France has great mineral wealth of prime importance to industry, namely, iron ore and bauxite. But she is not so well endowed as England and Germany in regard to power resources. French mines furnish only 50,000,000 tons of coal a year, which is equal to 65,000,000,000 kilowatt-hours of electrical energy. Water power contributes another 10,000,000,000 kilowatt-hours. But to satisfy all the power needs of France, at least another 30,000,000,000 kilowatt-hours must be produced. To make up this lack, France must import coal, especially from the Ruhr basin of Germany.

This is where the Schuman Plan—or European Coal and Steel Community—comes in. This scheme, for pooling the coal and steel resources of Western Europe, was first proposed in 1950 by Robert Schuman, then French Foreign Minister. A year later, the plan became the basis for a fifty-year treaty, signed by France, Belgium, the Netherlands, Italy, Luxembourg and Western Germany. The treaty provides for a single market for coal and steel among these countries. Its general aims are to decrease costs in the industries that hinge on coal and steel and to allow a better standard of living for the workers.

For the nations agreeing to the plan, it meant yielding a part of their sovereignty, or authority, to an over-all European administrative council. Some day the scheme may prove to have been the cornerstone of a united European community. Even as it stands, it is one of the most constructive efforts put forward to draw the European countries away from their narrow nationalist thinking.

French electrical equipment has also lagged behind demand. However, there are large electric installations in the Massif Central, in the Alps and on the Rhine. The Génissiat Dam on the upper Rhone, built after the Liberation, is one of the largest in Europe. It has a capacity of 3,000,000,000 kilowatt-hours.

Early in the 1950's, another powerful dam was being constructed on the lower Rhone at Donzère-Mondragon and Châteauneuf. Considered one of the most important public-works projects in West-

STANDARD OIL CO. (N. J.)

GATEWAY TO TARASCON

On the site of the Roman Tarasco, on the lower Rhone, is the medieval town of Tarascon, surrounded by thick walls. Part of this old gateway has been restored in modern times.

ern Europe, it meant removing as much earth as for the building of the Suez Canal. In time it will divert the waters of the Rhone for about twenty-five miles.

Next to England, France has ties with the greatest overseas territory in the world —10,000,000 square miles, about 24 times her own area. The population of these territories amounts to about 75,000,000, of which 48,000,000 are in Africa and 27,000,000 in Asia. Some of these lands are ancient colonies, the remnants of the colonial empire that came to an end in 1763. The territories include ports in India, West Indies islands and lands acquired since 1830 in Africa and Asia.

In 1946, the French Union, embracing all these territories, came into existence. However, the political status of the different territories varies. Some are departments (states), such as Algeria and the islands in the West Indies. Others are grouped in federations, such as Western and Equatorial Africa. Still others are protectorates, such as Morocco and Tunisia; and some, such as Togo and Camer-

**BLESSING THE SEA, NEAR BIARRITZ**

Mass is celebrated by the water's edge, near Biarritz, at the *Fête de la mer.* This is a traditional yearly blessing of the sea and of those who make their living by the sea.

PHOTOS, FRENCH GOVERNMENT TOURIST OFFICE

**THE BEACH AT SAINT JEAN DE LUZ**

Among the many popular vacation spots on the Bay of Biscay is Saint Jean de Luz, just south of Biarritz, another famous resort. Hundreds of cabanas (shelters for bathers) dot the sunny beach.

oun, are governed as United Nations trusteeships.

The economic resources of the French Union are tremendous, especially in agriculture, and they have hardly been tapped. At the same time, since about 1850, the French have spared neither effort nor money to develop the backward areas and to give their populations a modern standard of living.

Nevertheless, the defeat suffered in 1940 brought about unrest in some of the overseas territories. In 1946, a long struggle began in Indochina between the recognized government—Viet Nam, backed by the French—and a rebel government—Viet Minh—of communist leanings, backed by the Chinese Communists. The contest has drained the financial resources of France, adding an enormous burden to her other difficulties.

There has been trouble in Morocco and Tunisia as well. There, zealous nationalists have accused the French administration of thwarting their rightful growth toward complete independence.

Dark clouds thus loom over the future of France. But this is not the first time that she has passed through an anxious period of storm and stress, and she has always shown a remarkable ability to recover. Today signs of French vitality are not lacking. France faces her destiny with pride in her past and a firm determination to keep her colors flying.

By Robert Barrat

---

## *FRANCE: FACTS AND FIGURES*

### *THE COUNTRY*

A nation of west central Europe, it is bounded on the north by the English Channel, the Strait of Dover, Belgium and Luxembourg, east by Germany, Switzerland and Italy, south by the Mediterranean Sea and Spain, west by the Bay of Biscay and the Atlantic Ocean. Included among 90 departments is Corsica, an island off the Italian coast in the Mediterranean. Area, 212,954 square miles; population, 42,200,000.

### *GOVERNMENT*

The Constitution of the French Fourth Republic, which came into force December 24, 1946, guarantees the right of all citizens, men and women, over 21 years of age to vote. It establishes a Parliament consisting of the National Assembly and the Council of the Republic. The Council, elected by communal and departmental governing bodies, is largely advisory in function. The Assembly, elected by direct, popular vote for a 5-year tenure, is solely responsible for making laws. Both chambers elect a president of the Republic to serve for 7 years. He nominates a president of the Council of Ministers (premier) who is invested when his executive program receives the majority approval of the Assembly. Upon his investiture the premier selects a Council of Ministers, or Cabinet, which is also subject to Assembly approval. If the Cabinet receives from the Assembly a vote of no confidence or of censure, it resigns and the president nominates a new premier.

### *COMMERCE AND INDUSTRIES*

Agriculture: 34% of land under cultivation; 22% is pasture; 3% under vines; 20% under forests, and 21% uncultivated. Leading crops: beets, potatoes, wheat and oats. Fruit culture considerable, especially for production of wines and cider. Livestock: cattle, 15,720,000; sheep, 7,470,000; swine, 6,740,000; and others. Government encourages sericulture. Mineral production: coal, iron ore, crude steel, pig iron and rock salt. Other industries: electric power production, manufacture of cement, textiles, motor vehicles and machine tools. Imports: foodstuffs and wines, manufactures, raw materials such as rubber, coal, oil, rags and paper pulp and oil-bearing seeds. Exports: foodstuffs and wines; industrial raw materials; machinery, chemicals and other manufactured products; ores and metals; textiles and clothing.

### *COMMUNICATIONS*

Shipping: tonnage of merchant marine, 1951, 2,965,609; mileage of inland waterways, 5,261. Roads, 444,457 miles; railways (all state-owned), 25,630 miles. Telegraph cables and wires, 276,345 miles; telephone lines, 126,274 miles.

### *RELIGION AND EDUCATION*

Church and state separate, freedom of worship guaranteed. Roman Catholicism predominates; there are about 1,000,000 Protestants. Education, free and compulsory for ages 6 to 14, is under the Minister of National Education. Teacher training is provided by 152 normal schools. State and private primary schools, including nursery schools, number 84,785; state secondary schools, 979. Higher education: 17 universities; separate faculties attached to museums and other public institutions; technical colleges under various government ministries. Also, numerous trade schools on an intermediate level.

### *CHIEF TOWNS*

Population (latest census): Paris (capital), 2,725,374; Marseilles, 636,264; Lyons, 460,748; Toulouse, 264,411; Bordeaux, 253,751; Nice, 211,165; and 16 others with more than 100,000.

PHILIP GENDREAU

**DRAWING WATER FROM AN ANCIENT WELL IN THE TOWN OF LOUDEAC**

A farm woman of Brittany wears wooden shoes (sabots) and full, heavy skirts. Though she may work very hard, even in the fields, the expression on her face says that life is good.

# THE FRENCH SEA PROVINCES

## *Ancient Normandy and Romantic Brittany*

France has two provinces that jut into the English Channel. Of these, Normandy has been the home of an adventure-loving race from which William the Conqueror was sprung. When Viking Northmen descended upon these shores in the tenth century, the Danes called them "Normand," and the name has clung. Brittany is also a land of sea-faring people (though they are of different stock), a land of legend and scenic beauty, of quaint costumes and queer customs. This peninsula was once called Armorica; but when the Anglo-Saxons invaded England, the Britons fled across the Channel and in memory of their homeland called that part of France "Britannia Minor."

BRITTANY is a rugged promontory tempered by the salt winds off the Atlantic, a land of weather-bronzed fishermen whose blue and henna sails have tempted artists for generations. Its beliefs are half-Celtic, half-Druidic, although no natural barrier divides it from Normandy with its tall, fair-haired, adventure-loving people, so unlike most of the French because they are descended from the Norse Vikings who invaded the land in the ninth century.

The land of the "Normand," as they were called, had been inhabited by wild Gallic tribes to whom Christian missionaries came at an early date. Later a Roman provincial capital, it had been a feudal duchy of the bishopric of Rouen, conquered by King Clovis in the sixth century. When Hrolf of Norway (Rollo) seized Rouen, he compelled Charles the Simple, whose daughter Gisela he married, to make him Duke of Normandy. But when his proxy had to perform the ceremony of allegiance by kissing the king's foot, that ruddy Viking stood erect, lifted the royal foot to his mouth and toppled the king over backward, at which Hrolf's followers shouted with laughter.

From Hrolf sprang the dukes of Normandy and one of them was William I of England, known as William the Conqueror. So adaptable were the Northmen that they soon became more Gallic than the more civilized Gauls themselves, and zealously restored the very monasteries they had destroyed. William the Conqueror himself was present when the rebuilt church at Jumièges, west of Rouen, was consecrated in 1065. William, be it remembered, was the son of Robert the Devil and a maid of Falaise, and a famous tapestry at Bayeux depicts his conquest of England. One also recalls that Normandy, after having been united with England, then separated, was saved from English invaders by Joan of Arc, who was martyrized at Rouen in 1431. Rouen is now a great manufacturing town, although one may still find relics of ancient times. Throughout Normandy one still sees examples of the ponderous Norman architecture, as in the chapel of Mont St. Michel, a granite structure (just across from St. Malo) where abbey and fortress were once combined on this rocky island laved by a forty-eight-foot tide. Fortresses like that of Château Gaillard at Les Andelys once enabled the dukes of Normandy to hold back the kings of France. Normandy impresses the tourist as a land of chalk cliffs and half-timbered villages, of emerald fields and fragrant apple orchards reaching inland along the valley of the Seine. Cider is not unnaturally the favorite beverage of the countryside. Havre (The Haven) owes its fame as a port to the fact that it stands where the Seine, the water route from Paris, widens to seven miles before blending with the English Channel. Cherbourg, on the peninsula of Cotentin, is a renowned seaport with a vast breakwater. Dieppe, to the northward, was aptly named for the deeps beneath its cliffs.

The Bretons live chiefly along the coast, securing their living from the sea.

RAPHO-GUILLUMETTE

THE FISHERMAN'S WELCOME HOME

From a vantage point above the harbor of one of Brittany's many small ports, the wives of fishermen watch the safe return of their husbands' boats. Brittany is a sea-washed peninsula and many of its people make their living from the sea. The Breton women still wear their stiffly starched headdresses, decorated with embroidery, and their colorful aprons.

PHILIP GENDREAU

**TAKING ADVANTAGE OF A CLEAR AND BREEZY DAY IN NANTES**

An enterprising housewife calmly hangs out her wet clothes as the town hums with action on the other side of the canal. The well-worn cobblestone streets and sharp-gabled roofs show plainly that Nantes is an old and historic French city, where automobiles now travel on the streets once meant for carriages and saddle horses. Nantes is a port on the Loire River.

not the barren uplands. The old walled town of St. Malo, the gateway to Brittany, has a harbor protected by many islets, including Grand Bey where Châteaubriand lies in his grave. In this region and as far westward as Cape Fréhel there are bays in which the sea leaves wide expanses of sand at low tide; but for the most part the coast is wildly picturesque. Around Ploumanach there is as weird a stretch of wilderness as can well be imagined. The actual "land's end" presents to the Atlantic dangerous reefs, bold capes and rocky desolation. And yet Brest roadstead is accounted the finest natural harbor in Europe; for within its bottle-neck entrance, illuminated by five lighthouses, lies a harbor fourteen miles long by half as wide. Just beyond, in the bay of Douarnenez there is something every tourist ought to visit—the grottoes of Morgat, the largest of which can be visited only by boat with the passengers lying flat at the cave mouth. Here the waves have hollowed a cavern 150 feet long into which the blue light enters through the sea, and in the middle of this grotto stands a huge block of red granite, the "altar." The sight is impressive.

Where the coast bends sharply southeastward, it is protected by a chain of islands and becomes less rugged until it ends in sand dunes at the mouth of the Loire. It is here that relics of the Bronze Age and Neolithic remains are most numerous. The first people in Brittany to leave records behind them were the Armoricans, as they were called by the Romans. These Druidical people erected strange monuments to which the Bretons even to-day make journeys, superstitiously taking their cattle to be blessed. These monuments were of three kinds, dolmens, menhirs and cromlechs. The dolmen was a cairn rudely constructed of upright stones and roofed over by a capstone, and it is thought that in some prehistoric age it was used as a repository for the bones of the dead. Menhirs are single upright stones, possibly used to mark boundaries, more likely placed to do honor to those buried in the dolmens. At Carnac fully twelve hundred of these stones stand ranged in eleven rows, and at Erdeven near by are similar alinements. It is also believed that the tribesmen of those pagan times used to dance down these aisles, leading their victims to stones called cromlechs where the priests stood ready to make the sacrifices. At any rate, the place names in this region are largely derived from funeral ceremonies: Plouharnel means "the bone houses," Kerlescan, "the place of ashes" and Kermario, "the place of the dead." The Armoricans were vanquished in the fifth century by the invading Celts from Britain; but in the "pardons" of which we shall presently tell, there is more than a suggestion of a Druidical religion marked by an elaborate cult of the dead. The Bretons, living isolated from the rest of France and daily faced by the hazards of the sea, although a Christian people, cling superstitiously to certain pagan customs. To a mutilated Roman statue of a horseman at St. Marcel, for instance, the sick are brought on horseback.

The Breton is peculiarly religious. He has the cemetery in the middle of the town in order that the dead may hear the church services; and the great days of the year are the "pardons" when he believes his sins will all be forgiven and his bodily ills cured by the particular saint whose day it is. He therefore spends the early part of the day in pilgrimage and prayer. Penitents will kiss the stones and on their bended knees make their painful way to the spot where they believe the saint to be buried, and afterward will drink of the fountain that rises nearest his grave. But in the evening there is merry-making and the erstwhile devotee dances to the shrill music of the "biniou," the Breton bagpipe, or the concertina.

There is the Pardon of Rumengol, remarkable for the number of people who attend it and for their costumes. At Rumengol is a celebrated statue of the Virgin which the Bretons believe has the power to cure the ills of body or soul. This

PHILIP GENDREAU

**PAYING A FRIENDLY VISIT IN THE TOWN OF QUIMPER, BRITTANY**

On the Breton peninsula, where life in the small towns moves at a dignified pace and ladies still wear snow-white caps, the two-wheeled carriage is a practical method of travel.

RAPHO-GUILLUMETTE

**A VILLAGE IN THE HEART OF BRITTANY, DOZING IN THE SUN**

The stone houses sit close together, presenting an unbroken front. Almost everywhere in France, farming families live in hamlets, with their fields some distance away.

PHILIP GENDREAU

**A WOOD-CARVER OF BRITTANY CHISELS OUT A NEW FIGURE**

His neighbors and friends may have served as models for some of these scowling, smiling or saintly faces. With skill and experience he captures their changing moods and expressions.

BLACK STAR

**AN IMMACULATE COIF SETS OFF A GENTLE BRETON FACE**

The becoming coif is a fashion that has come down from medieval times. This one is typical of Brittany. Many old ways survive here, even the language of the Bretons' Celtic ancestors.

© E. N. A.

**FALAISE CASTLE** is of special interest to us. Looking from its windows, Robert the Devil, sixth duke of Normandy, first saw Arletta, the tanner's daughter, in the streets of Falaise town. Their son, who was born in the castle, was William the Conqueror. This town was badly bombed during the second World War so that few buildings remained standing.

SPECIAL PRESS

**THE GLORY OF JOSSELIN,** a little old town of south Brittany, is its "château," a fortified castle many centuries old. Its water-front is very grand, with high, strong walls and round towers rising from the living rock. In the old church is the tomb of Oliver de Clisson, a famous soldier of the 14th century. Washing is done in the placid River Oust.

© E. N. A.

GAILY DRESSED FOR CHURCH

On week-days this girl of Douarnenez is at work tinning sardines—an important Breton industry—but on Sundays she always wears the beautiful costume of her district.

is also called the Pardon of the Singers, and it obtained its name from a very old legend. It is said that a king of ancient Brittany, Gralon by name, threw his lovely daughter, Ahes, into the sea that he himself might escape from drowning. She became a siren, luring fishermen and mariners to their doom by her wonderful singing. Gralon heard it and was sorrowful, and on his death-bed asked the Virgin to deprive Ahes of her voice. This the Virgin said she could not do; but she promised that a race of sweet singers should come to the earth and that every year they should sing at the Pardon of Rumengol.

On the night of the twenty-third of June the Pardon of Fire is celebrated. On a hillside at St. Jean du Doigt, or St. John of the Finger, will be built a great bonfire. The peasants gather around it, excitedly getting scorched in their efforts to seize brands to carry away as charms—"Joy and good health from the blessed St. John!"

The Pardon of the Sea, which is the Fête of Sainte Anne de la Palude, is the greatest of all. Then the procession includes widows with extinguished candles, and survivors of wrecks with a small ship's model. St. Anne is the saint of all who lie beneath the sea or make their living in deep waters. Her story is full of that mystical meaning which the Breton loves. St. Anne, when young, was a much-beloved duchess in Brittany, and married a king of France. When the king found she was likely to become a mother, he drove her from home and she came down to the sea in great distress. But a "ship of glory" was provided for her, and the helmsman was an angel. He guided her to the Holy Land, where she gave birth to the Virgin Mary—or, some say, the Lord himself. When Anne was growing old, she longed for her Breton people and begged to be taken back, so the "ship of glory" came back, with the angel still at the helm, and her own people assembled

© Créte

PEASANT IN OLD-FASHIONED GARB

In Brittany most of the men now have their hair cut short, and the puffy breeches that were once commonly seen are worn to-day by only a few old men on festivals.

PHILIP GENDREAU

**A SHRINE AT ROUEN—TO JOAN OF ARC, THE MAID OF ORLEANS**

This statue of Joan stands near the place of her execution in Rouen. She led the French legions to victory over the English at Orléans and died at the stake, falsely accused of sorcery. The statue immortalizes the tragic moment when flames leaped up to destroy her, and shows the dignity and courage of the heroine who continues to inspire the land she loved.

CROOK

**FASCINATING OLD HOUSES** seem to nod to each other across the narrow streets of Quimper, capital of Finistère. Behind rise the modern twin towers of the old cathedral of St. Corentin, which was started about 1239. We are visiting Quimper at the right time—on market day—when the streets are thronged with women and men in a variety of costumes.

MC LEISH

**AT LOVELY OLD ROUEN,** in Normandy, Joan of Arc was burned, more than five hundred years ago. This picture shows the town as it looked before World War II bombings damaged many of its historic buildings. The ancient cathedral, with its graceful spire soaring above Rouen's rooftops, was seriously harmed, although it is not beyond restoration.

WIDE WORLD

AT OMAHA BEACH, A LANDING CRAFT AND BAREFOOT CHILDREN

On the Normandy beach where the Allied invasion of Europe began, June 6, 1944, French children turn the hull of a landing boat into a perch from which to view the now peaceful horizon.

on the shore to give her a welcome as their queen. But St. Anne would have none of this. "I give all my goods to the poor!" she cried; and she was as good as her word, ending her life in poverty.

There is a wonderful legend about the City of Is, so beautiful a city that when the people of France were seeking a name for their capital they could find nothing better to call it than Par-is—*the like of Is*—an ingenious but untrue derivation.

### *A City Under the Sea*

The City of Is was below sea level, but it was protected from inundation by walls and dykes with doors that could be opened for the water to flow out or in. The Princess Dahut carried the silver keys that unlocked those doors suspended from her neck. One night a stranger made his appearance and captivated the princess by his beauty and masterfulness. As soon as he got an opportunity, he snatched the keys from her neck, or (one version has it) she gave them to him; at any rate he made away with them and opened the floodgates. The sea streamed in; the waves mounting higher and higher, swamped the streets, houses and palaces, until finally there was left only the wide surface that to-day makes the Bay of Douarnenez.

For years the clergy used to embark on fishing-boats every year to say Mass over the drowned city, and it is still said that when the sea is calm and the weather is clear, the remains of a great town may be seen at the bottom of the bay, and the ringing of its church-bells can be heard.

### *Legend of St. Galonnek*

The feast of St. Galonnek is held every first of April, when "the time of the singing of the birds is come." St. Galonnek was a native of Ireland, a disciple of St. Patrick, and his heart was said to be "like a fresh spring of water, ever bubbling-up with blessing," hence the name Galonnek, which means open-hearted. At the age of eighteen, Galonnek crossed over to Brittany, and after many adventures came to a place where he seated himself on the doorstep of a house and waited for an invitation to enter; but its owner bade him go away. He went from house to house, always meeting with the same injunction to "Get up and begone," which in Breton is expressed by the word "zevel." Ever afterward that village bore the name of Plouzevel. In a neighboring village there was a poor widow who received Galonnek as if he had been her own son. To reward her he dug for water on her land and a fountain sprang up. Her land became rich meadow and cattle came to feed there. When the villagers saw this, they begged Galonnek to take up his abode with them and he did so. Living in a hut, he persuaded them to abandon their custom of lighting fires on the rocks to lure ships to destruction.

Later, when Galonnek was made Bishop of Cornouailles, he had many a struggle with the nobles on behalf of the serfs. His body lies buried in the Cathedral of St. Pol where its resting-place is covered by a granite slab. On that slab the Breton mothers lay their baby boys, praying: "St. Galonnek bestow on my child two hearts—the heart of a lion, strong in well-doing and the heart of a turtle-dove, full of brotherly love."

### *In Lace Cap and Velvet Apron*

We see the Bretonne at her best at a wedding. In some districts she wears a butterfly cap of fine lace, a velvet bodice and an apron of brilliant flowered velvet. First there is a civil ceremony at the mayor's office, then a church ceremony, where the bridal couple occupy two chairs at the altar rail with candles placed in front of them. If the wedding is a country one, there follows a feast in a meadow which everyone attends, especially the beggars. When old and young, rich and poor have feasted, the oldest woman may recite a litany for the dead. After that there may be several days of merry-making.

There is a considerable nomadic population in the province, including "sabotiers," the makers of wooden shoes, who go in groups to the woods to get their material, then divide into small bands to go through the villages and sell their

**IN OLD DINAN,** once a stronghold of the Dukes of Brittany, there are many queer, narrow streets, but none queerer or more ancient than the Rue du Jerzual, with its top-heavy houses of the Middle Ages. This street winds down very steeply to the Porte du Jerzual, one of the gateways that pierce the old town walls. Through this gate one reaches the River Rance.

© E. N. A.

**TIMBERED HOUSES,** built by the master craftsmen of the Middle Ages, border the River Seine at Caudebec-en-Caux, a sleepy town of Normandy. Centuries have given them an added richness of color. The church, dating from the 15th century, is one of the finest in the diocese. Caudebec was once an important fortress, which was taken in 1419 by the English.

© E. N. A.

**VIEW OF PICTURESQUE AVRANCHES, ONE OF THE OLDEST TOWNS IN NORMANDY**

Avranches dates from Roman times. It occupies a hill by the Sée in the department of Manche, while situated on the coast road from St. Malo to Granville it commands a delightful view of Mont St. Michel and its beautiful bay. Three churches and a town hall are among its most interesting buildings, and historical interest centres in the inscribed stone in the square which indicates the spot where in 1172 Henry II of England did penance for the murder of Thomas à Becket. Avranches has experienced several sieges, and suffered severely each time.

**A TRIO OF LIGHTSHIPS BACK IN HARBOR TO BE REFITTED**

Le Havre, at the mouth of the Seine, is one of the world's great harbors. A huge breakwater forms a great outer basin that supplements the natural inner harbor. There are docks, warehouses and modern service installations on a grand scale. The entire harbor area suffered tremendous damage from bombardment in World War II, but was rebuilt after liberation.

PHOTOS, STANDARD OIL CO. (N. J.)

**BUSY CORNER IN ONE OF THE OLDER SECTIONS OF LE HAVRE**

Transatlantic travelers seldom see much of Le Havre, for the express train is waiting at the dock when the ships come in, ready to carry the passengers to Paris. The city is well worth a visit, however. It has been important since the days of Francis I, who fortified it. There are fine, modern residential streets as well as business and industrial centers.

© UNDERWOOD & UNDERWOOD

**MONT ST. MICHEL** at low tide is an island of granite in a sea of sand. At high tide the real sea makes a real island of the picturesque mass save for the causeway that connects it with the mainland. At the base of the mount are strong fortifications. Next we would come to a little medieval town; and then to the beautiful 13th century monastery; and lastly, on the very summit, to the abbey-church of St. Michel. The monastery was founded in 709 and became very rich. That on St. Michael's Mount, a similar rock off the Cornish coast, was its dependency.

**A CALVARY,** or solitary cross of stone, wood or iron, is a very common sight at the roadsides and by the sea in Brittany. Many of them are wonderfully carved. This one, erected on the quay at Concarneau, looks across the waters of Concarneau Bay, that it may watch over the fishermen of the town while they are at sea. This is a centre of fisheries.

PHILIP GENDREAU

**A SHAGGY ROOF SHELTERS AN OLD FARMHOUSE IN NORMANDY**

The steep roof overhangs the building so that rain and snow will drip off away from the walls. Farmhouses like this are still in use among the hedgerows and apple orchards of Normandy.

wares. There are charcoal-burners, weavers of linen and wool, thatchers, rag-merchants, all leading a kind of gipsy life.

Tourists ought to see the great châteaux at Nantes and at Josselin, go boating on the silver Rance and go driving past the apple orchards, where perhaps they will hear the evening notes of the Angelus coming from some village church tower. The motorist will find both roads and inns surprisingly good; and there is a regular passenger service between Southampton and St. Malo.

It is related of that ancient seaport that in the sixth century a holy man called Malo (Maclow, Maclou, Machut or Maclovius) came sailing over from Wales in a stone dugout, and with a resident hermit named Aaron as audience, held religious services on the back of a whale. He then built a hut of the native granite and started to perform miracles. Druid competition in time drove him out, but by 680 he had been canonized; and though Charlemagne's warriors destroyed the city in 811, Charlemagne restored it. It was a warlike Bishop, Châtillon, who (in 1155) started the seaward-facing ramparts that remain to-day; and in time the church rubbed elbows with merchant-corsairs who cut cellars into the rock to hide their booty from the tax-collectors. The island city had to grow skyward since it could not expand far otherwise. In the days before it built its inner harbor, the receding tides left wide stretches of sandy beach exposed, and a dozen ferocious watchdogs were kept on guard at night. When the Bastion of Holland was built to overlook the sea and receive William of Orange, these dogs were put in a bomb-proof room which may still be seen.

In all, the corsair city took toll of English shipping to the number of 4,500 merchantmen and between 300 and 400 warships, and it took England and Holland together to subdue the rocky isle. Its flag saw Madras and Rio de Janeiro, and it was a son of St. Malo that gave Canada to France. But "my blood tints the banner of France," Châteaubriand the writer reminds us from over the doorway of his father's dwelling—now become part of a big hotel. Among the names in blue and white enamel that mark most of the streets and public squares we find that of Cartier, discoverer of the St. Lawrence; De Gournay, France's first industrialist; and Thévenard, her first cannon-founder.

St. Thomas's Gate was named for the Breton sailor's favorite patron and the gate was endowed with a shrine by a crew that declared the Saint had answered their prayer and saved them from an octopus that had clutched their boat. Another landmark is the palace of Anne of Brittany, who married King Louis XII of France in 1499 and thereby brought Brittany to the crown of France.

The old piratical days of St. Malo have long been past. The island city now broods, in its towering aerie overlooking the sea, amid the many souvenirs of its romantic past.

The Bay of Morbihan is said to contain as many islands as there are days in the year. When we look across the water from Tregastel we see the Isle of Avalon, to which King Arthur was carried to be healed of his grievous wound and where he is supposed to have died. But the Bretons say he is not dead, but only held a prisoner in an underground palace, from which he comes out occasionally in the form of a raven. Certain it is that there are ravens occasionally to be seen.

RAPHO-GUILLUMETTE

**RIVER FRONT OF HONFLEUR ON THE NORMANDY COAST**

Seaport and fishing town, Honfleur looks across the mouth of the Seine at its famous and much bigger rival, Le Havre, only seven miles away. Honfleur is on the river's southern bank.

PHILIP GENDREAU

**PEACE—A SCULPTURE ON THE ARC DE TRIOMPHE DE L'ETOILE**

Though the arch was begun in 1806, under Napoleon's orders, this relief represents the peace of 1815. *L'étoile* means "the star"—twelve avenues radiate from where the arch stands.

# A City of Enchantment

## *Paris the Capital That Charms the World*

Paris fascinates everyone who goes there, first for its historic and romantic interest and the beauty of its architecture, then because of its life of gaiety and learning and its cosmopolitan population. The city has been called the mind of France; certainly it has been a crucible of thought that has helped direct the civilization of the world. Paris is not alone a city of palaces but of gruesome slums; a vast fortress, it contains the loveliest of parks· it is a center of art and science, of fashion and allied manufactures. The Parisians themselves work hard, but they also play wholeheartedly: on a summer morning the floating swimming-baths of the Seine are filled with shop attendants, and the crowds along the boulevards make the evening merry.

PARIS is a city of quick tempo and architectural beauty and of unequaled historic interest. Let us review that history as in a quick-motion camera. Julius Cæsar mentions it in 53 B.C. when the tribe called the Parisii dwelt on an island in the Seine and their chief town was Lutetia. Not until the fifth century, when Roman power declined, was the name Paris used. St. Denis brought Christianity about 250 A.D., and the succession of leaders who followed included Clovis, King of the Franks, who expelled the last Roman official; Charlemagne, under whose successors of the Carolingian dynasty twelve townsmen once fended off besieging Norman pirates at the Petit-Pont; and the Capets, builders of famous churches.

Under Philippe Auguste, brother-in-arms of Richard Cœur-de-Lion, a girdle of walls was built to protect the city; Louis IX encouraged colleges and his chaplain Robert de Sorbon established one famous today. After the Hundred Years' War with England the feudal lords became more powerful than the kings themselves. Civil strife resulted and the city was occupied for a quarter of a century by the English. A few generations later the Italian campaigns initiated the Renaissance, and Italian artists transformed the medieval French fortresses into such beauty as that of the Louvre and part of the Palace of Fontainebleau. There followed Catherine de Médicis, the House of Bourbon, Cardinal Richelieu, who created the Académie Française, and under Louis XIV, "Roi Soleil," France became the great political powei of Europe, and Paris was ornamented with splendid buildings.

But after Louis XV came hard times, and Louis XVI saw the capture of the Bastille by a mob. Under the Convention royalty was abolished. Now came the Corsican, Napoleon Bonaparte, as First Consul. During the First Empire which followed, more than sixty new streets were laid out and two triumphal arches begun. Under the Second Empire many old sections were torn down and the Outer Boulevards of today undertaken. Paris was captured during the Franco-Prussian War; when the invaders retired, turbulent elements attempted to establish a Commune, and when they were defeated, tried to destroy the city. Later came World War I when the city was almost captured by the Germans and suffered from long-range bombardment and from air raids. During World War II, the Germans took Paris in 1940 and held it until the Allied liberation in 1944.

It is a far cry from the original village of savage huts to the great European capital of today. The city is laid out with intriguing irregularity, in a somewhat concentric pattern that begins with the Île de la Cité, midway of the Seine. The Grands Boulevards correspond to the ramparts of the fourteenth to seventeenth centuries which enclose most of old Paris. Outside, the ancient suburbs, or faubourgs, are enclosed by fine wide streets which mark the eighteenth-century ramparts; and outside these in turn lie suburbs which have been a part of Paris only since 1860. Of these, fashionable Auteuil and Passy lie to the westward, while the dwellings of the petite bourgeoisie occupy the remaining sides. To turn now and work inward, it is the west side faubourgs which are expensive—St. Honore, the Champs-Élysées and St. Germain. The shopping and theatre districts lie within the Grands Boulevards, especially on the north bank of the bisecting Seine.

*On the Île de la Cité*

One can but mention the most outstanding points of interest which might be visited in the course of a series of pilgrimages. In the Cité the Palais de Justice has endured in part for two thousand years, and on this site have been dispensed the justice of the Roman law and the Code Napoleon. The old clock on the corner tower was set up by Charles V in 1370. Several streets to the right we find the Cathedral of Notre Dame. We enter its vast, dim interior with reverence and examine the carvings that everywhere adorn it; then, from its balconied squat towers we have a view of the city. First we note in the distance the golden dome of the Invalides. On the Left Bank of the Seine cluster the University buildings and the principal part of medieval Paris. Now if we cross the river by the Petit-Pont, oldest of Parisian bridges, a bridge in Cæsar's time, we have the scene of the defense against the Vikings before mentioned. It is not far to the old church of Saint-Julien-le-Pauvre, which has altered little since the twelfth century. In this neighborhood the streets twist and turn and some of the house fronts loom clear from one narrow street to another, concealing dank-smelling courtyards and mysterious passageways. The Rue Saint-Jacques, however, lies straight because it is laid out along what was one of the mathematical Roman roads. During the Middle Ages students from all over Europe were attracted to this quarter, and one of the professors at the University of Paris up the hill to the southward was Abélard, who loved Héloïse so tragically.

*In the Latin Quarter*

From here we can walk to the Musée de Cluny, opposite which stands the façade of the Sorbonne, old and famous before our universities were founded. On a hill near by stands the Panthéon, of troubled history, in which are buried Jean-Jacques Rousseau and Voltaire. As we wander through the narrow old streets of the Latin Quarter, lined with bookshops and cheap restaurants, we are walking in the footsteps of many great scholars and writers of the past. We may end this day's walk with a stroll along the Boulevarde Montparnasse, where at times, as elsewhere in the Latin Quarter, art students and even those whose best work sells elsewhere string their paintings up between the trees, and save the art dealer's commission on scenes from Rouen to the Riviera.

A walk of only a few blocks will take us to the Luxembourg Quarter, where the Catacombs extend chill and dark beneath a vast area of the south and east of Paris. Here for two thousand years, human bones have been deposited and—amazingly!—a subterranean fountain bubbles forth. From the exit in the Rue Dareau one may easily reach the beautiful gardens of the Luxembourg, laid out in formal Italian style. The Palais du Luxembourg now houses the French Senate, and the Musée de Luxembourg is one of the best known galleries of modern French art.

*In the Luxembourg Quarter*

On our way back we may pass the Théâtre de l'Odéon, where many an actor, who later appeared behind the footlights of the Théâtre-Français, has trained. From here it is not far to the École des Beaux-Arts, where painters and sculptors of every nation have received their training.

On the opposite side of the Seine is the Louvre, which is worth many a visit, for it contains such world-famed works of art as the Venus de Milo, Mona Lisa and the Winged Victory, all placed most effectively. The Victory hovers

PHILIP GENDREAU

**LANDMARK: THE OBELISK IN THE PLACE DE LA CONCORDE**

From the spacious square, the beauty of Paris unrolls on every side. These buildings, on the north side, were once palaces. Between them is the Rue Royale, with the Madeleine at its end.

FRENCH GOVERNMENT TOURIST OFFICE

**PARIS IS NOTED FOR ITS FAMOUS STATUES**

The statue of Mercury on a winged horse, by the French sculptor Antoine Coysevox, adds to the beauty of the Place de la Concorde, one of the most beautiful squares in the city of Paris. It was in this square that Marie Antoinette and many others were beheaded during the French Revolution. In the background stands the obelisk from the temple at Luxor, in Egypt.

TRANS WORLD AIRLINES

**A STREET SCENE IN MONTMARTRE**

Paris is believed by many to be the most beautiful and fascinating city in the world. She is famous not only for her magnificent boulevards and parks, her art and culture, but for the intimate charm of certain sections of the city. Here the informally dressed citizens of Montmartre, in the northern part of Paris, do their shopping and greet each other as they pass.

PHILIP GENDREAU

**THE FABULOUS CHAMPS ELYSEES, LINED WITH TREES**

One of the most magnificent avenues in the world, the Champs Elysées stretches from the Arc de Triomphe de l'Etoile (from which this picture was taken) to the Place de la Concorde. The name "Champs Elysées" means "Elysian fields," the Paradise of Greek mythology. Horse-chestnut trees, which are a mass of white bloom in the spring, line the broad boulevard on either side.

**BETWEEN TWO ARMS OF THE SEINE, THE ÎLE DE LA CITÉ**

The boat-shaped Isle of the City, which we see here from an aeroplane, is the oldest part of Paris. At the near end of the island is the Palace of Justice, an almost square block of buildings. Among them is the Sainte Chapelle described in the text. We can recognize it by its high, narrow form, its gleaming roof and its little slender spire, alone amid all this massiveness.

© Aerofilms

**ON WHICH ARE MANY OF THE FAMOUS BUILDINGS OF PARIS**

To the left of the Sainte Chapelle is the Conciergerie, shown on page 300. Beyond the Palace of Justice, to the left, is the Tribunal of Commerce, and beyond that a huge hospital, the Hôtel Dieu, which was founded about 660 A.D. In the right background with an empty white square in front of it is the magnificent medieval Cathedral of Notre Dame.

BLACK STAR

**THE PALAIS DE CHAILLOT FRAMED IN THE EIFFEL TOWER'S BASE**

The palace consists of a terrace in the center, a large theater below and two vast wings. It houses several museums today. Hidden by banks, the Seine River flows between palace and tower.

with wings spread just above a long flight of steps. There are surely miles of corridors leading to hundreds of rooms. In the Musée de Peinture on the first floor one finds, among pictures only less well known, work by Titian, Raphael, Tintoretto, Veronese, Giotto, Fra Angelico, Botticelli, Andrea del Sarto, da Vinci, Murillo, Velasquez, Van Dyck, Rubens, Rembrandt, the Holbeins, Millet, Corot, Lorrain, Watteau, Fragonard—the list is endless! And these paintings are but one phase of the exhibits in the Louvre. During five centuries the kings of France contributed to this building.

Apart from the treasures it contains, the Louvre is one of the most interesting buildings in Paris. A palace of the French kings in the days before France became a republic, it is stately and graceful beyond imagination. It is much more beautiful than the other buildings of the city that were once royal residences—the Luxembourg, the Palais Royal or the Palace of the Elysée where French presidents have lived. As we turn from the busy streets into the quiet court of the Louvre, we cannot but be moved by the grandeur that surrounds us. There is only one building in Paris that equals the Louvre in magnificence and that is the Cathedral of Notre Dame, mentioned above.

To the west of the Louvre extends the Place du Carrousel, once a tournament field and later the square on which Napoleon reviewed his regiments. Beyond lie the gardens of the Tuileries; and from the courtyard of the Louvre, through these popular stretches of green, we may enjoy a vista across the Place de la Concorde, up the Avenue des Champs-Elysées to the Arc de Triomphe de l'Etoile, visible from nearly every point in Paris.

Paris is particularly happy in having been laid out in such a manner as to have an architectural picture at the end of every vista. From the circular Place de l'Etoile, twelve avenues radiate starlike.

Not far from the Louvre stands the Bibliothèque Nationale with its collection of over five million books—a mecca for research students. And from here it is easy to reach The Bourse (Stock Exchange) where pandemonium reigns from twelve to two. The Bourse de Commerce (Produce Exchange) is at the end of iron buildings called Les Halles where for centuries the great food markets have been held. At neighboring restaurants of the early nineteenth century Dumas the Elder, Gautier, Balzac and other famous writers consorted.

Starting from the Place du Châtelet along the Avenue Victoria one comes to the modern Hôtel de Ville, or Town Hall. It occupies the site of an earlier town hall, destroyed by the Commune in May, 1871. Behind the Hôtel de Ville is the Church of Saint-Gervais, where the singing of the famous Chanteurs of Saint-Gervais can be heard at certain festivals during the year. Nearby, according to tradition, the author Rabelais and the Man in the Iron Mask are buried.

The Place de la Bastille occupies the site of the great prison destroyed at the beginning of the French Revolution. Now it is the scene of the bizarre street fairs which are as much a part of Paris as the night life beloved of tourists or the races, attended by people of fashion. Here we are not far from the Gare de Lyon, from which, some fine day, we may make excursions to several famous places around Paris. But while we are still in the neighborhood, we might take a peek at the Ile Saint-Louis, where in age-old houses along the quays a colony of writers and artists live. In one of these Gautier used to foregather with Balzac and Baudelaire. But everywhere in Paris the old houses are being torn down and glittering apartment houses erected in their places.

FRENCH EMBASSY—INFORMATION DIVISION

**THE BOURSE IN PARIS WITH ITS SIXTY-SIX CORINTHIAN COLUMNS**

The Bourse, built in the style of the Temple of Vespasian in Rome, is the Stock Exchange of Paris. The French word *bourse* has become almost international in its meaning of an exchange.

McLeish

**GRIM PRISON THAT HAS PLAYED ITS PART IN HISTORY**

The Conciergerie, part of the Palace of Justice, is one of the most famous prisons in the world. Here were confined Queen Marie Antoinette, Robespierre and other great figures of the French Revolution. The bell of the square tower in the foreground sounded to warn people of the Massacre of St. Bartholomew in 1572.

PHILIP GENDREAU

**THE EIFFEL TOWER, GIANT IRON SENTINEL OF PARISIAN SKIES**

Rising to a height of 984 feet, the graceful taper of latticed steel, the Eiffel Tower, dominates the low-roofed expanse of Paris. Erected for the exposition of 1889 by the engineer Alexandre Gustave Eiffel, it became one of the city's most familiar ornaments. At the top are an observation platform, a television transmitter and a meteorological station.

PHILIP GENDREAU

THE ARC DE TRIOMPHE DE L'ETOILE AND ITS CIRCULAR PLAZA

The greatest triumphal arch in the world, it was begun on Napoleon's orders in 1806, though it was not completed until 1836. Under the arch is the grave of the French unknown soldier.

The Grands Boulevards that curve from the Place de la Republique to the Place de la Madeleine may be explored by bus. One must first secure a numbered ticket, then await one's turn. From the Place de l'Opéra, the heart of Parisian pleasuredom, where it is said you have only to wait long enough to meet everyone you know, one may turn into the Rue de la Paix, where the famous dressmakers have their small shops and one has costumes made to order after inspecting the models. While there are no window displays of gowns and hats, there are wonderful jewelry stores with windows to enchant the eye of the tourist. How many cafés there are with little tables under awnings!

The Place de la Concorde is one of the world's famous squares, and its loveliness is second only to its historic interest. To the north stretches a line of buildings designed by Gabriel, to whom much of the credit for the Palace at Versailles is due. From this point one can see a portion of the Eiffel Tower, and the Hôtel des Invalides under the dome of which Napoleon lies buried. To the east of the Place the Gardens of the Tuileries begin. Starting westward, we ascend the beautiful Avenue des Champs-Elysées, which in turn leads to the Place de l'Étoile.

Nor must we leave Paris without seeing the Bois de Boulogne, with its zoo, its race courses and open-air theatre; and the palaces and gardens of Versailles not far outside Paris, where there still remains something of the splendor of the Court of France in the days of Louis XIV when the palace housed more than ten thousand people. Here one finds a hundred matters of interest, from the Grand Trianon of pink marble with its open-air loggia designed for the royal pleasure to the trap-doors so built that banquet tables ready laid might rise from the underground kitchens.

Parisians at the time of the race meetings visit Chantilly, the little town (an hour's distance from the Gare du Nord) which has become the headquarters of numerous training stables. The Château of Chantilly—often called the Musée Condé—was the residence of the princes of the House of Condé, one of the most important families at the court of Louis XIV and his successors. The Château

PHILIP GENDREAU

**PART OF THE PLACE DU CARROUSEL, IN FRONT OF THE LOUVRE**

Formal gardens make a lovely setting for a Louvre façade and a monument to a French statesman, Léon Gambetta. The Arc de Triomphe du Carrousel and a Lafayette statue are nearby.

PHILIP GENDREAU

**BROWSING IN THE STALLS ALONG THE BANKS OF THE SEINE**

Old books and magazines, paintings, prints, stamps for the collector—all invite the passer-by to linger. The philosophic stall owners seem to care little whether they sell or not.

actually dates from the ninth century, when the helmeted Norse Vikings were trying to make their way up the Seine, although the buildings we see to-day were almost entirely erected by Anne de Montmorency, a famous general born the same year that "Columbus sailed the ocean blue." Here are various works of art belonging to the Bourbon and d'Orléans families. These works are ranked second only to those in the Louvre and at Versailles. Nor should one miss a glimpse of Compiègne. This historic town, which is on the River Oise, a little below its junction with the Aisne, has a Gothic Hôtel de Ville with museum and library and a palace built by Louis XV. The park is extensive and adjoining the gardens is the large forest of Compiègne. The town was the scene of some fierce fighting during World War I, and it is interesting to note that it was in a railroad car in the heart of the forest of Compiègne that the Armistice ending that war was signed in 1918. The car was used again in 1940 for the signing of the German-French Armistice.

When evening falls and Paris is jeweled with twinkling lights, we might visit one of the splendid theatres or the great Opera House. Or we might go to one of the less fashionable cafés, where we can sit among real Parisians. Here whole families listen to the music of the band while they drink coffee or fruit syrups and groups of friends come to the same tables night after night to talk and play games. This, too, is Paris.

# The Sunny Country of Spain

## *A Land Where East and West Have Mingled*

In the days when the adventurous Phœnicians sailed through the Pillars of Hercules at Gibraltar, Spain was the western limit of the ancient world, and it seems fitting that Columbus, centuries later, should have sailed from here to find the New World. His discovery gave Spain vast wealth and power, and widespread colonial dominions which are now no longer hers. It is a land rich in contrast, peopled by different races and bearing the marks of a long and stormy history. In some of the cities we shall find wonderful Gothic churches, and in others, palaces which are relics of the days when the Moors ruled most of the peninsula. To-day in Spain modern industrial life is developing side by side with medieval ways of living and working, and the result is a country where change and conservatism mingle.

A BRIGHT sunny land is Spain, full of color, romance and great possibilities. Cut off from France and the rest of Europe by the snowy barrier of the Pyrenees, the square Iberian Peninsula looks, on the map, like a geographical unit. But this square, apart from the strip on the west coast which is Portugal, is divided into many different sections. The Cantabrian Mountains in the north, those of Cuenca on the east and the Sierra Morena above the valley of the Guadalquivir mark off a high central tableland which is cut across by other hills. Here the summer nights are cool and the days hot, and rain falls seldom on the dry stony fields and dusty greenish-gray olive trees. Galicia in the northwest corner has a much more even, damp and temperate climate, while Andalusia in the south is semi-tropical and rarely sees snow except on the peaks of the high Sierra Nevada. The mountains of Spain are rich in minerals, and the river valleys fertile when irrigated, but it is not a land which yields its riches easily. The peasants of Estremadura or Aragón and even the carefree Andalusians must work hard for a living, and only in Catalonia does prosperity seem well distributed. But whether we are in medieval Segovia with its age-old Castilian ways unchanged, or bustling Barcelona, the most modern city in Spain, we are conscious of the charm and color pervading this proud and beautiful land.

The story of Spain reaches far back into that of the Mediterranean region. To the ancient Greeks, it seemed to be on the edge of the world, and Gibraltar was one of the Pillars of Hercules beyond which lay mystery. The Phœnicians saw that the land was rich and formed colonies to trade with the native Iberians and Celts. Cádiz, in the south, which the Greeks called the city of Aphrodite, "born of the foam," because of its splendor of white stone and snowy marble rising out of the blue sea, was the ancient Phœnician settlement of Gades and is, perhaps, the oldest town in Spain. Cartagena, on the east, was settled by men from the Phœnician city of Carthage, in Africa. The Romans took Spain from Carthage during the Punic Wars, and the land was more prosperous as part of the Empire than at any time since. The mark of the powerful Roman civilization is to be seen everywhere in Spain. Many of the city walls are built on Roman foundations and great aqueducts still exist—the one at Segovia is in use to-day. Toledo has the remains of a temple; Mérida was a Roman city, with a theatre, circus, baths, temples, aqueducts and bridges.

When Rome fell before the barbarian invaders in the fifth century, Spain was overrun first by the Vandals and then by the Visigoths, who came from Eastern Europe. The chaotic, turbulent rule of the Visigothic kings lasted about three hundred years, and the barbarians became an important element in the Spanish race. They adopted the language of their new country, and so modern Spanish is one of the Latin tongues.

BUSHBY

**A DEEP CHASM,** along the bottom of which rushes a turbulent stream, divides the old Moorish stronghold of Ronda from its suburb, the Ciudad. Three bridges, of which this is the loftiest, span the gorge. Along the edge of the chasm runs the public promenade. The brilliance of the skies in Spain makes sharp contrasts—dark shade and dazzling light

BUSHBY

**THE GATE OF JUSTICE,** the most generally used entrance to the amazing Moorish palace, the Alhambra, was built in 1338 by the Sultan Yûsuf. Its name arose from the fact that the kings of Granada sometimes sat under it to administer justice. The name Alhambra is Moorish and means "the red." This is a Red Palace rich in architectural splendors.

A SHEPHERD AND HIS FLOCK AMBLE ABOVE A STORIED TOWN

The mountains that rise abruptly on three sides of ancient Avila provide good pasture for thousands of sheep. Some herds are of Merino stock. Famous for its fine wool, the breed was first brought to Spain by the Moors. The shepherds have a pleasant occupation in summer, but in winter they must guard their flocks against hungry wolves.

PHOTOS, MONKMEYER

A GLIMPSE INTO THE MIDDLE AGES—THE BATTLEMENTS OF AVILA

Avila has known the tread of many adventurers and conquering armies. Early Phoenicians were driven out by Romans, and later the Moors invaded the land. During the eleventh century, King Alfonso VI started building thick walls for protection from the Moors. Although erected so long ago, the walls still surround the town like a great fortress.

The rich land attracted the Mohammedan Moors who were spreading along the north of Africa, and in 711 a number of Moorish warriors under a famous leader, Tarik, crossed over to Spain. The rock near his landing place was named after him, Gebel Tarik, the modern Gibraltar. A hard battle gave victory to the Moors, who easily subdued all the best of the disunited country, driving into the mountains of the north such Gothic warriors as remained unconquered. The new rulers introduced palm trees and all sorts of fruits, cultivated the land diligently, established industries and built schools, colleges and some of the grandest palaces, mosques and gardens in the world. The Alhambra and the Generalife at Granada were both originally Moorish palaces, and many of the cathedrals were first built as mosques.

The mosque at Córdova, within which

MONKMEYER

**THE MODERN OUTER HARBOR OF MALAGA, ON THE MEDITERRANEAN**

Breakwaters enclose the outer harbor of the wine region's busiest port. From the Andalusian valleys behind it, Malaga receives grapes, raisins, wine and olive oil which it ships out in great quantities. Founded by the Phoenicians, Malaga is a very ancient city. The harbor installations and the bullfighting ring in the foreground are modern touches.

**GOLD, SCARLET AND AZURE** are used here in a gorgeous decoration that has a haunting appeal. This is the alcove of the Captive's Tower in Alhambra, named after the beautiful Isabel de Solis, who was taken prisoner by Abu-el-hasan, Moorish king of Granada. Through the gracefully arched windows we see the Sultana's Tower and beyond it the Infanta's Tower.

© E. N. A.

**GRACEFUL PILLARS,** lifting up honeycombed ornamentation of the richest coloring, surround the Court of the Lions, the best preserved part of the Alhambra. The twelve marble lions which support the fountain show that the Moors of Andalusia were lax in their religion, for Mohammedan teaching forbids the use of living forms in sculpture or painting.

to-day is a church, was called the Wonder of Spain. It had a forest of columns, twelve hundred in all, of which several hundred remain; it had nineteen gateways of bronze and was lighted by over four thousand lamps burning perfumed oil. At Seville the Moorish palace of the Alcázar has a wall-carving so fine that it has been called a veil of lace in stone, and the Giralda, the famous belfry beside the cathedral, was the prayer-tower of the old Moorish mosque. All the Moorish buildings were beautifully inlaid with colored marbles, mother-of-pearl and rare woods; they were surrounded by gardens and courtyards where palms waved and oranges and myrtles bloomed and fountains, rising from alabaster basins, cooled the "hours of fire," as the hot afternoons are called in Spain.

But the Moors became too rich, quarreled among themselves and forgot to be vigilant against the remnant of fighting Goths who were gaining strength in the hard life of the northern mountains. Many petty Christian kingdoms were formed, and gradually their rulers began to press south and reconquer the country bit by bit. There came a time, in 1474, when the kingdom of León and the kingdom of Castile—the stronghold of old Spain, the haughty province from which come most of the grandees and nobility to this day—were inherited by a Princess Isabella, and she married Ferdinand, son of the king of Aragón. Thus at last Christian Spain was united and a final attack was made on the Moors. In 1492 Boabdil, last of the Moorish kings, surrendered to Ferdinand and Isabella his beloved royal city of Karnattah, which the Spaniards call Granada.

That same year Columbus, the Genoese sailor, with the help of Isabella set out on

**THE ALCÁZAR IS THE ALHAMBRA OF SEVILLE**

As the Alhambra is the glory of Granada, so the Alcázar is Seville's most glorious relic of Moorish days. It was begun in the twelfth century, but in later years Christian kings made many alterations. This beautiful shadowy archway, with its delicate tracery, leads to the part of the palace known as the "Sleeping Chambers of the Moorish Kings."

THE FAÇADE OF THE BEAUTIFUL ALCÁZAR PALACE

Here we see the principal doorway of the Alcázar and the fine carving of the façade. The palace as it stands to-day is largely the work of fourteenth-century architects, who, though employed by Christian kings, kept the spirit of the original Moorish design. The Alcázar continued to be the residence of the king of Spain whenever he visited Seville.

his first great voyage and discovered the West Indies. Six years later he sighted the coast of South America, and from this time onward gold and jewels, all the riches of the New World, poured into Spain. That is why the noble families of Spain have such wonderful stores of jewelry, and why images of the Virgin are studded with priceless precious stones.

Charles V, the grandson of Ferdinand and Isabella, was the first prince in Europe—King of Spain and Naples, Holy Roman Emperor and lord of Germany, Duke of Burgundy and the Netherlands and ruler of the New World beyond the seas. But the riches of the Americas and the magnificent energy of the Spanish nation were wasted in wars

**MOORISH ARCHES,** one beneath another, enchant the visitor to La Mezquita at Cordova, a great cathedral that was once a mosque. It was begun in 786 on the site of a Christian church, which had replaced a Roman temple. The interior, one of the finest examples of Moorish architecture, has a labyrinth of pillars in colored marbles, porphyry and jasper.

**IN GRANADA,** north of the Alhambra and across the River Darra, is the old, walled suburb of Albaicin, which was peopled by Moors from Baeza, after their city had been sacked by the Christians in 1227. Now the district is impoverished. Close by in the gipsy quarter, hillside caves are used for dwellings. The suburbs of Granada include a large area.

Rev. C. F. Fison

WEATHERED WALLS OVERSHADOW THIS CLOISTERED CATHEDRAL GARDEN

Tarragona Cathedral crowns a steep hill above the Mediterranean. It was built about eight hundred years ago, and its walls are hoary with age, but it is not nearly as old as the city itself. Tarragona was an Iberian settlement before the Romans occupied it in the third century before Christ, and made it one of their strongholds.

Nicholls

BY THE WELL IN A DELIGHTFUL COURTYARD OF RONDA

Though old Ronda on its precipitous crag is mostly Moorish in construction, we can still find traces of a yet earlier Roman occupation, especially in the castle, the walls and the gates. In this courtyard, too, the round columns with their carved capitals are certainly Roman, and so is the beautiful but rather battered well-head, with its fluted columns.

© E. N. A.

**FRAGRANT, JUICY ORANGES** grow everywhere in the sunny south of Spain, and those of us who have only tasted them when they have traveled overseas, can have no idea how delicious they are fresh from the tree. These women of Alora are grading the fruit and wrapping each separately. Anyone eating one of the oranges may see by looking at the stamp on the paper wrapping that it came from Alora. That picturesque old town, on a hill overlooking a fertile valley and surrounded by orange and lemon groves, is the centre of the orange trade in Malaga.

© E. N. A.

**MULBERRY TREES** are grown around Murcia, and their leaves are picked to provide food for the silkworms. This part of Spain is noted for its silk, which was first made here by the Moors in the 8th century. The white mulberry, a tree with white fruit, is the best kind for the silk industry. It is a Chinese tree, introduced into Europe in the 12th century.

THREE LIONS

**THATCHED HUTS ON THE OUTSKIRTS OF JEREZ DE LA FRONTERA**

Outside the sherry capital of the world, huts with stucco walls, mats of grass and rough woven cloth for doors serve as the temporary homes of a small community of workers. The rich fruit of the vineyards nearby and the special fermentation processes used in Jerez give the unique tang that has made sherry wine one of Spain's best-known products.

MONKMEYER

**A YOKE OF OXEN COMES ALONG TO HELP ON A DIFFICULT HILL**

Spain needs modern farm machinery badly. The few tractors in use are old, most of them small and unable to pull heavy loads. It is doubtful whether tractors can ever replace completely the faithful ox, horse or mule in Spain. Most of the agricultural land is hilly. Even the tractors that are easiest to maneuver get into trouble on the uneven fields.

SPANISH TOURIST OFFICE

**CASTLE LOOKS DOWN ON TOWN PUMP**

Estremadura (or Extremadura) is Spain's western region adjoining Portugal. It is a rugged land, inhabited as of old by rugged people. Many of the conquistadors of Spain's period of glory proudly boasted that they came from Estremadura. Pictured above is the city of Albuquerque, with the Castle of Cano on the hill and the town pump below, in the foreground.

to hold the great dominions of Charles and his son Philip II, and to make their subjects in the Netherlands renounce Protestantism. Spain's welfare was neglected; first the Jews, then the Mohammedans and finally even the Moors who had become Christians were expelled and with them went much of the country's prosperity, for commerce and industry were largely in their hands. In 1700 a Bourbon prince, Philip V, became king and the country was much under French influence. During the Napoleonic wars the whole peninsula was a battleground, for Napoleon deposed the rightful king and put his brother, Joseph Bonaparte, on the throne. Spanish resistance contributed to Napoleon's downfall, but when the country had its own king again things went badly. The dominions overseas slipped away; Cuba, Puerto Rico and the Philippines, the last of the western possessions, were lost as recently as 1899, and to-day once mighty Spain holds nothing outside the country but a few small islands, some colonies in Africa and a protectorate over part of Morocco.

Republican ideas agitated Spain throughout the nineteenth century, until in 1876 it became a constitutional monarchy, but labor troubles, disputes with the Catholic Church and war in Morocco combined to make conditions so unsatisfactory that finally in 1923 the Cortes, or Parliament, was dissolved and General Primo de Rivera formed a military directorate, which was followed by a civil régime not unlike Fascism in Italy. Early in 1930, Primo de Rivera resigned but unrest continued. On April 14, 1931, as the result of revolution, a republic was proclaimed, and King Alfonso and his family were forced to leave the country. A constitution separating Church and State, and containing several radical provisions was adopted but disorder con-

© UNDERWOOD & UNDERWOOD

**IN THE VINEYARDS** of Malaga, luscious Muscatel grapes hang down in purple clusters. Many of them are turned into the sweet wine for which the province is celebrated; a few are packed for export in kegs of sawdust; but most are dried, and turned into the famous Muscatel raisins. Manufacture of cane and beet-sugar is also an important industry.

© LEHNERT & LANDROCK

**SUNNY GOOD HUMOR** is a characteristic of the Spanish people, but combined with it is an easily roused and passionate temper. The women as a rule possess great charm of manner and often considerable beauty. They are usually small and, though their figures are graceful at the age of this smiling maiden, they are inclined to grow heavy with age.

tinued, and in 1936, bloody civil war broke out. Feeling ran so high that many atrocities were committed. Many towns were bombarded or damaged by bombs dropped from aeroplanes. Many famous old churches, palaces and other memorials of the past which had endured for centuries were damaged, as for example the Alcázar in Toledo. In 1939 the war was won by the Insurgents under General Francisco Franco, aided by German and Italian troops sympathetic to his cause. The task of bringing prosperity to war-torn Spain is a heavy one.

Local characteristics are so strongly marked that they are at times an obstacle to national unity. Catalonia with its industrial life is different from easy-going Andalusia, and has often agitated for home-rule; Galicia in the damp north is a striking contrast to the hot dusty plains of Castile. The Basques, inhabiting the corner of Spain by the Bay of Biscay, are a race whose origin may never be known; some authorities link them with the ancient Iberians, others consider them unique. Hardy and independent, they have their own language, which they say was spoken in the Garden of Eden, and their own customs, literature and songs. Apart from the Basques, the people of Spain have developed from the mingling of Iberian, Phœnician, Roman, Gothic and Moorish blood. Most Spaniards are dark-haired and dark-eyed, although here and there we may see fair-haired, blue-eyed persons whose Gothic descent is unusually pure. They are all well built and dignified of movement, and wear their clothes gracefully.

Formerly Spanish women dressed their abundant hair high, with a few flowers tucked in at the side and a fan-shaped comb at the back of the head, over which was draped a graceful mantilla of silk lace, black for street wear, white for festive occasions. So universal was this that it became part of the national costume; but old customs change even in Spain, and the beautiful, flattering mantilla, like the

BLACK STAR

**A VILLAGE PERCHES ABOVE A ROAD HIGH ON THE MESETA**

Most of Spain is a great plateau, or *meseta*, crossed by mountain ridges. In places it has a barren, desolate look, scorched by the sun in summer and beaten by howling winds in winter.

MONKMEYER

**LIGHTS THAT GLITTER ON THE SEA AT NIGHT TO ATTRACT FISH**

Bulbs with beams strong enough to penetrate down through the black Mediterranean waters at night are used to lure curious fish close to the boat. They are then easily caught.

richly-embroidered "manton," or shawl, is being more and more reserved for certain occasions, such as feast days and bull fights. The pretty custom of wearing flowers in the hair is still common. Spaniards love flowers, especially carnations, which may be seen growing in old tins or boxes on the balconies in the villages. The dress of the peasants varies according to the district, and some of the costumes are charming.

The better classes live in handsome residences built, in Moorish fashion, round a central court, or patio, which is gay with flowers and fountains. Few of the windows look out on the street, and these are usually protected by an iron grille called the "reja." When windows are on the ground floor, much courtship is carried on through the reja; when they are on a higher story the lover has to be content with sign-language and with sere-

**BRILLIANT COLORS** are not worn every day by the ladies of sunny Spain. In the south, especially, black is the usual color. Bright hues are reserved for holidays or the dance. This man is not wearing the typical costume. He has not even a "faja"—a sash like that worn by the three peasants of central Spain in holiday attire, shown on another page.

**BARRED WINDOWS** are numerous in beautiful Seville, where many of the buildings remain just as they were centuries ago, in the time of their Moorish builders. There is no glass in windows like the one in the picture, and we should see, if we walked down a narrow street of Seville in the evening, that they witness many a serenade and lovers' meeting.

TRANS WORLD AIRLINES

**ALL DRESSED UP FOR THE FAIR IN SEVILLE**

Seville, largest city of Andalusia, in southern Spain, treasures its romantic customs of a bygone era. During the annual fair, itself a gay relic, the young people don costumes of olden days and parade through the streets. Even the surrey with the canopy top is dusted off for the occasion and hitched to horses decorated with balls of yarn that are all the colors of the rainbow.

nading his lady to the accompaniment of his guitar, for Spanish women still live in a certain amount of seclusion—a legacy from the Moors. But "playing the bear," as window-courtship is called, is nowadays often superseded by dances and "dates" not so very different from those in the most modern lands of Europe and America.

In the days of Moorish supremacy and after, the eight provinces of south Spain —Almería, Cádiz, Córdova, Huelva, Seville, Málaga, Granada and Jaén—were all known as Andalusia. This district is mountainous in the south, where is the lofty Sierra Nevada range, but to the north lies the wide fertile valley of the Guadalquivir. Andalusia is much more like north Africa than like the rest of Spain. Indeed, scientists say it was once a part of Africa, separated from Spain by a narrow channel. Then, centuries and centuries ago, before man existed, two great convulsions occurred. The first raised the bed of the channel and joined Andalusia to Europe, and the

WIDE WORLD

**A BASQUE SHEPHERD AND HIS DOG TAKE THEIR EASE**

Nestled among rolling tree-covered hills, the sunny meadows of the Basque country pasture some of the finest sheep in Spain. The wool is of excellent quality, and the prosperous Basque shepherds take pride in Spain's position as one of the leading wool-producing countries in Europe. The Basque provinces are ringed round by mountains and sea.

© PHOTOCHROM

**A SPANISH GUITAR** is the perfect accompaniment to a Spanish song or dance, especially when the gentle clapping of hands or the gay clatter of castanets accentuates the rhythm. It is the guitar that has influenced the folk music, making rhythm its most attractive feature. The two women shown here in holiday attire are about to begin one of the favorite diversions of the countryfolk—a song that does not end until the singer's voice or her invention fails, for she makes up her words as she sings, employing frequent repetition.

© PHOTOCHROM

**A LADY OF ANDALUSIA** has sparkling black eyes and knows very well how to arrange her wealth of hair. Her white lace, scarlet blossoms and coal-black tresses remind us of the words of the old fairy tale—"As white as snow, as red as blood, and as black as ebony." On special occasions a Spanish lady arranges, over a high tortoise-shell comb, a handsome scarf of silk lace called a "mantilla." Sometimes it is black, sometimes, white, according to the occasion. An Andalusian belle has the advantage of beautiful scenery as a setting.

BLACK STAR

**RUFFLED SKIRTS AND HIGH-HEELED SLIPPERS ON HORSEBACK**

Spanish dancers are known everywhere for their fire and grace. Many festivals are held to keep the old dances alive; and young couples such as these vie with each other in intricate steps.

second separated it from Africa. It is a sunny land, warm in winter and hot in summer, with roses blooming all the year round. In its fertile soil almost anything grows, if only there is enough water. The Moors did wonders by means of irrigation, and modern irrigation projects are again making this the most fruitful part of Spain. Enterprising landowners have installed agricultural machinery and are employing modern methods of farming. Andalusia has great vineyards and olive groves, and produces some of Spain's finest oranges. It is rich in minerals such as copper and coal, iron, lead, manganese and sulphur. Everywhere, in the speech and the appearance of the people, in customs and in architecture, we see signs of the former Moorish domination. Most of the villages and the towns—Seville, Córdova, Martos, Almería, Ronda on its rocky summit, and above all, Granada—can show many houses and mosques, bridges, fortresses or palaces which were built by the Moors in the days of their pride and strength.

The soil in Catalonia and Valencia has nothing like the fertility of the rich lands of the south, but untiring industry has made these two provinces extremely productive. The sides of the hills are carefully terraced for cultivation and the river valleys are thickly seamed with irrigation canals. Spain is an agricultural, not a manufacturing country. Much the greater part of its area is given over to pastures and crops—wheat, barley, corn, grapes, olives, nuts and fruits of many kinds. In fact, only Barcelona and the surrounding district can be regarded as a manufacturing area. Here the cotton mills are busy with Spain's most important manufacture, and silk and woolen goods are also produced.

Catalonia is so different from the rest of Spain that it hardly seems to belong to it. Even the language, Catalán, is different from the Castilian spoken elsewhere. It is often said that the Catalonians have the brains of Spain. They are industrious and practical, and Barcelona, though one of the oldest cities, is modern and up to date, with good shops and thoroughfares and a busy, thriving population. The hydro-electric power used in its factories keeps it free from smoke and soot. Its position on the Mediterranean has made it a place of importance; it is Spain's greatest port, and its mariners were early famed for their en-

BLACK STAR

**DON QUIXOTE SUPPOSEDLY EXPLORED THESE WINDSWEPT PLAINS**

The windmills Quixote mistook for giants still dot the plains near La Mancha. Some of the land is still farmed in the primitive manner of Quixote's time, the wheat being cut by hand.

© E. N. A.

**A MOORISH ANCESTRY** shows itself in the features of this Murcian peasant girl, who stands at the door in holiday clothes. Murcia, the capital of the province of that name, seems to stand in a flower garden, so fertile is the country around. Taken by the Moors early in the 8th century, it continued until the middle of the 13th under Moorish princes.

© PHOTOCHROM

**EVERY SPANISH WOMAN** has a "manton de Manila," a silk, embroidered shawl of great beauty and often of great value, but she wears it only when she dances or on festival days. The shawl, with its knotted fringe, is folded across from corner to corner and arranged so that the point hangs in the front. The ends are crossed and brought over the shoulders.

terprise. But though the richest city in Spain, Barcelona is not concerned only with money-making. It is to the fore in literature, in music and in painting, while modern Catalán architecture is decidedly unusual. Museums, colleges and schools of art and science are well supported, and the practical nature of the education is seen in the fact that here the percentage of illiteracy is lower than in Spain as a whole.

The city is very beautiful and its old cathedral an unusually fine severe type of Gothic. In the cloisters of this stately building we may see geese kept as pets. The story goes that once during a siege Barcelona, like Rome in a similar plight, was saved by the cackling of geese, so these strange pets are kept as a reminder of the episode. The new Cathedral of the Holy Family is of modernistic Catalán design. There is a fine statue of Columbus at the harborside in memory of the fact that when he returned from America the Court was at Barcelona, and in the open square the king and the queen awaited him under a canopy of brocaded gold. Hither he came with his Indians, carrying the skins of rare animals, gold and other treasures, samples of the wealth to be found in the new country. Then the people fell on their knees and raised the Te Deum in gratitude.

Other parts of Spain dislike the hustle and bustle of Barcelona's businesslike methods, and there has been much conflict between ancient and modern. Outside of Catalonia, nobody minds missing a train, or gets excited if it is half an hour late. Pride and politeness, not hurry and immense efficiency, are characteristic of most Spaniards. They give perfect courtesy and expect it in return. Even a beggar asking for alms expects at least a polite refusal.

The life of the streets in old Spanish cities is colorful and fascinating. Peasants come to town driving mule-carts full of produce. A milkman leads his goats from door to door and fills each order by milking one of his animals on the spot. Everywhere government lottery tickets are for sale, and bootblacks are eager to remove the dust from one's shoes. Gipsy

MONKMEYER

**ENTRANCES TO UNDERGROUND WINE CELLARS IN SOUTHERN SPAIN**

When wine is aging, the temperature must be kept uniformly cool and so wine cellars are built underground for insulation. Throughout the wine-making districts of Spain, the countryside is dotted with wine cellars, their entrances peeking out from under humps of sod. Row after row of wooden casks line the cellars, and within the casks new wine is mellowed.

MONKMEYER

**AUTOMOTORS—TROLLEY-BUSSES—RIDE THE RAILS IN SPAIN**

While many countries are busily tearing up their car tracks, Spain is making good use of hers. Modern automotors, produced by an Italian company, run on rails between Segovia and Madrid.

TRANS WORLD AIRLINES

A PEACEFUL COUNTRYSIDE BETWEEN TOLEDO AND SEVILLE

On sunny Spanish hillsides, olive groves bear one of the country's most important crops. Although four out of every nine working people are employed in agriculture and forestry, Spain still does not produce enough foodstuffs for her own use. The trouble lies largely in the inferior quality of the land itself, too little rainfall and very primitive farming methods.

girls in bright skirts and shawls are a frequent sight. In hot weather, water is sold by the glass and the most familiar street cry is: "Agua, agua!" (Water, water.) Chocolate or coffee is served for breakfast with little cakes called "bunuelos," made of egg and flour mixed together and fried in oil. Butter is expensive and is not much used. Olive oil is used instead for cooking, usually unrefined and greenish just as it comes from the press. This and the garlic relished by the Spaniards give to the cooking a flavor all its own. Kid is a favorite dish; at picnics, which play an important part in this sunny, pleasure-loving, out-of-doors land, a kid is frequently roasted whole over a fire in the open air, but the Spanish peasant eats relatively little meat. Every part of the country has its own particular dish, which appears on most tables as part of the meal, and which in the case of the poorer classes may be the only food. There is an abundance of fruit—olives, grapes, oranges, strawberries, melons, peaches, apricots, pomegranates, dates and figs.

Although living poorly, the peasant is as a rule a cheerful, happy person. A light diet suits him; a poor home does not matter when he lives so much out of doors. Cigarettes are cheap—the Spaniard and his cigarette are inseparable—and so long as he has enough money to pay for a place at the bull fight, he is satisfied. But the new generation now growing up is demanding education and better living conditions.

Every baby born in Spain is named after some saint, and instead of observing birthdays, the people celebrate the day of the saint after whom they are named. On that day they keep open house, with cakes, candy, wines and cigarettes for all comers. At a wedding, the bride and groom are attended, not by bridesmaids and best

PHILIP GENDREAU

**GIBRALTAR COMMANDS THE GATEWAY TO THE MEDITERRANEAN**

Gibraltar, a heavily fortified rocky promontory at the southern tip of Spain, belongs to England. It was captured from Spain in 1704 and, in spite of many sieges, has remained British ever since. Gibraltar is connected with the mainland of Spain by a low, sandy isthmus. The ancients were awed by the great "rock" and dared not sail beyond it into the ocean.

TRANS WORLD AIRLINES

A DANGEROUS MOMENT—ALL EYES ARE ON THE BULL

In Madrid's vast arena (plaza de toros) some 12,000 spectators hold their breath as the already wounded bull charges toward the barricades. The bullfight has been for many centuries the favorite sport of the Spanish people and is attended with pomp and ceremony. The greatest of the matadors are national heroes whose entrance is acclaimed with the sound of trumpets.

man, but by two sponsors. Instead of little boxes of wedding cake, delicious sugared almonds are passed around.

Holy Week is a time of great religious observance, when people flock to the churches and cathedrals. Wheeled traffic is suspended in the streets and they are given over to processions arranged by the religious brotherhoods. The marchers wear long robes of white or black and their heads are hidden under tall conical blue hoods. They escort a number of platforms on which are reproduced life-sized figures of scenes from the Passion. At every halt a singer comes forward and chants a few lines, which the people take up and repeat until the procession moves slowly on its way through the city.

THREE LIONS

**WAYSIDE SCENE REFLECTS THE TIMELESS QUALITY OF SPAIN**

This peaceful scene near Old Castile might belong to another era, so far removed is it from the rush and confusion of today. The women of rural areas still bring their clothes to the river on washdays just as their mothers and grandmothers did before them. Water is always at a premium in Spain for it is scarce during droughts and uncontrollable during flood times.

MONKMEYER

**SAN ANTONIO BOULEVARD: A BUSY THOROUGHFARE IN MADRID**

Wide, handsome boulevards traverse modern Madrid, though the buildings have the florid touch of an earlier day. The old quarter—once an Arab town—clusters at the foot of the Alcazar.

### Pageantry of Medieval Splendor

On Maunday Thursday of Holy Week, it was the custom for the king and queen to wash the feet of twenty-four beggars, twelve men and twelve women. This was a stately church ceremony, preceded by a procession of soldiers and glittering officials, of nobles dressed in their best and ladies wearing the most precious jewelry. It was easy to pick out the nobles, or grandees, because they, and only they, wore their hats in the presence of the sovereign. After the service, the procession returned to the palace, where the beggars—all made neat and clean for the occasion—were waiting each with one foot bare. The queen, with a towel pinned around her, knelt before the women, and as the water was poured over the bare foot she dried and kissed it. The king did the same for the men. Then a dinner, often of twenty-four courses, was served by the king and queen to the beggars. It was not eaten then, but taken away by the grandees and duchesses and put aside with the wine, knives, forks, spoons and even the tablecloths for the beggars to take home or sell as they chose. A similar procession took place on Good Friday, only then the queen and ladies were in black dresses and mantillas. On this occasion, the king pardoned several criminals who were under sentence of death, after which the black ribbons on the warrants of execution were exchanged for white ones.

Then on Easter Sunday, Spain throws off the solemnity of Holy Week, the bells ring for joy, people come out in their best, and cafés and theatres are open day and night. In the afternoon rich and poor, old and young flock to the nearest arena to see the first bull fight of the season.

### Festival Time in Seville

The "feria," or fair, which is held annually, sometimes for a week, in most of the towns and villages, is a great occasion. Seville, the charming capital of old Andalusia, is especially delightful in festival time. Then visitors from all Europe, as well as gaily dressed peasants from the smiling country roundabout, fill the streets and enjoy the gaiety of the spring season.

Madrid, the capital of Spain, is a city of wide and beautiful avenues, fine streets and imposing public buildings, but it has not the natural advantages of most Spanish cities. It stands on sandy hills in the midst of a rocky, treeless, grassless plain which is cold in winter and hot in summer. It owes its importance to the fact that the Emperor Charles V ate far too much and so had gout. The only place where his tiresome legs were free from pain was in the dry mountain air, so he lived chiefly in Madrid when he was in Spain. Its austerity appealed to his son Philip II, who made it the capital and built for himself near by what has been called the gloomiest palace in Christendom. This is the Escorial—palace, church, monastery and tomb in one. Dedicated to Saint Lawrence, it is built in the shape of a gridiron, and is so vast that it has fifteen gateways and hundreds of doors. To-day it is famous for its valuable collection of rare books and great pictures, and many people go out from Madrid to see it. Members of the royal family are buried here—kings in a black and gold vault under the High Altar, along with queen consorts who have been mothers of kings, and the other queens in a vault apart. Madrid suffered terribly during the Civil War.

### The Fascination of Old Spain

Spain is full of beautiful churches and palaces—Moorish, Gothic and Renaissance. Her old towns and cities are as picturesque as any in Europe; an artist knows not where to begin. Everywhere one meets the instinctive courtesy of the people, from grandee to peasant, and the Castilian speech is music in the ears. Perhaps the fascination of the Spanish land lies in its varied scenes and peoples. Few countries combine such different regions as cool Galicia, sunny Andalusia, proud Castile, vigorous Catalonia and all the contrasting provinces which have each contributed to Spain's past greatness and present development.

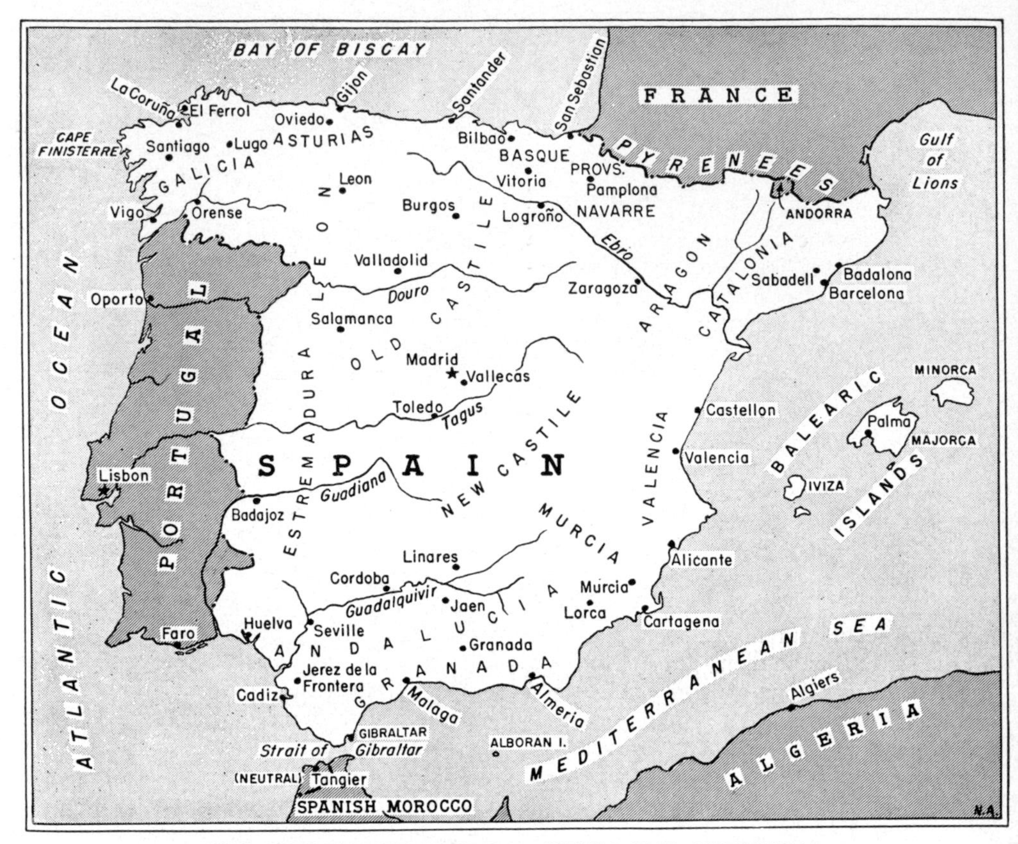


THE IBERIAN PENINSULA—SPAIN AND PORTUGAL

## *SPAIN: FACTS AND FIGURES*

*THE COUNTRY*

Bounded north by Bay of Biscay, France and Andorra, east by the Mediterranean, south by the Mediterranean and the Strait of Gibraltar, southwest by the Atlantic and west by Portugal and the Atlantic. Area of continental Spain, 189,392 square miles; including island provinces in the Canaries and Balearics, 194,232 square miles; total population, 28,286,518.

*GOVERNMENT*

Spain, which had been a constitutional monarchy since 1876, was proclaimed a Republic in 1931. In 1936, a revolt broke out against the Republican Government and developed into a civil war; a Nationalist Government, headed by General Franco, was proclaimed by the rebels. In 1939, the Loyalists, supporters of the Republic, were defeated and Franco became dictator of Spain.

*COMMERCE AND INDUSTRIES*

Eighty-four percent of the land is in pasture, fallow or under cultivation. Leading crops are wheat, barley, oats, rye, rice, oranges, olives, potatoes and tobacco. Livestock, 37,101,000 head, including 25,921,000 sheep. Leading minerals are hard and soft coal, lignite, iron ore, lead, iron pyrites, potash, zinc, tin, wolfram and copper. Leading manufactures are cotton and woolen goods and cement. Fisheries are important; leading catches are sardine, tuna and cod. Leading exports: tin, iron and wolfram ores, cork, hides, salt, fish, vegetables, citrus fruits, wines, potash, olive oil and mercury. Imports: cotton, cereals, potatoes, sugar, coffee, tobacco, wood products, nitrates, machinery, automobiles, petroleum and coal.

*COMMUNICATIONS*

Length of railways, 11,068 miles; roads and highways, about 69,000 miles; telegraph lines, 25,577 miles; 591,948 telephone sets; international and domestic air service.

*RELIGION AND EDUCATION*

Roman Catholicism is the established church; there are about 26,000 Protestants. Primary education, free and compulsory; 5,511 primary schools with 4,221,438 pupils; 119 secondary schools with 212,210 pupils; 12 universities with 46,926 students.

*POPULATION OF CHIEF CITIES*

Madrid (capital), 1,511,695; Barcelona, 1,285,920; Valencia, 534,866; Seville, 390,755; Malaga, 295,757; Zaragoza, 271,587; Bilbao, 235,508; Murcia, 220,290; Granada, 174,663; Cordoba, 164,415; Las Palmas (Canary Islands), 151,411.

# BEAUTIFUL PORTUGAL

## *The Home of Pioneers by Land and Sea*

On a map of the Iberian Peninsula, Portugal looks like a part of Spain, and indeed there are no great natural barriers between the lands; the boundary line is purely political, and in olden days the two countries were united. Yet the Portuguese are quite different from the Spaniards and speak a language of their own. In the fifteenth and sixteenth centuries they were the pioneers of Europe, carrying their flag to the ends of the earth and winning for their motherland a vast colonial empire. To-day Portugal has lost most of those vast possessions and has suffered years of political unrest, but still it remains a strikingly beautiful land of flowers, green meadows, wooded hillsides, winding streams and fragrant uplands.

THERE is an old saying that "Europe is the best of the four quarters of the globe; Spain is the best part of Europe; Portugal is the best part of Spain." Yet few people know enough about Portugal to understand the reasons for that extravagant-sounding claim. Everyone has heard of the beauty of Cintra, and we associate Lisbon with one of the most terrible earthquakes ever known (1755), but we forget that the exploits of the Portuguese explorer, Vasco da Gama, rival the achievements of Columbus, and that Portugal was once the greatest pioneering power in Europe; nor do we realize what an exceptionally picturesque and beautiful land this western part of the Iberian Peninsula is.

Until the twelfth century, Portugal's history was that of Spain; the Iberians who originally lived there were conquered first by the Carthaginians and then by the Romans, who left an indelible stamp upon the land. From roads and aqueducts to the speech of the people, the Roman inheritance is still evident. Barbarian tribes of Northern and Eastern Europe—Vandals, Suevi, Alani and Goths—overran Portugal as they did the rest of the Peninsula, and after them came the Moors from Africa. The modern kingdom of Portugal began as a small principality which extended only from the Minho to the Mondego; it became independent of the Spanish kingdom of León in 1143. With the help of many bands of crusaders from England, Flanders and other parts of Europe, the Moors were gradually pushed south until the boundaries of Portugal came, in the middle of the thirteenth century, to look much as they do to-day. It was the mingling of Iberians, Romans, barbarian tribes, Moors, Jews, English, Dutch and, later, Negroes from Africa which produced the Portuguese nation. King John I laid the foundations of the great maritime empire which his son, Henry the Navigator, was to establish. Men like Bartholomew Diaz explored and colonized the west coast of Africa, pushing farther and farther until the Cape of Good Hope was reached in 1488. Ten years later Vasco da Gama reached India by sailing around Africa, and for eighty years Portugal was mistress of the southern and eastern seas. But in 1580 the Spanish king succeeded to the throne of Portugal, and by the time (1640) the Portuguese revolted and set up their own king, their country had lost its great eastern dominions. Brazil, which had been discovered incidentally, remained a Portuguese colony until 1822, but Portugal never recovered its position as a European power. Since 1910, when the monarchy was overthrown by a revolution, the country has been slowly trying to evolve a stable republican government, but the present régime is a military dictatorship as the president's power depends on the army. Of the colonies, only a few scattered possessions in Africa, India, China and the Malay Archipelago are left. The Azores and Madeira in the Atlantic are an integral part of the republic.

With an area of nearly 35,000 square miles, Portugal occupies a sixth of the Iberian Peninsula. It is not divided from

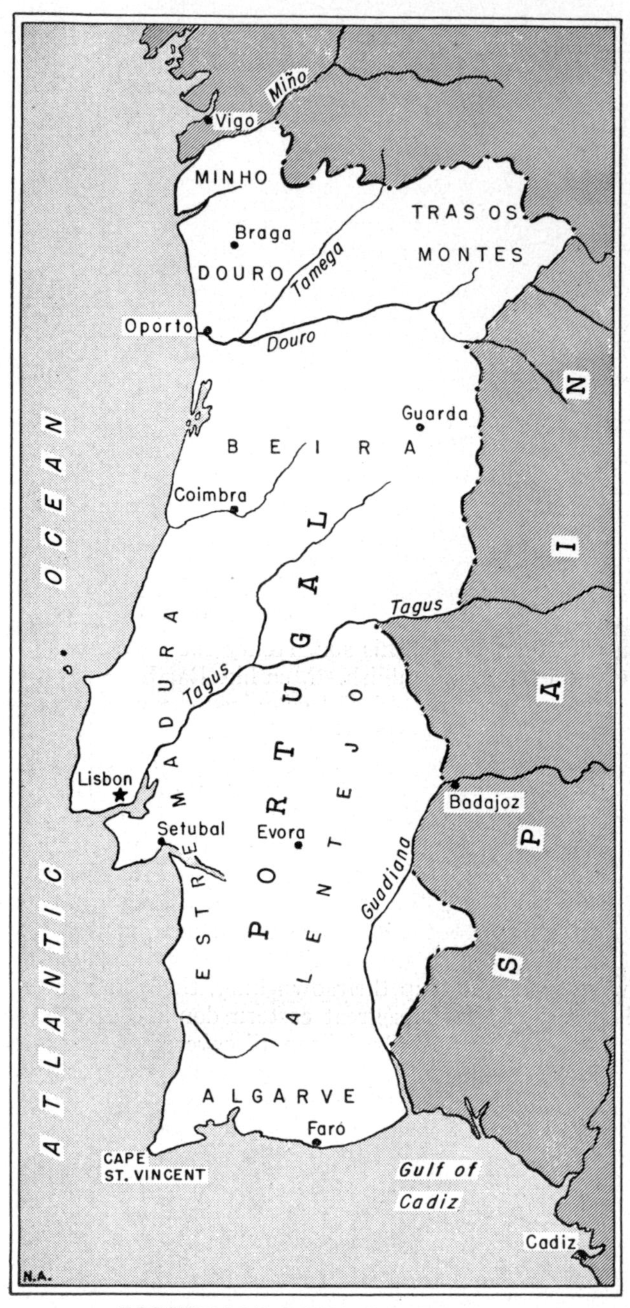


PORTUGAL'S LONG COASTLINE

Spain by any natural barriers; its low mountain ranges are but prolongations of Spanish ones, and all its important rivers rise in the neighboring country The Tagus and the Douro are the two chief streams, and they divide the land into three distinct sections. The northernmost includes the two provinces of Entre Minho e Douro and Tras os Montes, above the Douro; the central district between the Douro and the Tagus includes Estremadura and Biera, and the southern provinces of Algarve and Alemtejo lie south of the Tagus. The name "Alemtejo" means "On the Other Side of the Tagus." North of the Douro is the most mountainous part of the country; the Serra da Estrella cuts across Biera, and in the south the Serra de Monchique marks off the old Moorish province of Algarve. Though adjoining Spain, a country that suffers in the summer from too great heat and an insufficient rainfall, central Portugal has a most delightful climate with plenty of warm sunshine and cool breezes from the Atlantic Ocean to temper the heat. These winds bring just enough rain but not too much. The northern provinces are far more rainy than Alemtejo and Algarve, which are almost as dry and tropical as North Africa. Most of the coastline is low, with two or three bold headlands and many sand dunes. A little above Lisbon the scenery becomes wildly beautiful, and from here to the Minho River on the northern boundary stretches the loveliest part of the country. The valley of the Douro is terraced with vineyards, while on the moorlands, or "campos," above the Tagus grow sweet-smelling shrubs, such as cistus, which has a white flower like that of the sweetbriar rose and wild flowers of colorful beauty.

Courtesy, Mundet Cork *Corp.*

**WORKMEN ENGAGED IN STRIPPING BARK FROM CORK TREES**

Cork is the dried outer bark of an evergreen tree grown largely in Spain, Portugal, Algeria and Italy. Some is now being grown in California as well. The outer coat is replaced in a few years, and a cork tree may be peeled every eight or ten years without damage to the tree. The cork improves in quality with successive peelings.

TRANS WORLD AIRLINES

**THE MONASTERY OF THE JERONIMOS IN LISBON**

This magnificent structure is considered by many to be the finest example of Portuguese national architecture. Located in Belem, a suburb of Lisbon, it was begun about 1502 by the order of King Manuel, the Fortunate. The church (shown here), which is more than 300 feet long and 80 feet wide, is decorated with a great wealth of beautiful and interesting sculpture.

CASA DE PORTUGAL

**TREES OF STONE THAT FLOWER OVERHEAD**

Living stone, shaped laboriously and skillfully long ago by the loving hands of artisans, creates a perfect harmony. The curving and interlacing branches glorify the vault of the sacristy in the church of the Monastery of the Jeronimos. In this room are kept the sacred utensils and vestments used in the services in this great monument of Portuguese art and piety.

**SHEER BEAUTY AND POETRY IN STONE**

The graceful arches of the Royal Cloister of the Monastery of St. Mary of the Victory at Batalha are pure and breath-taking in the loveliness of their Gothic style. The monastery is actually a monument to the freedom of Portugal. It was begun, in fulfillment of a vow, by King John I of Portugal sometime after his victory over John I of Castile at Alajubarrota.

PAN AMERICAN WORLD AIRWAYS

**FISHING FLEET ON THE BROAD TAGUS RIVER NEAR LISBON**

Groups of fishermen in small, swift boats are seen all along the coast of Portugal. When setting out for tuna, they draw a barrier of nets across the boats, and drive the fish toward it. Then the sport gets violent. The men grip tight the rigging at the very edge of the boat and, yelling with excitement, cast harpoons at the struggling, writhing fish.

TRANS WORLD AIRLINES

**YELLOW DOMES OF THE BIZARRE CASTLE OF PENA NEAR CINTRA**

Built about a century ago by a German prince, the Castle of Pena is an imitation of a medieval fortress. It incorporates nearly every known form of architecture. The castle's minaret stands higher than the sentry wall. A roofed gallery adjoins a Gothic turret. Yet it is beautiful from a distance, its fantastic silhouette shrouded in soft sea mist.

Nearly every plant of tropical and temperate lands will and does grow in Portugal, and in spring the countryside is covered with a gorgeous display of flowers. Pine trees and palms, oaks and cactus plants thrive almost side by side. Despite the fertile soil, agriculture in some parts is more backward than it should be, though this cannot be said of northern Portugal, where every bit of good land is carefully cultivated; there wheat, corn, rye, potatoes, oats and beans are all raised, and the vineyards are famous. The green beauty of the provinces above the Tagus contrasts with the arid landscape in the south. Here grow olive trees and cork-oaks, and the soil is no less fertile, but water is scarce. On many a farm we come upon an old water wheel of the type the Spaniards call "noria," and it is turned by a blindfolded donkey who trudges round and round in a circle, raising water from the well in little jars which empty into trenches leading to the fields.

Along the coast, many Portuguese are fishermen. Sardines are plentiful and so are tunny fish, which we call tuna. When a school of sardines is sighted, there is great excitement in the fishing villages

TRANS WORLD AIRLINES

**A HOUSE OUT OF THE FIFTEENTH CENTURY**

The new-old city of Lisbon is famous not only for its beautiful monuments and buildings but for the many picturesque sections that are a joy to those who love to explore picturesque places. One of the most striking of the old buildings is the House of Pointed Stones, which belonged to the son of a Portuguese viceroy of India in the fifteenth century.

EWING GALLOWAY

TRAFFIC SPANS THE STEEP-SIDED DOURO RIVER ON TWO LEVELS IN PORTUGAL'S SEAPORT TOWN OF OPORTO

Oporto, second city of Portugal, stands near the mouth of the rapid and treacherous River Douro. Most of the city is built up the sides of the northern bank, and many of the streets are too steep for vehicles. Its architecture shows the same Moorish influence as other Iberian cities.

WIDE WORLD

**PLENTY OF ROOM FOR MASS DRILLS OR ANY KIND OF BALL GAME**

Sports spectacles in the huge modern stadium just outside of Lisbon attract thousands of cheering fans. Colorful national festivals are also held in this vast structure.

TRANS WORLD AIRLINES

**BREATH-TAKING GARDENS SURROUND THE CASINO AT ESTORIL**

Estoril is a seaside resort only a short distance from Lisbon. The center of fashionable life is the Casino. Its perfectly kept grounds are the delight of anyone who loves flowers.

TRANS WORLD AIRLINES

A FARMER AND HIS PATIENT DONKEY POSE FOR THE CAMERA

In rural Portugal, where life moves at a moderate pace, there is always time to stop for a picture or to exchange a friendly word with a traveler, especially in the heat of the day.

BLACK STAR

**ON THE WAY HOME FROM THE FISH MARKETS IN LISBON**

The cobblestone streets in the capital of Portugal are picturesque. They are also sloppy, so the housewives wear flat shoes to help keep their balance on the slippery stones.

and hundreds of little boats with high pointed prows put out from shore. They come back loaded to the gunwales, and the sardines are sold in the streets by men who wear specially made tin hats with wide, deep brims to hold the fish. The rest of the catch goes to the big factory at Setúbal, below Lisbon, to be canned and exported.

The two great cities of Portugal are Lisbon and Oporto. Lisbon is the capital, and the center of southern Portugal; it is very beautifully situated on rising ground above the "golden-sanded" River Tagus. An old writer considered that Lisbon was intended by nature to be the "Emporium of Europe" because of its good harbor on the Tagus and its position as the westernmost port on the continent. It is one of the fine cities of Europe, with splendid boulevards as well as picturesque alleyways and colorful houses painted any shade from blue to pink. The motley crowds which throng its hilly streets are endlessly fascinating. The city-dwellers as a rule wear dark clothes of ordinary European type, but the many country people who come to town to buy and sell flaunt bright costumes in great variety, and on feast days any street scene is a kaleidoscope of color.

Oporto, farther north, is also delightfully situated on the steep banks of the River Douro, near the seacoast, and its

HENLE FROM MONKMEYER

**PORTUGUESE WOMEN TEST QUALITY THROUGH THEIR FINGERTIPS**

Gossip or a joke does not interfere with the task at hand, sorting beans. Beans are a staple article in the diet of most Portuguese people. The handknit shawls, stockings and lace edgings worn by these women suggest that their hands know many other skills. Bean-sorting is probably only a part-time occupation for them, an interlude in their cares as housewives and mothers.

© Cutler

TO MARKET, TO MARKET, TO SELL A SMALL PIG

There are certain days when only animals are sold in Portuguese country markets, and then everyone with pigs, donkeys, oxen or other farm animals to sell journeys to market with the four-footed merchandise. This little old farmwife has set off with a switch to keep her small white porker moving, and a string on its leg to keep it from wandering off.

THE GREAT PALACE OF PENA CROWNS THIS STEEP MOUNTAIN TOP HIGH ABOVE BEAUTIFUL CINTRA

Built in the nineteenth century for the use of the royal family, the palace looks like one of Portugal's medieval castles. From the dizzy height of its windows and battlements we may gaze upon one of the best views in a country of fine landscapes. The forest-covered cliff drops away sharply, and far below lies the town of Cintra, famous throughout Europe for its beauty. Southeast of Cintra is the valley of the Tagus, which widens out to form the harbor of Lisbon, and on the hills by the distant river rise the buildings of the capital.

Emilio Biel & Co.

**COIMBRA IS THE INTELLECTUAL CENTRE OF PORTUGAL**

Over six hundred years ago—in 1306—Coimbra became a university town. To it come boys from all over Portugal, from the Portuguese colonies and from Brazil. Everywhere in the town are the students, wearing the black costume and long full cape which have been worn by Coimbra scholars for generations. This is one of the university buildings.

name means "the Port." Two headlands overlook the city; one is crowned by the archbishop's palace, and vineyards clothe the other. Down from the many vineyards that line the river come the picturesque little wine boats, each with one mast and a big square sail, and four or five casks of wine amid ships. There is a big trade also in salt codfish; Portuguese ships are frequently seen on the Newfoundland Banks and barques laden with cod arrive from Norway and are unloaded by porters, both men and women. These men are a bare-footed, bare-chested, black-whiskered and indescribably dirty crew, and they rush up the short street leading to the Exchange, carrying their loaded baskets on their shoulders. The women carry huge loads of the fish on their heads, and scarcely ever steady the baskets with their hands. Ox-carts and automobiles compete for room on the narrow streets.

Portuguese roads used to be bad and traveling difficult, which may partly account for the fact that a country with scenery as lovely and towns as old and quaint as those of Portugal is so little known to the foreign tourist. Beautiful Cintra, near Lisbon, and the district around it are of course familiar but there are also fortified Valença do Minho, on the northern frontier; ancient Braga and Vianna do Castello; Coimbra, the old university town; Batalha, with its convent; Bussaco, in the centre of beautiful woods; Beja, with its ancient castle; and Moorish Evora. The famous port wine which was the foundation of Portugal's trade with England was first shipped not from Oporto but from Vianna do Castello, and this fascinating little old town was a bustling seaport in the days of discovery and empire.

Wherever one goes, the beautiful costumes brighten every village and Portugal is a delight to those who love the picturesque. The peasant's everyday clothes are not particularly striking, though grace of body is evident even under rags and tatters, and faded colors often blend into strange harmonies. But on holi-

BLACK STAR

**PORTUGAL'S GAY FESTIVALS ARE BASED ON ANCIENT CUSTOMS**

Costumed farmers ride frequently to town to attend religious festivals. Wherever these colorful processions go, music mingles with the scent of rosemary scattered in their path.

BLACK STAR

**FUTURE FISHERMEN MAKE SMALL TALK AT THE VILLAGE FOUNTAIN**

Nazarre fishermen are recognized throughout Portugal by their tartan shirts and black caps. Their children, wearing the same gay plaids, love to play at the splashing village fountain.

© E. N. A.

**VINTAGE TIME IN PORTUGAL,** which lasts from the end of September to the middle of October, finds the vineyards crowded with men and women gathering the ripe grapes. Their baskets, when full, are emptied into great vats on wheels, which are slowly drawn to the wine press by stolid, wide-horned oxen with decorated yokes. The vehicles used by the peasants of Portugal have for wheels great disks of wood, the ungreased axles of which creak discordantly. Much of the wine travels to the coast (see the following page) to be stored until ready for export.

WAYMARK

**THE RIVER DOURO** flows through the Paiz do Vinho, the "Wine Country" of Portugal, and for many miles of its course the steep banks have been laboriously cut into terraces on which grow the vines. The wine produced here is called "port" because it is shipped from Oporto (known in Portugal as Porto), "the Port," to which it is carried in odd flat-bottomed barges, usually with enormous rudders. Some of these boats can be seen in the picture. The men who pilot them need to be very skillful, for the course of the Douro is broken by reefs and rapids.

days, both men and women dress in the gayest and brightest colors.

A woman living around Oporto will wear a bright kerchief over her head, and maybe a queer little round black velvet hat—a legacy from Moorish days—tilted over one eye. Another bright kerchief, crossed over and tied at the back, will form her bodice, and her apron will be wondrously embroidered in many vivid colors. The working women are fond of investing their savings in gold and silver filigree ornaments. They also like to wear gaily embroidered "money-pockets" at their waists, and these give a redeeming touch of color to the most drab and well worn dresses. They rarely wear shoes and stockings while at work, but in the evening they don bright magenta stockings and black, painted shoes, and are then dressed for going out of doors. Their habit of carrying on their heads everything, including the baby, gives them an excellent carriage and fine figures. It is astounding to see what heavy loads they carry with apparent ease. They like full, swinging skirts, and their walk is proud and free.

The "festa" dress of the fisher-girls is gorgeous in the extreme, but in everyday life they are generally content with fewer, though still vivid colors, which make of any crowd an attractive picture. When they are at work on the shore, cleaning fish and hanging pieces of cod to dry in the sun, they wear enormous straw hats with high crowns and wide brims. Country women, coming to market sitting sideways on their donkeys, with laden panniers swinging at each side and often a festoon of flapping fowls behind, present a distinctly picturesque appearance. But their menfolk surpass them, for the farmer rides to town on his mule, with a high peaked saddle and cumbrous stirrups tipped with brass, and with his rolled

TRANS WORLD AIRLINES

**A SYMBOL OF PORTUGAL'S GLORIOUS PAST—THE TOWER OF BELEM**

From this spot on the Tagus River, near Lisbon, Vasco da Gama is said to have set sail in 1497 on the voyage that was to win Portugal a fabulous empire in India. He now lies buried in the chapel. The tower itself was not built until 1520. Its dungeons are flooded with every tide; and in the past, many prisoners died locked within these dark, watery cells.

HENLE FROM MONKMEYER

**WHERE FARMERS SPREAD THEIR PRODUCE ON A MOSAIC PAVEMENT**

The market place in Caldas da Reinha is paved with mosaics as are most of the streets in this city that was built with a lavish hand. Queen Leonor founded it in 1485 because she thought the waters of its warm sulfur springs had cured her. It has been a fashionable spa ever since for wealthy patients seeking cures. The name means "the queen's hot springs."

LONG

**CINTRA, IN PORTUGAL,** is so beautiful that an old Spanish proverb says "To see the world, and yet leave Cintra out, is verily to go blindfold about." Here we stand near the Sabuga fountain, and look over the houses to a rocky height crowned by the ruins of a Moorish castle. Cintra, once a royal residence, has two famous palaces.

© CUTLER

**HOLIDAYS** and carnival time are gay days in Portugal, for then women and girls wear their gala clothes—skirts, aprons, bodices, kerchiefs and slippers all bright with embroidery. This sober little boy and his rainbow-clad sisters are from Vianna do Castello, in north Portugal, where the peasant costumes are most colorful and picturesque.

cape, displaying its lining of bright blue or crimson, strapped in front of him. He wears a smart jacket and fine sombrero hat, and is altogether an imposing figure. In other walks of life the costumes of the men are interesting rather than picturesque. If a sash is worn round the waist it may be black, crimson, scarlet, magenta or blue. Sometimes there is a loosely knotted kerchief also, which either tones with the sash or contrasts with it daringly.

The striking peasant costumes well express the strong artistic sense of the Portuguese, which also shows itself in superb medieval architecture of churches and convents, in the making of fine lace and in the lines of everyday pottery. Beautiful tilework for decorating houses and public buildings has been a national industry since Moorish days. The people are musical too, and have a natural genius for story-telling. The background of adventure and discovery in their history gives them a fascinating storehouse of folk tales, and in the past there have been great poets well able to use that rich material. Though Portuguese and Spanish have both developed from the Latin tongue, the speech of one land is unintelligible to people of the other, and it is as reasonable to expect a Portuguese to understand French as to think that he can automatically comprehend Spanish. As a language, Portuguese has a greater variety of expression than Spanish, because in bygone days many Arabic, Dutch, French and English words became incorporated with it; it is very harmonious and perfectly adaptable to any style of writing or speaking. With such natural advantages, there may again rise another dramatist like Gil Vicente, or another poet with the powers of Camoëns, who wrote his great epic, the Lusiads, in the early sixteenth century to commemorate and extol the epoch-making voyage of Vasco da Gama.

---

## *PORTUGAL: FACTS AND FIGURES*

### *THE COUNTRY*

Bounded on the north and east by Spain, on the west and south by the Atlantic Ocean. Area, including the Azores and Madeira Islands, 35,490; population, 8,490,455. Continental area, 34,254; population, 7,902,590.

### *THE GOVERNMENT*

In 1933 a new constitution was adopted, establishing a dictatorship on a corporative basis. It provides for a president, and a Council of State to advise him, and two assemblies of 120 members each—a National Assembly, elected by heads of families regardless of sex, and a Corporative Chamber, chosen through guilds.

### *COMMERCE AND INDUSTRY*

Agricultural and forest products are the most important. Wheat, corn, oats, barley, rye, rice, French beans and potatoes are the country's principal crops. Vineyards abound, and the making of wine is the chief industry. Forest area, comprising 19% of the total, includes oak, pine, cork-oak and chestnut. Cork is the second largest industry; 232,109 metric tons of cork products were exported in a recent year. Much olive oil is produced as well as resin and turpentine. Fishing for sardines and tuna fish is important, and great quantities of canned sardines and tuna are exported each year. Mineral deposits include coal, pyrites, lead, copper, tin, wolfram, titanium and other ores, but production is slight. Manufactures: cotton textiles, sardine-packing, decorative tile and chinaware, embroideries and handmade lace, superphosphate of lime. Principal imports: raw cotton and cotton goods, iron and steel, wheat, motor vehicles, coal and coke, sugar, dried codfish, ammonium sulfate, coffee, hides, gasoline, dyes, corn. Principal exports: cork and cork products, wine, wolfram, canned sardines and tuna fish, olive oil, resin, pyrites, turpentine.

### *COMMUNICATIONS*

Railway mileage, 2,240; about one-third state-owned. Telegraph line mileage, 6,557. Telephone mileage, partly state-owned, 215,-730. Main ports, Lisboã (Lisbon) and Porto (Oporto).

### *RELIGION AND EDUCATION*

Roman Catholicism is dominant, but all denominations have freedom of worship. Primary education is compulsory, but the percentage of illiteracy is about 50%. In a recent year there were 679,671 enrolled in primary and elementary schools, excluding special and technical schools. The 3 universities—Lisbon, Coimbra (founded 1290) and Porto (Oporto).

### *CHIEF TOWNS*

Population, 1940, Lisboã (Lisbon), the capital, 709,179; Porto (Oporto), 262,809; Coimbra, 35,437; Setúbal, 35,071; Braga, 29,875; Evora, 21,851; Ponte Delgada, 21,048; Faro, 19,695. The number of emigrants in a recent year was 21,892, of whom 14,143 went to Brazil.

# ISLES OF THE MEDITERRANEAN

## *From West to East in the Great Inland Sea*

For centuries the isles of the Mediterranean have been the meeting-place of different races. Old costumes and customs, the ancient ways of East and West, still linger here. The islands have played a vital role in the annals of commerce; they have played as prominent a part in the history of warfare from the very earliest campaigns. The strategic importance of the Mediterranean islands in World War II can hardly be overestimated. They have served as stepping-stones of conquest and as citadels that have withstood a determined foe. The conquest of Crete by the Germans endangered the position of the Allies in the Middle East; the dogged resistance of Malta helped to pave the way for the Allied triumph in North Africa. Sicily, the largest of the islands, is the subject of another chapter; here we shall see something of Sardinia and Corsica, the Balearics, Malta, Cyprus, Corfu and Crete.

THE Mediterranean seems a magic sea, so vivid is the blue of its waters and so golden its sunshine. Not the least of its enchantments are the islands big and little which break its blue surface here and there. The Balearics are numbered among Spain's fairest provinces, while Corsica is a mountainous, rugged land with a wild beauty all its own. In Italian Sardinia the colorful costumes of by-gone days are still worn on occasion, and rocky Malta with its hoary fortifications is reminiscent of the time when it was the feudal stronghold of the Knights of St. John. Eastern influence is strong in the Greek isles of Corfu, Crete and Cyprus, though Cyprus belongs to Great Britain nowadays. All these islands have been meeting grounds for different races, which only increases the fascination of each beautiful spot.

The Balearic archipelago is situated off the east coast of Spain, and the three most important islands are Majorca, Minorca and Iviza. They have been ruled in turn by Carthaginians, Romans, Vandals, Moors and Spaniards, and in the eighteenth century France and England each gained temporary footholds. The British left their mark upon Mahón, which they made the capital of Minorca, but outside of it the Balearics are essentially Spanish to-day.

The Majorcan climate is almost perfect, never too hot nor too cold. The only thing lacking is a good water supply; rains are infrequent and the islanders have had to terrace their fields and build reservoirs to conserve and use every drop that falls. The many old-fashioned stone windmills are used not for pumping water but for crushing olives. Everywhere in the Balearics grow the olive trees, with delicate gray-green leaves and thick gnarled old trunks. Fine big melons, oranges, lemons, figs, almonds, peppers and other vegetables, and carob beans—which grow on trees—are luscious products of the islands. Besides the ancient industries of farming and fishing, the island of Minorca manufactures shoes, which it sends to Spain for sale. Perhaps on account of this industry, the Minorcans wear shoes instead of the alpargatas or rope sandals of the other islands.

Corsica is less idyllic than the Balearics. It is a part of France, but lies nearer to Italy, and its people speak an Italian dialect. Imagine an island with mountains rising steeply from the blue waters of the Mediterranean—an island possessing great forests of pine and chestnut, hills covered with vineyards, olive orchards and lemon groves, and above, wild stretches of uncultivated rocky ground where the sweet-flowering scrubby growth called "maquis" makes the air fragrant. That is Corsica, a land of troubled, bloody history and terrible vendettas, and famous as the birthplace of Napoleon. Its story is very confused and distressing, especially since the end of Roman rule in the year 469, when Northern barbarians and Eastern Mohammedans alike began to attack

**THE IONIAN ISLANDS** lie off the west shores of Greece and Albania. The largest and most important of them is Corfu, which was colonized by Corinth in the eighth century B.C. Standing now with our backs to Corfu city, we are looking across the entrance of the large inlet that was probably the ancient harbor. Canone lies in the centre, and the cypress-clad island behind it is the Scoglio d'Ulisse (Rock of Ulysses), which was believed by the ancient Greeks to be the ship that, having carried Ulysses to Ithaca, was turned to stone by Poseidon.

**MAJORCA,** the largest of the Balearic Islands, with its orchards and gardens and vineyards, is a most attractive place. The climate is delightful, and the soil yields the usual Mediterranean flowers and fruits. The Balearic Isles, lying off the coast of Spain, so resemble the mainland that this lane with its picturesque setting might well be in Andalusia.

EWING GALLOWAY

**A MIRROR FOR THE TOWERS OF A BAROQUE CATHEDRAL**

Bastia, fortified port and chief city of Corsica, was once its capital. The Cathedral of St. John the Baptist in the background is in the old section, north of the modern city and port.

it, and rival Corsican barons fought each other. The Italian city of Genoa claimed the land, and France supported now Genoa and now the Corsicans, who might more than once have made good their independence had they been able to stop quarreling; finally in 1768, Genoa ceded the island to France. Since 1815, it has been a French department (state).

The appalling misgovernment and confusion of centuries encouraged the vendetta, or blood-feud. When a man could not hope for justice from the authorities —and often there were no authorities— he took matters into his own hands and killed his enemy. Whereupon the relatives of the dead man would take their weapons and hunt the assassin down. The feud might go on until scores of lives were lost and both families wiped out. Since the island became French, the vendetta has been partially eliminated.

Ajaccio, the capital, is a delightful seaport surrounded by mountains. The streets are lined with palms and orange trees and the houses painted in gay colors. The house where Napoleon was born is still to be seen, but to reach it one must run the gauntlet of a mob of beggar-children who are eager to act as guides.

The Italian island of Sardinia is about seven miles south of Corsica, and like it is a mountainous land, wild and desolate in spots. There are many fascinating ruins of strange dwelling-houses and temples built long ago in the Bronze Age. The Sardinian peasants are a simple primitive race, short of stature, with dark hair and eyes; they speak different dialects, as their ancient speech has been influenced by both Italian and Spanish. In Roman days Sardinia was a great source of food supplies, and galleys carried load after load of golden grain from Sardinian harbors to the Roman markets. After Rome fell, the Vandals conquered Sardinia and then it became part of the Byzantine Empire. The Saracens attacked it constantly, until they were finally defeated by the Pisans, who in turn were driven out by the Spanish king of Aragon. In 1720 Savoy and some other parts of

KEYSTONE

**A CORSICAN IN HIS FRENCH BERET SMOOTHS A BLOCK OF MARBLE**

The rock under the workman's chisel and hammer may be fashioned into a statue or used in a building. Marble with delicate veining and granite are quarried in the mountains of Corsica.

© E. N. A.

**ON THE ISLAND OF MALTA,** which lies in the very middle of the Mediterranean Sea, there are no streams because the rain sinks into the porous soil. Except in time of drought, the land is fertile. The winter gales are very destructive, and the summer heat is intense; but, on the whole, the climate is favorable and the inhabitants have good health. Malta has the distinction of naving been one of the most bombed targets of World War II. The island has lived, in fact, in a state of siege. The bravery of the people under continued fire won the admiration of the world.

© E. N. A.

**FORTIFIED VALLETTA,** the capital of Malta, is a great port of call and the chief British naval and coaling station in the Mediterranean Sea. Its strong walls testify that it was equally important in ancient days. Built upon a promontory that juts out into a large inlet on the east coast, it has a fine harbor on each side. Here we see the entrance Grand Harbor. From 1530 to 1798 Malta was the home of the Knights of St. John of Jerusalem, or Knights of Malta. In 1942 King George VI bestowed the George Cross upon the island, for the people's courage under Axis raids.

PIX

SUNNY DAY IN OLIENA, SARDINIAN HILL TOWN

From the bridge, the street winds on up past tile-roofed houses that have almost no windows. Oliena is in central Sardinia, in a region of vineyards. Nearby there are strange, prehistoric towers of stone, called nuraghi.

Italy were combined with the island and called the Kingdom of Sardinia, which in 1861 became the core of united Italy.

The Sardinians have escaped to some extent the standardization of costume and custom that is so noticeable among more sophisticated peoples. A kilted shepherd from the southern Sulcis might have stepped out of the Middle Ages, and in the Barbagia, or eastern interior of the island, we find people whose scarlet and white costumes also remind us of the pageantry of past ages. Each peasant community has its distinctive patterns, colors and embroidery, and the styles in head kerchiefs are delightfully various. The men wear a peculiar stocking-cap called a "berretta," the end of which falls to the shoulder and serves as a pouch. These beautiful, valuable old costumes are nowadays worn only on Sundays and special occasions. On the Campidano (or plain), in the mining district of the south and in the cities, Cagliari and Sassari, ordinary modern European clothes are the rule, and as communications become better and better, the medieval styles are sure to disappear.

From Sardinia we shall voyage to the British island of Malta, that lies south of Sicily in a most strategic position. Valletta, the capital, is built upon one of the finest harbors in the Mediterranean, and is an important naval base. But Malta has not always been a British possession. Like Sardinia, it has many very ancient ruins, in this case built by men of the Stone Age. Before the sixth century B.C., it was a Phœnician colony, and the Maltese of to-day are descended from those settlers of long ago, whose language they still speak. Carthaginians, Romans, Arabs, Normans and Aragonese all governed Malta without vitally changing the character of the people. The Knights of St. John of Jerusalem were an ancient military and monastic order which fought against the Mohammedans during the Crusades and for years afterward. They were driven from the Holy Land to Cyprus and Rhodes and eventually, in 1530, to Malta. There they made a stand against the Turks and were victorious in the great siege of 1565. The Grand Master of the Order, Jean de la Vallette, built and fortified Valletta and the Knights ruled Malta until Na-

PIX

LABOR IN VAIN—THE LOOSENED SOIL WILL SOON WASH DOWN

Farmers on Sardinia work long hours to eke a living out of land that is mountainous and denuded of the forests that once held the topsoil in place. Digging the hillsides means barren gulleys next year. Only about a fourth of the island is actually suitable for planting, chiefly in the lowlands. About half can be used as grazing land for sheep, goats and cows.

Courtesy, British Information Service

**REBUILDING RAID-DAMAGED STRUCTURES IN MALTA**

Although Malta suffered more than 2,500 air raids in World War II, the repairing and rebuilding of the island never stopped. There are many natural bomb shelters cut deep in the solid rock foundations and after each raid, civilians would climb out to clean up the damage. The people of Malta received the George Cross for their heroism.

poleon drove them out. Malta later became a British possession. The island won imperishable renown in World War II, when it withstood over 2,500 Axis air raids. In 1942, the George Cross was conferred on the island fortress by King George VI.

The city of Valletta, laid out on a rocky promontory, is fascinating. The beautiful old palaces of the Order of St. John remind us of feudal days; we can almost imagine that a proud red or black-robed Knight with an eight-pointed white Maltese cross upon his breast will presently step from one of the massive doorways, though such medieval figures disappeared from Malta well over a century ago. Malta owes its importance to its location on the trade route between eastern and western Mediterranean lands.

Corfu long ago was a great commercial city because it lay just off the Greek coast, yet not far from the heel of Italy, and Greek ships on the way to Italy and Sicily always put in there. It was settled before 700 B.C. by men from the Greek city of Corinth, and was called Corcyra in those days. It was an independent city-state until the Mediterranean world became Roman, and belonged to the Byzantine Emperors after the Roman Empire split apart. In the Middle Ages the Venetians governed it longer than did any other power, and during much of the nineteenth century it was a British protectorate. Now, along with the other Ionian islands, it is part of Greece.

It has been called the most beautiful of the isles of Greece, and indeed it is an enchanting spot. The mountains of the

PIX

**A PLEASANT TASK IN A VINEYARD ON CRETE'S GENTLE HILLS**

The vineyard worker is washing grapes in a sievelike pail by dipping it into a tub of water. The grapes will then be spread out and allowed to dry into raisins. Crete is an island of vineyards and olive groves. Its chief exports are olive oil, wine and raisins. Most of the people are of Greek origin and are skillful at tending grove and vine.

PIX

**LOUTEROS, TINY HILLSIDE VILLAGE ON THE ISLAND OF CYPRUS**

This sleepy little settlement is on Morphou Bay on the north coast of the "copper island" as Cyprus has been called. The tile-roofed cottages seem to cling precariously to the steep slopes.

northern part are bare and rugged, but the fertile valleys are covered with the gray-green of countless olive trees, the brighter green of vineyards and the very dark green of tall conical cypress trees. White-walled houses stand out sharply against the foliage, and over all is the intensely blue sky which seems to belong to Greece. Close at hand the Mediterranean sparkles in the sun. Olive oil, fragrant honey and many fruits are the products which the farms of Corfu send to other countries.

Crete, which also belongs to Greece, is another beautiful and pleasant land, extremely fertile, picturesque and interesting. It is a long narrow island, and serves to divide the Ægean Sea from the Mediterranean. As we read in the chapter Relics of Ancient Man, it contains many remains of long-vanished civilizations, which are among the oldest and most extraordinary known to us. In later years the island was a Roman province, and eventually the Saracens conquered it. Venice ruled it during four centuries, then the Turks seized it and in spite of many revolts maintained at least nominal power until 1909. In 1913 the island was incorporated with Greece, but in 1941, it fell to the Germans. After the war it was restored to Greece.

Most Cretans are of Greek origin and

belong to the Greek Orthodox Church, and the towns resemble those of Greece. But at Candia, the old capital, there are massive fortifications, old breakwaters, warehouses and fountains bearing the winged lion of St. Mark, the symbol of Venice. The long Turkish occupation has also left its impress; mosques with their white minarets gleam above the blue harbor at Canea, which is the capital today.

The beauty of Crete is more stern than soft and its pleasant valleys are shut in by rocky, inaccessible, snow-covered mountains. One of the highest was called Mount Ida by the ancient Greeks, and a deep gorge on its slopes was venerated as the birthplace of Zeus. In some places the mountains suddenly open out as though by magic, and there before us lies a wide flat plain walled in by hills, with olive orchards on all sides and the fruit of the vineyards golden in the autumn sunlight. Crete sends many basketsful of fresh grapes to Greece and Egypt, and crate after crate of fine raisins to more distant parts of the world. Along the harborfronts of the north shore, raisins by the yard are spread to dry in the sun. Citrons, too, are to be seen along the docks, cut in half and soaking in brine before being shipped. With citrus fruits, olives and grapes, Crete is typically Mediterranean.

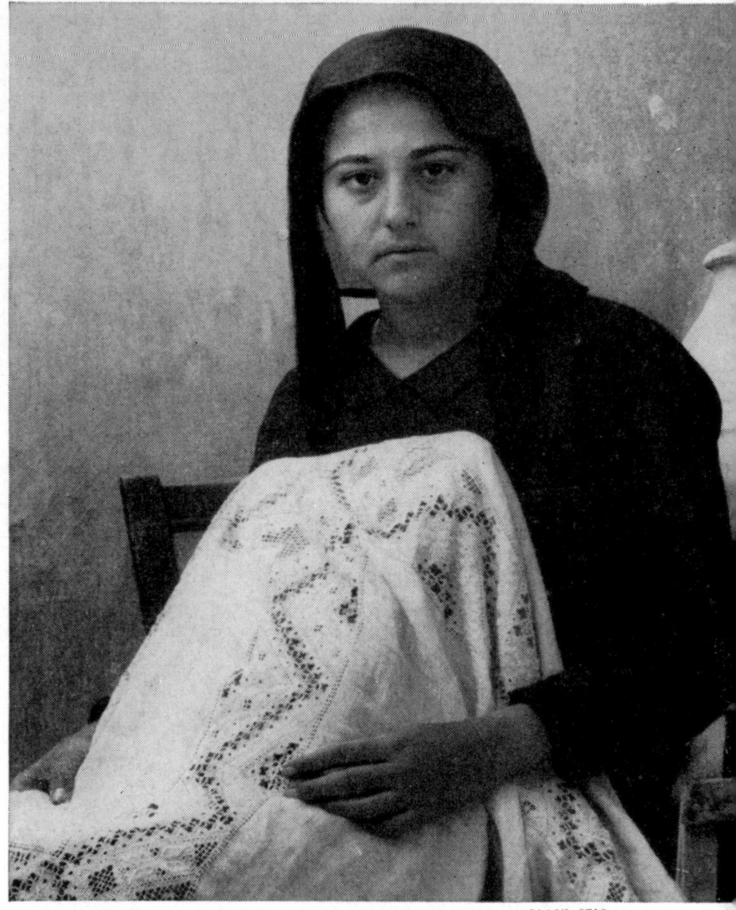

BLACK STAR

**CYPRUS EMBROIDERER AND HER WORK**

A needlewoman of Lefkara exhibits the embroidery for which her town is noted. Work and hands are both beautiful.

Both the Greeks and the Phœnicians colonized Cyprus, the most eastern island in the great sea, and it was conquered by Egyptians, Assyrians, Persians and Romans, for everyone coveted its copper mines. Some say that the island was named for the copper found there—others, that copper takes its Latin name, *cyprium,* from the name of the island.

Be that as it may, Cyprus is a famous spot, and has seen more stirring history than its sleepy life suggests today. The Byzantine emperors and the Saracens were its rulers after the Romans, and in 1191 Richard Cœur-de-Lion, on his way to the Holy Land to fight the Third Crusade, took Cyprus from the Byzantines and sold it to Guy de Lusignan. This knight was theoretically king of Jerusalem, but the Saracens held Jerusalem, so Guy sailed to Cyprus. His successors ruled it for three hundred years, and under them it was brilliantly prosperous. Churches, abbeys and castles were built, the ruins of which bear mute witness to

THE SUN SHINES BRIGHT ON A SPANISH ISLAND

Majorca, the largest of the Balearic Islands, in the Mediterranean, is about 120 miles from Spain. The climate is pleasant and mild, and in many parts of the island the vegetation grows luxuriantly. Grapes for Majorca's light wines are cultivated in sunny vineyards on terraced slopes above the sea. Large orchards of figs, oranges and olives are also carefully tended.

PHOTOS, AMERICAN EXPORT LINES

A JEWEL-LIKE CITY OF THE MEDITERRANEAN

Palma, the capital of Majorca, is located on the Bay of Palma on the island's south coast. The city, built around its excellent harbor, is beautiful and picturesque with its Moorish architecture and colorful tiled roofs. The Gothic cathedral (at right of picture) was under construction from 1322 to 1601; it contains the tomb of King Jayme II of Aragon.

IVAN DMITRI FOR AMERICAN EXPORT LINES

**MAJORCA WOMEN, BEAUTIFUL EVEN IN AGE, SORTING ALMONDS**

Not many years ago life was serene on Majorca and living was cheap. The island was a refuge for men and women of many countries who wanted to escape, at least for a time, the pressures of modern existence. Artists went there to paint, writers to write. What we call progress is bringing many changes to the island, but these women have not lost the old serenity.

their former splendor. Then the Venetians occupied it, but the Turks took it from them, and the British took it from the Turks, so now it is a colony of Great Britain and cares little for its ancient glory.

The forests which furnished timber for Greek and Egyptian vessels have disappeared, and there is little shade on the rocky hills of the great central plain. Cyprian peasant women are hard-working; if they are not busy in the fields or in the house, they may be seen doing jobs as different as making lace and breaking rocks for new roads. The lace of Lefkara goes all over the world, and Cyprus is known also for its hand-woven cottons and silks. Modern industry disturbs the easy-going atmosphere very little, even though up-to-date methods are used in extracting copper from the slag heaps of ancient mines, and asbestos is conveyed from the craggy peak of Mount Troodos by an aerial railway. The activity of the mines seems less typical than the drowsiness of the cafés in Famagusta or the quiet peace which envelops the white buildings of Greek monasteries in the mountains.

---

## *ISLES OF THE MEDITERRANEAN: FACTS AND FIGURES*

*BALEARIC ISLANDS (Baleáres)*

Group of 15 islands off Gulf of Valencia: Majorca, Minorca, Iviza, Formentera and 11 islets. Total area, 1,935 square miles; population, 422,089. Governed as a province of Spain; capital, Palma (on Majorca) has a population of 136,814. Religion, Roman Catholic; language, Spanish. Products: olives, olive oil, grapes, almonds, oranges, figs, carob beans, green vegetables, shoes, filigree work.

*CORSICA (Corse)*

Lies due south of Genoa and 51 miles west of Italian coast. Area, 3,367 square miles; population, 267,873. Governed as a department of France. Chief towns: Ajaccio, the capital, population, 37,146; and Bastia, 52,208. Religion, Roman Catholic; language, Italian dialect. Chief products: olive oil, wine, honey, gallic acid, chestnuts, citrus fruits, cereals and mulberries.

*SARDINIA (Sardegna)*

Lies 7 miles south of Corsica. Area, 9,196 square miles; population, 1,273,714. Governed as a department of Italy. Chief towns: Cagliari, the capital, 141,573; Sassari, 55,373. Religion, Roman Catholic; language, Spanish and Italian dialects. Products: lead, zinc, salt, timber, cork, tanning bark, charcoal, olive oil, wine, almonds, wheat, oranges, lemons, cattle, cheese and tuna fish.

*MALTA (Colony of Great Britain)*

Three islands (Malta, Gozo and Comino) lying 60 miles south of Sicily. Total area, 122 square miles; civilian population, 312,447. Administration by a governor, Council of Government and National Assembly for local affairs. Capital, Valletta (on Malta), 18,666. Religion: Roman Catholic; languages, English, Italian and Maltese. There are 118 primary, secondary and technical schools with about 48,000 pupils; 1 university and adult education classes. Imports: wheat, flour, sugar, coal, textiles, petroleum products, metal goods. Products: wheat, barley, potatoes, green vegetables, grapes and other fruits, hides and skins, cotton and cotton goods, lace, filigree work and cigarettes.

*CORFU (Corcyra)*

Lies 2 miles off the Greek coast, at the Albanian border. Area: 229 square miles; population, 105,226. Governed as a department of Greece; capital, Corfu, 30,706. Religion: Greek Orthodox and Roman Catholic; language, Greek. Products: olive oil, honey, grapes and other fruits.

*CRETE (Candia)*

Lies about 60 miles southeast of the Greek mainland and 110 miles southwest of Asia Minor. Area: 3,235 square miles; population, 463,458. Governed as a part of Greece. Chief towns: Canea, the capital, 35,237; and Candia, 54,541. Religion: Greek Orthodox and others are tolerated. Products: olive oil, soap, cheese, citrus fruits, raisins and grapes. For a time during World War II, Crete was occupied by the Germans, but it was returned to Greece when peace was made in 1945.

*CYPRUS (Colony of Great Britain)*

Lies 40 miles south of Asia Minor and 60 miles west of Syria. Area: 3,572 square miles; population, 492,297. Governed by a governor and an Executive Council. Chief towns: Nicosia, the capital, 38,669; Limassol, 25,803; Famagusta, 19,451; Larnaca, 15,828; and Paphos, 6,275. Religion: Mohammedan and Greek Catholic; languages, Greek dialect, Osmanli Turkish, French and English. Greeks and Mohammedans have their own schools; total elementary enrollment, 62,000. Products: barley, wheat, olives, olive oil, raisins, cotton, potatoes, cheese, sponges, gypsum, copper, asbestos.

# Index for Volume 1

# COLOR PLATES IN VOLUME I

# INDEX FOR VOLUME I

*(General Index for entire work of 7 volumes may be found at the end of Volume 7)*

**A single star before a page number marks an illustration; two stars are placed before color-plates. The repetition of a page number, first without a star, and then with a star, shows that there is an illustration on the page, in addition to an important text reference.**

## C



## D

PRINTED IN THE U. S. A.

ARCTIC
OCEAN
Ellesmere I.
GREENLA
Bank I.
Victoria I.
Baffin Bay
Baffin I.
ASIA
Bering Strait
Yukon River
Mackenzie River
Great Bear Lake
Great Slave Lake
Davis Strait
Hudson Bay
Bering Sea
Aleutian Islands
R. Nelson
L. Winnipeg
Vancouver Island
ROCKY
NORTH AMERICA
Columbia R.
Missouri R.
R.
Great Lakes
St. Lawrence R.
Newfoundl
MTS.
APPALACHIAN MTS.
Azo
Colo. R.
Rio Grande
Miss. R.
ATLANTI
Bermuda I.
Gulf of Mexico
Bahama Is.
West Indies
Cuba
Hawaii Islands
CENTRAL AMERICA
Caribbean Sea
OCEAN
PACIFIC
Panama Canal
Orinoco R.
Gilbert Is.
EQUATOR
Amazon River
Phoenix Is.
Solomon Is.
Marquesas Is.
Madeira R.
São Francisco R.
ANDES
SOUTH AMERICA
New Hebrides
Society Is.
OCEAN
New Caledonia
Fiji Is.
Tuamotu Archipelago
Paraná R.
MTS.
NEW ZEALAND
Falkland Islands
Strait of Magellan
Cape Horn
Drake Strait
ANTARCTIC CIRCLE
Weddell Sea